Breaking Open

Breaking Open: Reflections on Italian American Women's Writing

edited by
MARY ANN MANNINO

and
JUSTIN VITIELLO

Purdue University Press
West Lafayette, Indiana

Copyright 2003 by Purdue University. All rights reserved.

Printed in the United States of America

Library of Congress Cataloging-in-Publication Data
Breaking Open: Reflections on Italian American women's writing/compiled by Mary Ann Vigilante Mannino and Justin Vitiello.
  p. cm.
  Includes bibliographical references.
  ISBN 1-55753-243-5 (alk. paper)
   1. American literature—Italian American authors—History and criticism. 2. Women and literature—United States—History—20th century. 3. American literature—Women authors—History and criticism. 4. American literature—20th century—History and criticism. 5. Italian American women—Intellectual life. 6. Italian American women—Biography. 7. Italian Americans in literature. I. Mannino, Mary Ann Vigilante, 1943– II. Vitiello, Justin.

PS153.I8 R44   2003
810.9′9287′08951—dc21   2002036801

For Nunzio Pernicone, Professor of History, whose sponsorship of the 1999 Philadelphia conference at Drexel University on Italian American Women Writers made this book possible.

Contents

MARY ANN MANNINO
Introduction   1

JUSTIN VITIELLO
What I Wanted to Ask and Say Where and When This Book Was Conceived . . .   19

CONTRIBUTORS

HELEN BAROLINI
Difference, Identity, and Saint Augustine   31

MARY CAPPELLO
Breakage and Beauty   43

RITA CIRESI
Toward a New Catholic Novel: The Italian-American Woman Writer and the Church   51

LOUISE DESALVO
Breaking the Jar/Mending the Jar   59

RACHEL GUIDO DEVRIES
Until the Voices Came   73

DIANE DI PRIMA
Recollections of My Life As a Woman   91

MARIA FAMA
La Carta Parla   109

SANDRA M. GILBERT
Adventures on the Hyphen: Poetry, Pasta, and Identity Politics   137

MARIA MAZZIOTTI GILLAN
Shame and Silence in My Work   153

DANIELA GIOSEFFI
Forging into the American Mainstream since the 1960s:
On Being a Woman Writer with an Italian Name   177

JOSEPHINE GATTUSO HENDIN
A Usable Past: Writing to the Hybrid Future   195

CAROLE MASO
Notes of a Lyric Artist Working in Prose: A Lifelong Conversation
with Myself Entered Midway   215

MARY JO BONA
"But Is It Great?": The Question of the Canon for Italian American
Women Writers   239

FRED GARDAPHÉ
The Double Burden of Italian American Women Writers   265

EDVIGE GIUNTA
Speaking Through Silences: Ethnicity in the Writings
of Italian/American Women   279

MARY ANN MANNINO
Stains of an Immigrant Past: Inherited Habits of Being   301

JUSTIN VITIELLO
Beyond Tautologies?: Poetics of Female and Feminist "*Italianità*"
in Four Anthologies of Italian American Women's Literature   323

About the Contributors

Helen Barolini is the author of seven books, two of which have appeared in Italy in translation. Her many stories and essays have appeared in numerous publications and collections.

Mary Jo Bona is an associate professor of Italian American Studies and English at SUNY, Stony Brook. She is the author of *Claiming a Tradition: Italian American Women Writers* and editor of *The Voices We Carry: Recent Italian American Women's Fiction*.

Mary Cappello, professor of English at the University of Rhode Island, is the author of *Night Bloom* (Beacon Press). She is currently at work on a collaborative project with photographer Paola Ferrario to document the lives of new immigrants to Italy. Ferrario and Cappello are recipients of the Lange-Taylor Prize from Duke University's Center for Documentary Studies.

Rita Ciresi is the author of three novels (*Remind Me Again Why I Married You*, *Pink Slip*, and *Blue Italian*) as well as two short-story collections (*Mother Rocket* and *Sometimes I Dream in Italian*).

Louise DeSalvo is the Jenny Hunter Endowed Scholar for Creative Writing and Literature at Hunter College. She has published 14 books, among them, *Vertigo* and *The Milk of Almonds*.

Rachel Guido deVries is the author of *Gambler's Daughter* (Guernica Editions, 2001), a finalist in the 2001 Paterson Poetry Prize; *How to Sing to a Dago* (poems, Guernica Editions, 1996); and *Tender Warriors*, a novel, (Firebrand, 1986). Recent work has appeared in the *Paterson Literary Review*, in the anthologies *Don't Tell Mama* (Penguin, 2002), and in *The Milk of Almonds: Italian American Women Write About Food and Culture*, (Feminist Press, 2002). She teaches creative writing in the Humanistic Studies Center of Syracuse University.

Diane di Prima is the author of 40 books of poetry and prose. Her work has been translated into over 20 languages. She lives in San Francisco, where she writes, and teaches privately.

Maria Fama is the author of three books of poetry and the producer of poetry videos. Her poems, short stories, and essays have appeared in numerous publications and have been in several anthologies. Fama lives and works in Philadelphia.

Fred Gardaphé directs SUNY, Stony Brook's Italian/American Studies Program. His books include *Italian Signs, American Streets: The Evolution of Italian American*

Narrative, Dagoes Read: Tradition and the Italian/American Writer, Moustache Pete is Dead!, and *Leaving Little Italy*.

Sandra (Mortola) Gilbert is a poet, a critic, and professor of English at the University of California, Davis. Her latest publications include *Kissing the Bread: New & Selected Poems 1969–1999* (W. W. Norton, 2000) and an anthology entitled *Inventions of Farewell: A Book of Elegies* (W. W. Norton, 2001). Forthcoming are a chapbook, *The Italian Collection*, and a critical study, "Death's Door: Mourning, Modernity, and the Poetics of Memory."

Maria Mazziotti Gillan is director of the Poetry Center at Passaic County Community College in Paterson and of the Creative Writing Program at Binghamton University–SUNY. Her latest book of poetry is *Italian Women in Black Dresses* (Guernica). She edits the *Paterson Literary Review*.

Daniela Gioseffi is an American Book Award winning author of 11 books of poetry and prose. She has been a professor of creative writing and world literature at various universities including New York University, Long Island University, and Brooklyn College, CUNY. She has published innumerable poems, novels, stories, interviews, and reviews in leading literary magazines and has won two New York State Council for the Arts grant awards in poetry.

Edvige Giunta is associate professor of English at New Jersey City University. She is the author of *Writing with an Accent: Contemporary Italian American Women Authors* and *Dire l'indicibile: Memoir di autrici italo americane*, and co-editor of the anthologies *The Milk of Almonds: Italian American Women Writers on Food and Culture*, and *Italian American Writers on New Jersey*.

Josephine Gattuso Hendin is professor of English and Tiro A. Segno Professor of Italian American Studies at New York University. Her novel, *The Right Thing to Do*, won an American Book Award from the Before Columbus Foundation in 1988–1989 and was reprinted by The Feminist Press in 1999. She is the author of *The World of Flannery O'Connor* and *Vulnerable People: A View of American Fiction Since 1945*. Her literary essays have appeared in The New Republic, Harper's Magazine, American Literary History, and other publications.

Mary Ann Mannino is a visiting assistant professor at Temple University. Her book, *Revisionary Identities: Strategies of Empowerment in the Writing of Italian American Women* was published in 2000. Mannino is also a poet and fiction writer. She is the 2001 recipient of first prize in the Allen Ginsberg Poetry Awards.

Carole Maso is the author of nine books including *The Art Lover, The American Woman in the Chinese Hat, Ava, The Room Lit By Roses*, and *Beauty is Convulsive: The Passion of Frida Kahlo*. She is professor of English at Brown University.

Justin Vitiello was born in New York City in 1941. Of Neapolitan origin, he has dedicated most of his adult life to understanding his ancestors' homeland and to building cultural bridges between America and Italy. This is his twenty-first book. Among them are works of poetry, essays, scholarship, and translations.

Mary Ann Mannino

Introduction

When I was a child, I was American during the week and Italian on weekends and holidays. Weekdays, I attended a private Catholic school with girls who, judging from their last names, appeared to be distantly related to Irish, Polish, or German settlers. As far as I knew, none of the girls in that school, surely not my preppy friends there, was the daughter of an immigrant like I was. Those girls were what my parents called *merigani*. During the week, because my mother, the daughter of immigrants but born in America, had attended public school and had learned about proper nutrition, I ate broiled lamb chops with a baked potato and spinach with butter much more frequently than I ate macaroni.

On the weekends, however, we visited my aunt, uncle, and cousins—my father's family, who had just arrived in America after World War II. My father, who had immigrated in 1913, had not seen his favorite sister in years. Because of their limited schooling, neither could write letters in Italian. All those years, they had not communicated.

At first, no one at my aunt's house spoke English. Later, when some could, they didn't because it was much easier for them to speak Italian, which everyone who crossed their threshold, except me, could also speak. (My mother, in her desire to assimilate and get ahead, did not encourage me to learn the dialect she and everyone else spoke.)

At my aunt's house we ate homemade pickled eggplant, Italian cookies, *bacala* on Christmas eve, *zeppoli* on St. Joseph's day, and ricotta pie at Easter. We even made fruit-flavored cordials for my cousin's wedding. There my aunt and cousin warded off the evil eye with oil and water. There my dad and the other men played Italian card games, *briscola* and *scopa*, and, in the summer, *bocce* in the driveway because the backyard had no grass. It was one huge garden where eggplants, tomatoes, and peppers grew.

In that house, everything was in order. Everyone seemed to know what was to be done and how to do it. There were rules of behavior, and there was laughter, food, heated conversation, and much hugging. However, somehow, strangers who came knew by my silence that I didn't quite fit. They would scowl at me and ask in Italian who the American was. They had to be reassured that despite my appearance, I was indeed part of *la famiglia*.

The way I ate cantaloupe provides a concrete example of the different cultures forming my identity and how I moved between them. During the week, if I had cantaloupe with my mother or if we were in a restaurant at the seashore and had cantaloupe for breakfast, I received one-half cantaloupe, skin on, with a spoon to eat it. On the other hand, if I were at my aunt's, my cousin Elena and I peeled the cantaloupe, sliced it thinly, and it was eaten with a knife and fork. At the time, it never occurred to me that there was anything significant in the eating of cantaloupe. All I knew was that how I ate cantaloupe depended on where I was.

My location determined how I acted in many other areas, as well. When I was a child, it was easy enough to learn the rules for two places and to act accordingly. As I became a teenager, these differences were harder to keep in separate boxes. Dating, fraternity parties, family christenings, studying, smoking, family visits, drinking, overnights, and funerals all took on enormous weight. Something as simple as a kiss or as exciting as a dance at the U.S. Naval Academy had the potential of turning me instantly into a *puttana* or a nerd. At sixteen, neither label appealed. My task seemed to be to succeed in America, stay at the top of my class, go to an Ivy League university, become a professional, and marry an educated man, but not associate too much with *merigani* and certainly not adopt any of their attitudes toward success, relationships, child care, religion, and especially the family. Trying to balance two conflicting worlds consumed my days. Even after I married, there were still no simple choices. A decision to go to a movie with my husband and leave the children with a baby-sitter was made by evaluating and then selecting one value system over another.

Much later, when I took my first course in creative writing, I found, to my surprise, that many of my stories focused on my schizophrenic existence. My short stories were sometimes about Italian immigrants trying to make it in the land of opportunity and other times about bored, middle-class Americans questioning America's claim that wealth equated with happiness. I was doing what writers seem compelled to do—order conflict by turning it into words on a page. I tried to control my confusion by capturing it in language and by making something beautiful out of the everyday as my grandmother did turning flour sacks into aprons and dandelions into salad for dinner.

When I was in school, I thought my life unique because it did not resemble the lives of the people I met there. My mother had encouraged me to attend, but not to participate. In this book, I now have a family of sisters whose lives are similar to mine in that each of us has been encouraged to go far but never leave home. So many of us who have moved just a short distance away from the world of our parents take "home" with us neatly packed in the suitcases of our minds. We neatly fold the old ways and old traditions and place them next to the new. We stow away the guilt if we don't cook, the guilt if we are divorced, and the memories of holiday food, the men playing cards, the laughter rising up with the cigar smoke, the love and security we once had when we didn't think there were any implications to eating cantaloupe.

This book, a portmanteau of past and present, is significant because it brings together twelve widely published Italian American women authors who write about the people and places that have influenced their works. So many write about the ways an emotional connection to their Italian American family and the longing for independence intersect in their creative endeavors. In addition, this book includes essays by five scholars who discuss the field of Italian American women's literature, which has burgeoned exponentially since the publication of Helen Barolini's first anthology of Italian American women's writing, *The Dream Book*, first published in 1985 and republished by the Feminist Press in 2001.

In the Introduction to the original text, Barolini states that the Italian woman at the time of mass immigration was "the core of the family, upholder of its traditions and transmitter of its values" (Barolini, p. 12). She suggests that because of this role, women had a harder time in the New World than men did. Success in America necessitated modification of cultural codes and change. Barolini writes that according to tradition,

> the one thing . . . a woman must not do was change. Since everyone leaned on her for support, she was supposed to be permanently accessible and permanently unchanging. She could not exist as an individual with autonomous needs and wishes, for that would have undermined the common good" (Barolini, p. 11).

The daughters of immigrants, the Italian American writers, have not been content to continue this pattern that generates respect but limits individualization. Educated in America, they seek self-actualization. Barolini suggests that "in denying the value of the mother's role they lay upon themselves a heavy and terrible conflict" (Barolini, p. 11).

Herein lies the challenge: How does one go far without leaving home? How does one become part of America without leaving Italy? Perhaps by making a space for balance. Perhaps by boldly insisting on the legitimacy of the in-between and the beauty of the hybrid as an American reality. Perhaps by writing a literature that accurately portrays lives enriched by a fusion of cultures. I want to suggest that this is happening and has been happening since the publication of *The Dream Book* and the connections between writers that it made possible.

Apropos, Justin Vitiello proposed long ago just such a self-determined new literature. He suggested a literature of "ascent" as an alternative to "conformity to the mainstream" or "ethnic provincialism" in "Off the Boat and up the Creek without a Paddle" (Vitiello, p. 42). Vitiello recognized that each work of Italian American literature would be a unique blend of two cultures. The exact combination of Italian and American parts would be determined by the individual author. Vitiello suggested that "our young and still shaky cultural edifice" would be left "for us to redecorate, rehabilitate, redesign, or construct anew—for ourselves..." (Vitiello, p. 30).

After reading *The Dream Book*, Italian American women writers, in a unity of purpose, began to work together on new projects and to construct anew a literature of their own, weaving their unique visions into American literature. This literature, connected to the Italian and American traditions, often addresses issues that arise out of identities formed by multiple and conflicting values. The writers are women whose roles as wives, mothers, lovers, and daughters have long been considered of lower status in the Italian and the American cultures. This realization gives rise to writing strategies of resistance. Their works question assumptions about woman's nature and the societal placement of women, and insist that women determine their own desires and their own identities. Born in America, they feel the need for education and the pull of self-actualization. However, their heritage is Italian, and deep within lie the ancestral voices demanding allegiance to the code of *omertà* and to a view that it is the burden of women to carry and transmit an ancient culture.

Although Italy has changed drastically in the intervening 120 years since the mass migration of southern Italians began in 1880 and, in particular, in its attitudes toward gender roles, for the writers, Italy is the country and the culture that the immigrants left. Their writing frequently reflects identities that are amalgams of nineteenth-century Italy and twenty-first-century America, which is, in many ways, an uneasy blending.

When discussing this new literature, the writers often use images of breakage to explain what they are doing in their lives and in their work. Their claim to a legitimate place in American literature involves the splitting open of themselves, as well as the breaking apart of the canon they wish to enter. Only the shattering of rigid literary forms and traditional codes of behavior will allow the necessary new growth to develop. The assumptions of Italian culture in the nineteenth century that would keep women in the silence of the home, as well as the traditional models of American literature that would have no room for working-class narratives emerging from oral tradition, or for women struggling to find a place of empowerment, must be destroyed to accommodate their voices.

In discussing this transition from the oral tradition of storytelling in Italy to the written stories of Italian Americans, Fred Gardaphé suggests that the immigrant experience is very much alive in the written word. He says of the writing process, "one gets what one needs to write by listening. By listening to the past inside oneself, a writer stays in tune with his or her oral tradition" (Gardaphé, p. 302). Gardaphé sees Italian American writing as an extension of a past oral tradition and insists that the ancestral voices are a part of it.

William Faulkner, in attempting to understand the American South, also was concerned with the ways that oral tradition and a people's history shape their present choices and determine their future condition. Faulkner recognized that within the individual, reverberations from the past continually struggled with present desires. Paying tribute to this ongoing process in his Nobel prize acceptance speech, Faulkner identified the subject of his writings as the human heart in conflict with itself. Each writer in this book uniquely combines aspects of Italian cultural history—stories and warnings—passed on orally with the structures and styles of American literature learned in school to record different aspects of Italian/American life. Often these stories are about internal conflict caused by a dual existence.

For Barolini, the individual as Outsider becomes a traditional American theme and a way to present a new American writing. In discussing her literary opus, Barolini writes, "I thought of my work as in the tradition of the most American of literary tropes, the Outsider theme" (p. 38). Barolini explains that her novel *Umbertina* was "an American novel about what it is to become an uneasy American, first by physical transplantation and then by spiritual birth, but in any case American" (p. 39). She argues against the charge of the literary mainstream that "so-called ethnic writers" do not write universally if they use material that reflects their ethnic origins. She insists that because she was formed in the English language and its literature, she is "a part of American writing undivided by mainstream or minority rankings" (p. 41). She demands the right to use her own material and voice while conveying "values from difference as well as from conformity" (p. 41).

Mary Cappello suggests that the outsider status of immigrants leaves an indelible mark on the psyche of their progeny. Cappello's writing is an attempt to make room in American literature for the absent immigrant voice. She believes that it is necessary "to break old forms and attempt to create new ones that can accommodate the unspoken" (p. 45). She explains that "the desire to achieve breakage . . . has to do with the conviction that my immigrant ancestors found no objective correlative for their passion, for their longing" (p. 45). In her memoir, *Night Bloom*, she incorporates the writing of her mother and her immigrant grandfather, thus physically demonstrating the breaking open of memoir as a literary form to include often-excluded voices and perspectives.

Like Cappello, Rita Ciresi sees breakage as part of her aesthetic. She suggests that the characters in contemporary Italian American women's fiction break rules. They are transgressors who are "grappling with choices: between good and evil, and right and wrong"(p. 53). Of her own stories, she writes, "I liked characters who dared to do wrong, and do wrong, and do wrong—until they got into so much trouble they had to get down on their knees and pray for mercy" (p. 56). She claims that misbehavior is the "stuff of good stories," but transgression is a daily occurrence for immigrants and for their descendants who commit cultural sins with frequency and whose multiple offenses perpetuate Outsider status. It is in her writing, the telling of Italian American stories of transgressing women, that she redeems the cultural sins of the immigrants. Her character, Rosa Salvatore in *Blue Italian*, leaves the enclave of Pizza Beach against the wishes of her parents and marries a Jewish man because she wants a better life. Instead of bliss, transgression brings her multiple losses. Rosa's choice to continue forward despite her pain and not return to her mother's house mirrors and redeems the immigrants' physical and cultural journey.

Louise DeSalvo explains the transgressive position of Italian American academic women succinctly when she writes "as an Italian American, I am an outsider to privileged culture . . . my critique of British imperialism in my work on Woolf is rooted in my personal history and in the fact that my people were colonized" (p. 61). Although she knows little about her family's immigrant past because her parents tried to assimilate and buried their history, "perhaps because it was shameful," she acknowledges that her grandfather's "journey here, to the United States, . . . has made [her] work as a writer, as a thinker, possible. . ." (p. 60). She sees her identity as inseparable from her Italian ancestors and her American education.

When DeSalvo indicates that no one in her family talked about *la miseria*, "as if being unable to work was your fault," she addresses the shame and the code of *omertà*. As one who has written about her sister's suicide, her mother's depression, and her father's anger, she has violated that code. She asserts, "I am quite certain that my grandfather would not have liked that I have written about my family" (p. 67). Despite her recognition of her transgression of her grandfather's code, she was able to continue writing, having been inspired after reading other Italian/American women's writing about working-class lives and family secrets, in particular, Carole Maso's *Ghost Dance*. DeSalvo was impressed with what Maso said about "the potentially healing power of art" (p. 64). For DeSalvo, writing is a "series of breakings and mendings, a shattering of the writing self that was, a repairing, through writing, of something in [her] life that needed fixing" (p. 70).

Rachel deVries also sees her writing as a way to heal injuries: "I think we are a sad people, full of loss and grief and beauty; it is in the making of art perhaps that our sadness is best translated" (p. 81). She, too, has been influenced by the other Italian American women she has read, in particular, Diane di Prima and Denise Nico Leto. She writes that she carried Diane di Prima's *The Calculus of Variation* with her when she traveled, "reading only a few paragraphs, sometimes even just a few lines, before I was transported to a place of translation within me, so that my own pen would now rush along the pages of my journal and later become poems of my own" (p. 85). DeVries suggests that in seeing her life reflected in the writing of another Italian American woman, she gains the insight to explore her own identity, to name herself, and to write for all to read.

Diane di Prima sees her life and her work as intimately intertwined. Her memoir, *Recollections of My Life as a Woman*, suggests that although she left home at eighteen to become a poet, moved to Manhattan, and lived a bohemian lifestyle, her early years with her immigrant grandparents influenced the way she responded to life, and that response determined what she wrote. Her memoir begins with an acknowledgement to her grandmother: "My earliest sense of what it means to be a woman was learned from my grandmother, Antoinette Mallozzi, and at her knee" (p. 91). Di Prima suggests that the role of women in an immigrant household was to take care of men and respond to their needs rather than to their own. Although di Prima lived an alternative beat lifestyle, she continued to hold firm to immigrant values. Members of her immediate family were and continue to be her highest priority, even above her art. Even at her most rebellious, she is still a traditionalist in certain intimate relationships, selflessly providing food, housing, warmth, and care to her family, many friends, and acquaintances. Her notion of womanhood seems to incorporate and rebel against the values of *serietà*.

Like di Prima, Maria Fama can write, "As a writer, as a woman, and as an Italian American, I believe I stand on the shoulders of my foremothers"(p. 113). Fama then explains how her illiterate great-grandmothers had a rich oral tradition from which she learned "the prayers, the proverbs, the tales, and the songs—which Nonna Mattia had known by heart" (p. 118). Although her essay describes her journey from the childhood stories of Italy told by her great-grandmother Mattia, which were important influences to her own personal exploration of Italy later in her life, Fama explains, "I belong to both cultures"

(p. 125). She illustrates this doubleness with poems written to claim her identity as both Sicilian ("Picking Apricots with *Zia Antonia*") and American ("The Captain of the Safeties"). Her poem "I Am Not White" confronts the racial implications of Sicily's many invasions. Fama explains that even though she lives in America and is an American, she is Sicilian in a bodily way. Her dentist has informed her that her teeth reveal a mixed racial heritage. Another poem, "Tablecloth," demonstrates the way a handmade tablecloth, which represents women's work and women's value, can travel across the ocean and grace a spring table in an American town house. Fama's poems celebrate the way "culture, like language, is flexible and ever changing" (p. 125).

Sandra Gilbert, too, turns to Italy "again and again in poetry and more generally in that struggle toward self-discovery of which poetry is a crucial element for [her]" (p. 144). For Gilbert, Italy holds several kinds of meaning, which determine her identity as a person and as an artist. Her poems "Grandpa" and "Kissing the Bread," generated by a desire to dramatize a mysterious heritage, are filled with questions and speculations about her ancestral culture. In *Mafiosa* and *Leeks*, Gilbert reveals the effect on her of the negative way Italian American has been culturally constructed. Running from all the American connotations of Italian, in "Leeks" the speaker imagines herself to be "a red-haired freckled / Presbyterian girl" who hums "Rock of Ages," has inherited a house in Brattleboro, Vermont, and has "never drunk red wine, / never tasted olive oil" (pp. 151–152). Other poems imagine Italy as a "lost Eden" or as a symbol of something always desired and "therefore perpetually remote . . . even inaccessible" (p. 144).

Like Gilbert, Maria Gillan expresses ambivalent feelings toward being Italian American. Although born in America, she did not speak English until she entered school. Apropos, she claims that her work "springs from shame and silence . . . a shame so strong, so overwhelming that [she] spent the first twenty-five years of [her] life unable to speak" (p. 157). Her early shame appears in many of her poems because she tries to "convey the emotional truths of [her] life in [her] work" (p. 198). Poems like "Public School No. 18, Paterson, New Jersey," "Learning Silence," and "Growing Up Italian" dramatically illustrate the ways that public school teachers and the Dick and Jane readers validated a set of mores that placed Gillan and her immigrant parents outside American culture. She writes, "I knew their world was so far removed from mine, it might just as well have been on Mars; yet it filled me with longing to be those people, to be blonde and cute and middle class" (p. 159).

Like DeSalvo, Gillan appreciated British and American literature taught in school. Until she was forty, her poetry was "very much in imitation of the poets [she] read in school" (p. 162), writing that she now sees as an attempt "to erase [her]self." Although in her early years she internalized the American view of Italian immigrants and their families and was ashamed of everything Italian including her name, she later realized that the Italian part of her identity was rich, beautiful, and had influenced all that she did. She demonstrated her change in awareness by reclaiming the name Mazziotti.

Her work gives an honest emotional portrayal of her early shame and silence and her subsequent triumphant pride in herself as "some hybrid creature, neither fully American nor fully Italian" (p. 167). Her poems lay open the trauma caused by an educational system that teaches children to hate themselves and adults to perpetuate this self-denigration.

Daniela Gioseffi found that having a long Italian last name was somewhat of a handicap when she first began her literary career. She notes that her emotional response to life, which she attributes to the influence of her immigrant father, is reflected in both her poetry and her performance pieces. It marked her work as different from the more emotionally restrained writers who seemed to dominate literary styles during her college days in the 1960s. Gioseffi believes her father's dramatic readings of literature when she was a child inspired her to express her feelings in writing and acting. Gioseffi's opus, though passionately celebrating the hard work and devotion of her father to his family, also rebels against the constraints he wanted to impose on her because she was a woman. Her poem "For Grandma Lucia La Rosa, 'Light the Rose'" questions the traditions of patriarchal culture that would limit the freedom of women while listing the ways that American culture placed limits on the accomplishments of Italian/American men.

Although Josephine Hendin does not claim she was ashamed of being Italian American, she does say:

> I wrote about American literature and culture for *The New York Times Book Review*, *Harper's Magazine*, *The New Republic*, and popular and academic journals, but I had kept the code of *omertà*, never writing about the practices and ways of the world in which I had grown up (p. 199).

She says that in writing her novel *The Right Thing to Do*, she was forced to confront her relation to an Italian American past. Writing that novel became ". . . more for me than shifting forms from criticism to fiction. . . . It involved an awakening of the voices, ethos, and emotions of my childhood that had formed [me]" (p. 200). The Sicilian father and the American daughter in the novel clash over issues of power and independence, which Hendin sees as reflecting upheavals in American culture. She suggests that these quarrels of the 1960s "left the power of authority and family connections foundering in a culture of experimentation" (p. 201).

For herself, she claims the family "is not only the bulwark against the competitive strife of the larger culture, but also the crucible in which cultural changes are registered in intensely personal and dramatic form" (p. 208). It is "the experience of unrest within the family" where her focus as a novelist has been (p. 209).

Hendin also believes that her writing has been directly influenced by "a style of expression that seemed natural to [her]. . . . This expressive style borrows from traditions of Italian folk storytelling," which emphasizes communication through illustrative tales (p. 209). She recognizes a difference in the writing of Italian American women from that of the men. She believes that the

> qualities of *serietà* that encompassed women's shrewd understanding of their situation, ability to manage inventively within it . . . readily expanded into a desire for self-realization and self-expression that often was accompanied by frustration, depression, and despair" (p. 202–203).

Although male writers do not seem to recognize this thwarted ambition, women's literature is filled with rebellion and depression. According to Helen Barolini, although the mother in men's writing is the giver of unconditional love and sacrifice, in women's writing the difficulty of that task is revealed. Hendin explains:

> For the Italian American woman writer, the clash between authority and freedom, silence and speech, loyalty to family and the craving for escape from its confines are all richly dramatic subjects that have cultural resonance (p. 207).

The articulation of a connection to these specific Italian American themes is not as easily found in the writing of Carole Maso, but if one looks carefully, it is there. Although *Italianità* is absent in her piece, like the other writers in this text, Maso's writing "is propelled by the desire to be reunited with lost, unremembered aspects of self and world" (p. 225). However, for Maso, that desire must address reality's "inaccessibility to us and to our modes of expression" (p. 220–221). Like Cappello, Maso finds it necessary to break with the traditional forms of writing if she is to give voice to her desire. Because Maso believes "we have witnessed the demise of the belief system that made Jane Austen's confidence and coherence possible," serious writers must discover "what forms might be opened up by our particular predicament" (p. 230). In her discussion of her novel *The American Woman in the Chinese Hat*, Maso describes the way the form of her work is imbricated with the subject matter:

> Inner emotion transforms the outer world into a fever dream, a hallucination where images from the exterior world are thrust into strange, glowing relief and reflect a verisimilitude, a portrait of the outer world as we can know it, and a private, interior, symbolic reality (p. 227).

The five literary scholars who are included in this work all agree that the defining factor of Italian American women's writing is its ethnically gendered exploration of relationships with the world and with the self. Mary Jo Bona, author of the first book-length critical study of Italian/American women's literature, *Claiming a Tradition: Italian American Women Writers*, suggests that although Barolini's anthology was instrumental in "placing Italian American women writers on the map for the first time in American literary history," much work must still be done to develop a definitive body of literature that both represents Italian American women's experiences and is widely recognized (p. 250). Instead of blaming outside agents such as editors and the general public for neglecting these writers, Bona suggests that Italian American writers and critics alone are responsible for constructing an Italian American literary canon. Bona praises the work that has been done and indicates that writers and critics currently "are in the process of defining this body of literature, exploring its greatness, and insuring the reproduction of this work" (p. 252). She records the many recent critical studies in the field and the success scholars have had securing the reissuance of out-of-print literary works: "In fact, Italian-American critics have been at the forefront of the workaday tasks of making such books as Barolini's available in paperback and accessible to students and a general reading public" (p. 252). Bona celebrates the increase in scholarly interest in Italian American women's writing and argues that scholarship is necessary for wider recognition.

Fred Gardaphé insists that it has been female creative writers much more so than the males who have developed the field of Italian American literature by first crossing the boundary between traditionally private and public spaces and becoming "the organic intellectuals of their ancestral culture" (p. 269). He mentions the pioneering work of Helen Barolini as well as that of poet Rose Romano, who, in addition to her own creative projects, "launched *la bella figura*, a literary journal devoted entirely to writing by Italian American women" and founded *Malafemmina* Press (p. 273). Romano's press published the chapbooks of several women writers and was instrumental in disseminating and preserving their writings. Gardaphè suggests that the field has grown so rapidly because many creative writers also have done important critical work.

One such critic and creative writer, Edvige Giunta, is interested in the way ethnic writers, pressured to acculturate, produce literature that "simultaneously verbalizes and silences ethnicity" (p. 283). Giunta believes that "a thinly disguised accent" not only reveals ethnic identity but also "dramatizes the cultural conflicts at the heart of the experience of hyphenation" (p. 284). Giunta notes that in the writing of women this conflict may be expressed in language that is "acquiescent and rebellious at once" (p. 285). In Agnes Rossi's *The Quick*, Giunta's finds Marie Russo's inability to connect with her ethnicity "at the core of her psychological and cultural displacement" (p. 290). Giunta argues that it is in the language—in the way Rossi chooses to write—that she reveals her own "accent": "The vanishing of the ethnic identity is rendered through abrupt narrative shifts, textual fractures and narrative gaps, as well as lack of narrative unity or final closure" (p. 288).

As we move, in time, further and further away from the immigrant experience, traditional markers of that culture, what we call *Italianità*, often disappear altogether from the writing. Critics are forced to ask if literature written by Italian Americans but missing many of the more obvious Italian American signs can still be read as distinctly Italian American.

My essay proposes that Italian American literature can be distinguished by certain habits of being manifest in the characters in fiction and the speakers in poems that suggest a connection to ancestral voices. For Italian Americans, the collective ancestral voice becomes a powerful internalized censor of everyday action. This voice, whose message has been influenced by the immigration experience, can be found in the super-ego of characters or speakers even where there is no indication of Italian American writing except the writer's ethnicity. Because the uprooting of emigration was traumatic for those who experienced it, often these immigrant voices, filled with anxiety, instill fear in their progeny. As cases in point, I examine Rita Ciresi's novel *Blue Italian*, Mary Cappello's memoir *Night Bloom*, Maria Gillian's poem "The Voices Inside Us," and Maria Fama's poem "Tablecloth." I am interested in the behavior of characters and speakers because I believe that long after the immigrant experience is forgotten, ways of responding to the world—that is, with fear or low self-esteem directly related to the immigrant experience—remain. I believe that because of this psychically inherited response, Italian American literature will continue to have distinguishing characteristics when it no longer specifically embodies overt *Italianità*.

In order to gain a comprehensive view of Italian American women's literature, Justin Vitiello examines four anthologies that contain the works of Italian American women: *The Dream Book, Il Viaggio delle Donne, la bella figura,* and *Curaggia*. The writings within them, he suggests, "redefine concepts of selfhood, American pluralism via multicultural consciousness, radicalizing gender identities, and the poetic justice of a more inclusive canonicity" (p. 335). He acknowledges the importance of *The Dream Book* as the "literary or historical frame of reference for the three subsequent anthologies," and he suggests that recurring themes appear in all:

> the ambivalence—or schizophrenia—that growing up as a child of immigrants entails in one of the most Americanizing . . . institutions, school, where the English language is imposed as the *sine qua non* for human status; (2) the conditioning of second-generation young people to conform and be lily-white; (3) their deeply psychosomatic shame for failing to be so; (4) their intimate sense of security at home (i.e. their ethnic and linguistic pride) versus their visceral and physical angst among Anglo-Saxon faces; (5) their internalized guilt for being special and their shame-faced rejection of their roots; (6) their awareness that Anglo culture has managed to teach self-hatred; (7) The revindication of ethnic pride years later when Italian Americans finally get fed up with being targets of Mafia stigmatizing; (8) the explosion of rage as a guilt-ridden but cathartic epiphany in which the dignity of heritage is reaffirmed in a militant way: the discovery of an empowered voice (pp. 341–342).

Vitiello praises the writer's diverse interpretations of these themes, noting that the works within the four anthologies re-envision ethnic origins and identity not as autonomous and fixed states but as relational developed by constant negotiation and reinvention.

Gloria Anzaldúa, a writer and theorist, in attempting to explain the position from which Chicana women write, uses the term *mestiza consciousness* to describe the constant reinvention that occurs within writers and that is reflected in their works. Vitiello recognizes this same negotiation taking place in Italian American women's writing. Anzaldúa, whose family lived in Texas for several generations but retained strong cultural ties to Mexico, points out that "the coming together of two self consistent but habitually incompatible frames of reference causes *un choque*, a cultural collision" (Anzaldúa, p. 427). However, Anzaldúa believes that in attempting to synthesize the disparate aspects of identity, the writer "has added a third element which is greater than the sum of its severed parts." The third element is a new consciousness—a *mestiza* consciousness—and though it is a source of intense pain, its energy comes from continual creative motion that keeps breaking down the unitary aspect of each new paradigm (Anzalduá, p. 429).

In writing literature that reflects our diverse concepts of what it means to be Italian American women, we continually re-envision our history breaking down past definitions of ourselves and creating new, more complex selves. In insisting that our works be recognized as legitimate American literature, we redeem ourselves and the immigrants who have helped form our identities.

Works Cited

Anzaldúa, Gloria. "*La conciencia de la mestiza*: Towards a New Consciousness." In *American Feminist Thought at Century's End*, edited by Linda S. Kauffman. Cambridge, Massachusetts: Blackwell, 1993.

Barolini, Helen. Introduction to *The Dream Book: An Anthology of Writings by Italian-American Women*, edited by Helen Barolini. New York: Shocken Books, 1985.

Gardaphé, Fred. "From Oral Tradition to Written Word: Toward an Ethnographically Based Literary Criticism." In *From the Margin: Writings in Italian Americana*, edited by Anthony J. Tamburri, Paolo A. Giordano, and Fred L. Gardaphé. West Lafayette, Indiana: Purdue University Press, 1991.

JUSTIN VITIELLO

What I Wanted to Ask and Say Where and When This Book Was Conceived...

The summer of 1977, after I had taught a course at Temple University in Philadelphia on the literature, anthropology, and history of the Italian Diaspora, two things happened in Rome (where I was about to teach in that institution's program abroad) that sunk me deeper into the fields of Italic Studies:

1. I was delighting in the company of my Roman Communist friends and in the tepid evening at their favorite open-air trattoria near the Tiber when one *compagna* turned to me and blurted, *"ma, te, non sei italiano?"*

    "No, vedi, sono d'origine napoletana, ma nato a New York."
    "Eccezionale!" she persisted, *"quindi, sei ITALOamericano!"*
    "Giusto."
    "Allora, come mai parli italiano così bene?"
    "Bob," I shrugged, *"l'ho imparato a scuola."* At that moment, while I had studied and taught about the racism, bigotry, and persecution Southern Italians had encountered in United Italy since

1860 or so and in the United States since the 1880s, I underwent an epiphany that came not from my gray matter but from my medulla oblongata. Sure, as a scholar I knew that, as early as 1909, the "distinguished scholar and critic" Giuseppe Prezzolini had expressed a widely held Italian view that the major obstacle to sociocultural relations between Italy and America was the Mezzogiorno migrant. But, while I was raised to take pride in my origins—the cradle of the Renaissance and my grandfather's anarchist roots on the slopes of Vesuvius—I was still "fulminated" by my friend's quip, which was unanimously seconded by all our other progressive convivialists.

2. This episode, from which I emerged, luckily, without any scars (shame, rage, rancor, desire for cultural vendetta), but with a deeper sense of irony and self-irony regarding other people's ignorance in perceiving me and my *paisans* as WOPS, was also one of the inspirations for my first consciously Italian American work, a semi-autobiographical novella called *Confessions of a Joe Rock*. Therein, for the love of the dialects, or "little mother languages," I had grown up hearing and speaking in and around New York City as a child and juvenile delinquent, I created a protagonist whose father was Neapolitan but whose mother (unlike my German American one) was Puerto Rican. Integrating the Black speech to which I was exposed via rock-'n'-roll and my gang and work experience, I tried to interweave diverse traditional and subversive linguistic forms of my ancestral and acquired cultures.

Ever since that fatidic summer, I have committed myself to building a tri-bridge connecting Italy, Italo-America, and the United States. Perhaps, not surprisingly, I have found that the hardest ramps to reinforce are those between Italy and Italo-America. My cultural activism is not so arduous when I deal with students who take my courses on Italy, especially Sicily, and Italo- and multicultural America. They are surprised but happy to learn that, for instance, spaghetti and meatballs ain't Italian, there is no such thing as Italian cuisine (it's all regional, *vero è?*), Sicily has been for centuries the epicenter of major civilizations, and Italo-Americans are not Italian. No, my job is most frustrating when I encounter Italo-American artists, scholars, and intellectuals who insist on telling me what Italy is all about—occasionally in terms of mysterious somatic substances, abstractions, blatant errors, and even disinformation.

I must confess my major problem regarding these searchers for identities and truths in the Old Country: I suspect that they are groping not via anthropological and historical evidence but through illusions falsely rooted in filial pietism, nostalgia, and feel-goodism. These survival-guilt phenomena originating in what our immigrant relatives transmitted to us as obsessions for having "killed" those loved ones left behind in Italy have led to complex-ridden and unconscious states of anxiety accruing from those rites of passage, better termed traumas of uprooting (usually as expulsion for radically economic and/or political reasons). Consequently, related forms of culturo-pathology have taken fairy tale, Manichean courses—all good or all evil—that the disease of nostalgia generates. Therefore, convincing certain Italian Americans that they need to emancipate themselves from "incestral" ghosts before understanding who they were and are is a challenge similar to dancing through minefields. . . .

I suggest that the psychosomatic effects of traumatic migratory experiences are what most writers in this book—representative, I would venture to say, of most Italo-American authors, male or female—are still undergoing and, in the best instances, grasping creatively. With few exceptions, they know little of Italy and its languages, histories, and cultures, so they cannot verify if their images of their land of origins have anything scientifically (where *sciens* means "knowing realities") to do with that most complex of territories at the dead center of the Mediterranean. Thus, most Italo-American artists and critics, in this anthology and elsewhere, undergo various nuances of pride in being ersatz Italian, ambivalence about being so, shame and rage about suffering the stigmata of such a grandly illusory but prejudice-targeted identity, confusion as to a distorted memory of a past that mostly never existed, and affirmation of a pseudo-history that is, simultaneously, too glorious (see the Renaissance) and too sordid (see the Mafias).

For these reasons, and many more that it would take tomes merely to describe, I would argue that we should cease using terms like *Italian American* and *Italianità* to describe and analyze the eruption of creativity and knowledge we peoples of Italic background, especially women in the context of this book, have caused and witnessed in the last two or three decades. Let's face it: Most of us are still hyphenated and so much more American than Italian. Why not be honest? We are Italos! Ouch! Call "home"! They'll tell you so! Second, because the *sfumature* of the term *Italianità*—if you know your history—harkens back to a Mussolinian myth that the Duce coupled with Romanità to glorify his brand of fascist, imperialist, and racist propaganda to "create"—ex nihilo, ahistorically—the third and, fortunately ephemeral, Roman Empire. That is to say, *Italianità*, under Fascism, was a crucial, mystifying catchword evoked to bamboozle, homogenize and force Italians, who have never been of one race, to mobilize as cannon-fodder, baby-breeders, and one more fake Master Race, allies—virile, "naturally"—of the Nazis to boot.

Really, I do not think this historical context is what Italo-Americans want as a frame of reference while we continue to render and affirm our own ethnopoetics by creating it via every work of art and science we produce. Herein, it is best to become *genuini come il vino*. We are more than 90 percent American in our vision of a mythical, hopefully non- or anti-fascist Italy. Or, should I say mythical Italies, mostly Abruzzese, Neapolitan, Calabrian, Sigey? . . . Unless we are or become bilingual, live in Italy and know its contemporary history and culture, and can write novels like Umbertina (i.e., works of art truly rooted in an experiential and cultural knowledge of Italy), let's confess: Our Italies are mythic. Why not? All cultures, civilizations, and literatures originate in myths! They are, as the Greeks knew, the navel stones of creativity.

With various airs cleared, I can proceed to the questions I wanted to ask at the February 2000 Drexel University conference—"Italian American Women Writers"—where we conceived this book. But first a digression. At that occasion of the genesis of the nonparochial literary and scholarly activity that is the substance of this book, Professor Nunzio Pernicone, a major historian of Italian and Italo-American radicalism, graciously presided. Alas, he was too gracious, fielding the predictables: "Why are we Italian Americans the only (sic) ethnic group left that can be stereotyped in mass media? Why don't we get together like the Blacks (or against them)? Why the Mafia mystique? The Sopranos?" and so on. . . . At one point, I waxed rude, urging the indulgent in self-victimization to write for us bibliographies regarding the rich heritage of Italy and Italo-America, to invite us to lecture and do poetry readings, slide presentations, whatever, at their cultural centers. The result? Ongoing silence.

This kind of wallowing in a staged self-pity, a form of *omertà* that shields denial of one's own responsibility to become informed about one's heritage and the refusal to take the time and concerted effort to know Italian languages and cultures, has a long history that deserves many volumes to interpret and develop in creative and scientific terms. Furthermore, this perhaps Sisyphean toil would involve rectifying many filial pietistic pseudoworks of history, sociology, and literature our first- and second- and even third- and fourth-generation *paisans* have spawned. But instead of trying to separate the wheat from the chaff here, I would prefer to voice, softly, issues that should be critically addressed in continuing dialogues this book hopefully raises in its search for aesthetic, epistemological, and metaphysical truths.

1. Is there, in truth, a consciously constructed, unified female and/or feminist ethos/aesthetics of *Italianità*? Why and how or why not and how not? Should there be one anyway? If it does exist, can it be authentically rerooted in Italy and rerouted in the United States? How does or will it relate to marginal and mainstream cultures in both countries? If it does so, what are its literary, historical, and political consequences? Besides, "naturally," the self-interest and possible sellout some of us already in new culture clubs are wrapped in to self-aggrandize. . . .
2. Let us say that there is a truly unified poetics endemic to the context of this book. Is it genuinely rooted in anything recognizably Italian? Or should it best be considered and evaluated only as part

of American cultural and literary canons? Whatever the case(s), I would like to pursue the following issues Socratically.

a. If such a unity exists in literary and historical terms, does it because the major Italo-American women writers have worked together in a school, by empathy, or on their own to self-redefine their tradition(s) via identifications with a mostly invented, not remembered, cultural ethos/aesthetics?

b. What of their literary praxes? Do they assimilate with, border on, or even reflect the artistic heritages of Grazia Deledda, Sibilla Aleramo, Maria Messina, Elsa Morante, Maria Luisa Spaziani, and Amelia Rosselli? Not as far as I know. Ergo, do not these praxes have to be valorized, in precise terms, for what they contribute to an Italo-American women's Naissance?

c. If there is no unified poetics in the context in question, what has brought about the emergence of so many fine Italo-American women writers in so many publishing venues of poetry, fiction, essays, memoirs, and mixed-genre works? Bona fide literary schools? Friendship? Creative emulation? Cliques? Love-hate? The politics of culture? Or just some good writing in individualistic, American terms?

d. Finally, what criteria exclude lesser-known women authors of our ethnicity from our still submainstream? What generates divisions and, yes, cultural mafias (which abide in all ethnic literatures) in our schools and affinity groups? What should we make of those female writers who still do not "fit" in our anthologies and journals but only in their own creative universes? Perhaps we two editors of this book, willy-nilly, have included here some authors who will sink into oblivion and omitted others who will last, like Keatsian beauty, forever. How can we rectify such probable abuses of editorial power?

3. These questions direct me to another key reflection related to Italo-American women's self-inventing and creating of a unique literary tradition. How do they connect to and treat the mainstream Anglo culture? In ways that are Manichean, demonizing,

polemical, confrontational, oxymoronic, assimilational, bordering, nonexistent, irrelevant, revolutionary? Can the ancestral cultures they invoke in mythic dimensions be reconciled with modernist and postmodernist literary movements?
4. Whatever the state of the art of Italo-American women's literature, criticism, and scholarship—which, I believe, in this book are represented fairly well—how are they related to that of their male counterparts? Let us forget, as di Donato urged, the Macaroni Joes, and, I would add, the *paisans* who have sold out to old and new trends, and focus on the situation today: how do men and women authors of Italian descent support, resist, ignore, betray, back stab, lionize, and patronize and matronize each other? In cultural and editorial terms, do the "boys" still oppress the "girls"? Are some women complicit with this putative game at the price of cultural pimps' and procuresses' promotions? Or do they rebel effectively, creating integral, nonreactive alternatives? Is there a good chance that inter-gender dialogue in this context can eradicate or, at least, undermine our Old Boy and New Girl Clans so that quality work can receive the critical attention it deserves in Italo-American and mainstream venues?
5. Finally, I want to address specific issues raised at our Drexel conference and elaborated on in this book. Again, I try to do so maieutically (i.e., as a Socratic midwife), asking questions to encourage free, but parthenogenetic responses.
    a. Why do so many Italo-American writers—of whatever gender—still believe that aesthetic values related to ethnicity, religion, and family are like alcoholism (i.e., in the bloodstream) when, simultaneously, these artists strive for creative liberations, often in postmodern styles?
    b. Why do some of these writers still harp on themes of shame, rage, and pride *in re* somatic substances, myths, and the feel-goodism that perpetuates victimization when, instead, they could concentrate, so positively, on the country where the Renaissance bloomed and where complex civilizations—ancient, folk, medieval, modern, and contemporary—still exist.

c. Why can't most of us Italo-American writers overcome guilt, shame, nostalgia, and facile pride in our past, which by now is a pseudoheritage, and focus on the real literatures and histories of those Italic territories where so many dignified folk cultures, the ones closest to our backgrounds, have existed and still endure in part? By doing so, we could relate to and write about ways of life (not lifestyles) that are so much more conservationist and ecological than the mainstreams some of us strive to kow tow to, and, thereby, contribute to the consumerist poisoning of the globe. In other words, why are some Italo-American artists and intellectuals trying to become successful by conforming to a New World Order that is blighting and exterminating our ancient and living cultures?

d. Apropos of these traditional civilizations, so many of the writers included in and referred to in this book develop—as a dominant, positive image of cultural revalorization—the immigrant mother or grandmother. She, often counter to sociohistorical evidence, emerges as the empowering matriarch, openly rebelling against the Master of the Roost to pass on to future generations of women-to-be writers strong female, even feminist, identities—including nonheterosexual ones. *Olé!* But how can this phenomenon be analyzed in more social-scientific and literary critical terms, above all, when so many scholars and writers are still bound to pietistic notions of *la via vecchia, serietà,* and other protohistoric essentialisms? How can the matriarchs, super-conditioned to uphold patriarchy, be seen as unambiguous models of transgressive behavior and sexual liberation, especially when they were and often still are, to a great extent, complicit with the male-dominated, even mafiosa, society by teaching sons they have always been naturally better than daughters?

I am often tempted to rewrite and remake history—my own, my families', my peoples'—in the way I would have wanted it to be, reinventing and reliving Pirandellian masks and illusions to make myself feel better and to perpetuate hypocrisies and deceptions. But when I face squarely the psychic and metaphysical implications and consequences of such Orwellian doublethink and doublespeak, I confess merely to the attempt to create myths in fiction and poetry, not to that of devising any objective truths. As Ignazio Silone said in Fontamara, it is always crucial to call bread *bread* and wine *wine*. For some reasons hidden in the dark nights of my putative soul, his metaphors still inspire me to tell truths through art and science.

As a poet, I insist on exercising my inalienable rights of imagination. But, as a scholar, I must sift out the various truths—mythic, narrative, anecdotal, legendary, historical, even political—and tell them, with humility and skepticism, to avoid mystifying confabulations and blurrings of lucid distinctions vis-à-vis the various categories of human knowledge. That is what secular humanism, one of the greatest triumphs of Western culture, means. So, as some major presses are now publishing Italo-American works of, unfortunately, still uneven artistic and scientific qualities, I ask myself why some of us *paisans* are not more rigorous in affirming the highest literary and scholarly standards we can imagine and uphold, why we continue to mire ourselves in *cafonate* by perpetrating clannishness, why we often persist in contributing to the infamous stereotyping of us as buffoons scurrying to jump like toadies into literary mainstreams that, like Rachel Carson's silent springs, are irrevocably polluted. . . .

Mah! Basta! We need not compromise with any currents of mainstream or marginal cultures that seduce us to sell out, factionalize, self-aggrandize. Why should we? We have prime examples in this anthology of what we, mostly women, can contribute to the revitalization of multicultural American literature and scholarship beyond dominant and parochial philandering. Although all editorial choices and "cultural wars" are political, I would submit that, here, we editors have, resisting the Machiavellians and imperialists in our midst and at our gates, made the most honest, impartial, catholic, democratic decisions possible about what is worth publishing as exemplary in the given field. Struggling to overcome the implications of Fitzgerald's ending to *The Great Gatsby*—"So we beat on, boats against the current, borne back ceasely into the past"—and transcending our own personal literary tastes, we offer this book as a collection of essays to be valued in and of themselves, creatively and scientifically, and as a challenge to other *paisans* to produce the best of our art, culture, and knowledge.

Notate bene: As an existentialist "condemned to skepticism"—especially regarding my own assertions—I entertain the following doubts: by the time this book goes into print and on the market, the Italy a few of us know today will have changed radically. It will have become more and more American in what many critics of globalization see, not only as ethnocide, but as universal homogenization leading to onmicide. My peasant and shepherd friends in Sicily will be dying or dead. Their children, for whom they have sacrificed their ways of life to send to college, will have adopted lifestyles in neurotic, greedy rhythms with the Consumer Revolution—that major upheaval of the twentieth century which, according to Pier Paolo Pasolini, has transplanted the pseudo-Marxian ones.

Yet future anthologies, like this one, I hope, will continue to ask questions about the "eternal verities" that Faulkner spoke of in his 1949 Nobel prize–winning speech. In the heretical spirit of the great medieval French poet François Villon, they will query: "Where are the snows of yesteryear?" And they will demand answers regarding crucial questions to ensure the survival of arts, humanities, and sciences: "Where will the new flowers grow?" Let us grow with them! And make them grow healthier!

Contributors

Helen Barolini

Difference, Identity, and Saint Augustine*

I was thinking of the early church father Saint Augustine as I set out for Bordeaux, a place I imagined as a center of equanimity (unlike Augustine's Hippo) for its association with Michel de Montaigne, famous son and once mayor.

I admired the tolerant long view of Montaigne as much as I did not the constrictive one of the saint. I thought of Augustine as having given classicism the final push over the edge as the fifth-century World hovered on the brink of transition. After roistering through life the natural way, sated, he found later and more exquisite enjoyment in penitence and conjured up the dogma of original sin to inflict on his contemporaries and all Christendom for millennia to come. He gave the Western psyche guilt and remorse. Harsh he was after his conversion: Antifemale, antinature, antipleasure.

Is it now sign of my own abandonment of a certain recklessness of thought that in coming of age I have come home to Augustine? Not to his church or its dogma, nor to any church or dogma, but to the wide sweep of Augustine's prospect of life and our place in it as individuals.

In a world beset by ethnic divisions and hostility and unspeakable cleansings, it seemed problematic at best, in November of 1992, to

---

*Barolini, Helen. CHIAROSCURO. © 1999. Reprinted by permission of The University of Wisconsin Press.

attend a conference entitled "Interculturalism and the Writing of Difference" at the University of Bordeaux. I had been invited to participate in the section addressing Italian American literature. I liked the fact that writers from the so-called ethnic or minor groups were being perceived and studied as writers of difference—that opened a range of interest quite overlooked in American criticism where difference is often interpreted as simply making writers marginal.

"Common sense," says literary scholar Henry Louis Gates, Jr., "reminds us that we're all ethnics." Another truth should be just as obvious—that the relevant standard by which to judge writing is excellence, not national origin or gender.

My own belief is that any writer from a marginalized position is writing in the most American of traditions—that of the Outsider. So the conference was enticing, at the same tune that it was troubling. Should there be such an emphasis on difference at a moment in history when traditional unities of nations are coming apart on the basis of ethnic differences? The French playwright Bernard-Henri Levy has decried nationalism that deteriorates into tribal passions and produces opposition to all "Others" save one's own tribe. Speaking of a united Europe, he feels the best hope for Europe's future is integration. "But Europe is exactly what people don't seem to want today. They want identities. The great modern and murderous delirium in Europe is the folly of ethnic identity."

Stories of confusion and conflict proliferate, in Europe and in the United States, indeed in the world. "Catholic Indians Try to Reconcile 2 Traditions" reads a newspaper headline on a story of Native Americans trying to retain their native traditions as well as a religious identity. The son of slain radical Jewish leader Meir Kahane is reported as saying that killing Arabs is natural. The PEN American Center holds a symposium on how authors write through their cultural backgrounds, in which the question of ethnic identity, as opposed to some notion of "universality" keeps popping up. Letty Cottin Pogrebin speaks poignantly as both female and Jew of her feeling of "Otherness" in America as she examines her entwined background, attempting to integrate an identity that will be enabling rather than restrictive.

My own persuasion is that I can be no other than an American writer since I was born here and write in English; that I write also of Americans of Italian origin should not keep me from being a strand—thin perhaps and less brilliantly colored than others—but; nonetheless a strand in the total pattern of a many-hued national literature.

Along the way, I embraced my heritage, married an Italian writer, lived in Italy, learned the language, and intensified my writing and thinking as an American. Because she had never had the experience of living abroad for an extended time, I could understand Toni Morrison saying at the 1986 International PEN conference in New York City that at no moment of her life did she ever feel as though she were an American. On the other hand, no matter how out of place in the culture one might feel as a disaffected American, sooner or later there comes to the expatriate—even James Baldwin!—the inevitable realization that the language and the culture of birth constitute the homeland after all.

Thinking back, I am transported to my childhood, growing up in Syracuse in a house on James Street named for the land-buying grandfather of xenophobic Henry James. When the question of nationality came up on forms we children had to fill in for school, or for the YWCA, or for going to summer camp (and there were such forms in those days), I never knew what to put: was I American or Italian? My name certainly had a foreign sound, but there was no doubt that I had been born in the state of New York, and my parents, too. Though the records said I was American, from the start my soul wasn't persuaded.

I was a bookish child and my ambition to be a writer was at odds with my family. I did not live in a household of books being thoroughly read and then discussed and everyone keeping diaries like most American writers of my generation. I was not; say, a Eudora Welty who was read to "in every room of the house," whose fantasy was fostered by book-loving parents, and whose goals were not only praised but also obtainable in the Anglo-American context of who she was.

Names are powerful signals. Fifty years ago author John Fante, in his classic story "Odyssey of a Wop," wrote that when still a school boy he matched the sound of his surname against that of other Italian names only to be relieved that people could think he was French. Here is what

Dorothy Bryant, novelist and author of *Miss Giardino,* wrote me when I was compiling *The Dream Book:*

> Calvetti is my maiden name, and the childhood of Miss Giardino is my mother's childhood: I had another Italian name (Ungaretti in a first marriage) after that one. Under neither of those names was I accepted as an artist . . . I wonder if one of the reasons so many Latin women's "identity" is veiled by a WASP name is the necessity of escaping from everything else that may be imposed upon a woman along with that Italian name.

An Italian American surname sets up, I am still learning, barriers of prejudice in those circles of American literature that are hard to penetrate under the best of circumstances. Our names are an immediate signal of difference; Francesca Vinciguerra's strategic move to Frances Winwar was an ethnic change of identity rather than the gender one of George Sand, the Brontës, and George Eliot.

As black skin is what Henry Louis Gates, Jr., terms the "epidermal contingency" of African American writers, so Italian Americans seem to have a nomenclatural contingency. In my own life I went from one signaling surname to another when I married an Italian author and he and Italy became my education.

I began to understand that I could not be as centered in national identity as Antonio Barolini surely was. His name did not marginalize him or make him prone to labels; he was supremely at ease with the fact of his calling as a literary person without having to question his right to be, or whether he was odd to be. Italian literature was his unquestioned patrimony; and when he practiced it, he was automatically part of it. I began to see that American literature was not automatically mine; at best, perhaps, I could belong to a subgroup, as in being picked for a second-best sorority because of my background.

I was left with questions: How does one gain the attention of an excluding publishing world? Can Italian American women become writers out of the intercultural tensions of their lives? How do they use their individual selves narratively to oppose or understand the Otherness not only of the dominant society but of their gender opposite and even their family? What are the strategies to free the self and yet retain a rich tradition?

The price for admittance into our literature was to become a facsimile Wasp, a pact entered into by those past writer-critics Lionel Trilling and John Ciardi, both from ethnic backgrounds they wanted to get beyond. Lionel Trilling, a writer and professor of English literature at Columbia University, well assimilated into a world removed from his Jewish origins, personified the passage from "ethnic" to "in." It was he who objected that writers like Alfred Kazin were "too Jewish," too full of lower-class vitality and experience. It was Trilling to whom Saul Bellow successfully gave the lie when he created the Jewish novel, opening the way for the rest of us.

John Ciardi was of the Trilling persuasion that a homogenized "universal" American voice in the literature was, preferable to a rich mix of diversity. Ciardi, the one token Italian American in the American Academy of Arts and Letters, was reticent about his background until after the ethnic awakening. Then he rediscovered it in himself to the extent of being on the editorial board of several short-lived Italian American magazines, even though he discouraged authenticity in other Italian American writers.

In my own youthful lack of inner fortitude it hadn't occurred to me that they—Trilling, Ciardi, and the real Wasps—were wrong. The burden was made mine: either take on an ersatz Wasp veneer and become one of a whole nation of Huck Finns and Daisy Millers no matter what the blood said, or form a strong enough personal identity with which to oppose the blandishments.

But what was *my* identity? In Italy I was American, but here in the States I never was sure.

Now in a world fraught with many more drastic problems of identity than a literary one, we have to ask the question, What is Identity, after all? And does it matter? Don't we all, as in James Baldwin's pan humanistic view, contain each other: the male in the female, the female in-the male; white in black, and black in white? Is it really our life mission to stalk, to hunt down, to try to catch what is only a will-o'-the-wisp—that elusive notion of who we are that keeps beckoning us like a lure?

For if the journey through life is to maturation, then it is toward becoming a self, a distinct individual: realizing an identity. The main obstacle to overcome is dependence on authority in whatever guise-parental, religious, societal; political, literary. Such strength requires a buildup of one's inner core—that personal sense of and confidence in one's very identity.

This is in a way the tragic catch-22 of life. We have our mandate, but it is a vexed one: we cannot ever claim to have reached a perfect identity.

Idem, the same, is the Latin, root for Identity. *Identidem = idem et idem* again, and again the same. Identity, thus, is the fixed sameness and stillness that Saint Augustine attributes only to God, the eternal nonchanging: "who art not another in another place, nor otherwise in another place: but the same and very same, and the very selfsame."

Is it not hubris of the most extreme to fixate on a personal Identity, a tribal Identity, a national identity? Perfect sameness can only be an attribute of God.

A fixed sameness is not meant for us, the evolving.

Living in the world with each other, in time and space, we change, move, diversify, put our Self up against the Other to know ourselves and know we are all the Other. Just by living we impinge on each other. We invent each other, are part of each other's transformation. Our humanness is based on our difference. That was Montaigne's paradox when he said the most universal quality is diversity. Some four hundred years later, American scholars like Noam Chomsky suggest that "diversity might be structured into the human experience," that unity through homogenization—or universality—"betrayed a profound misunderstanding of the human condition." But just because we are human, we fret against that condition and covet what is God's—perfect stillness and repose and sameness in Identity. Only death gives that. Life is not a realization of identity after all, but always alterity.

Recognizing difference might, at least for Americans, soften the impact of the so-called Identity Crisis which we are supposed to transit in adolescence. It would sort out the problems inherent in too strict a reading of "ethnic identity." Ideally it would eliminate ethnic conflict and cleansing in the world if the reality is diversity and there can be no fixed Identity in a temporal world, where all is flux and change and re-formation.

And *that*, perhaps, frustrates us the most—i.e.; *never* completing the quest for Identity, which is sameness, which is God-and so we rage at Difference which is ourselves.

As the Spanish poet Antonio Machado put it; there is a rational faith, an incurable belief of humankind that Identity = reality, as if everything must necessarily and absolutely be one and the same. "But the other refuses to disappear . . . it is the hard bone on which reason breaks its teeth."

Only partially, at a great remove, can the still, calm center which is the God within be experienced through the deep meditation practiced by Yogis. But that is precisely a relinquishing of self-identity a stopping of reflexes and processes and cognitive thought.

What we could instead be working for and toward, with all the creative tension at play in differences and similarities, is an Ecology of Opposites. Indeed, without contraries there is no progression. Ecology as a network of interdependent relationships. Creativity is the force that deals with a changing reality as an individual emerges from a family or national or religious identity into the newness of self. Creative ethnicity uses one's background as a point of departure and is outward facing, evolving, tolerant, adaptable. Above all, it allows for self-definition, yet is not exclusive of relationships with other groups.

For me, the seeds of doubt regarding identity that had been planted in America evolved and bloomed in Italy. When I stood at the full-length windows of our Rome apartment, I looked down into the gardens of Palazzo Barberini where fierce Puritan John Milton (who in England inveighed against Catholics) had been the gracious guest of Cardinal Barberini; and I thought about the lesson of accommodation, easing myself out of being just this or just that and letting myself drop into the humanist perspective which was Milton's in Rome.

Finally, with my youngest daughter, namesake of the mysterious "foreign" grandmother of my childhood with whom I had never been able to speak, I drove to Calabria. It was mid-August; while my

Northern Italian husband and Roman friends shuddered at the unchicness and discomfort of such an undertaking, I went to find where my immigrant forebears had come from. Years later the figure of my grandmother emerged in *Umbertina,* my first published novel. I thought of my work as in the tradition of that most American of literary tropes, the Outsider theme. The Outsider, whether Hester Prynne or Huck Finn or Lily Bart or even the bleak and uneasy suburban characters in Cheever stories, makes up the strongest part of our literature. *Umbertina,* I felt, was an American novel about what it is to become an uneasy American, first by physical transplantation and then by spiritual birth, but in any case American.

My surprise was in my book's being received as ethnic. Did ethnic, mean not American, or was it code for "marginal," out of the mainstream? It is important to me as a writer that the name on the spine of my book *is* Italian, and that I am writing something different from the stereotypes of Italian Americans. But does that make me marginal?

Toni Morrison has said that unlike some Jewish or Southern authors who despise being labeled, she does not mind being called a Black writer, or a Black Woman writer. "I've decided to define that, rather than having it be defined for me," Morrison said. "I understand that they were trying to suggest that I was 'bigger' than [Black woman writer], or better than that. I simply refused to accept their view of bigger and better." And I refuse marginal.

It's the strategy adopted by Ralph Ellison when he says in *Invisible Man,*" I am invisible because people refuse to see me. . . . I myself did not become alive until I discovered my invisibility."

I know now that it's the premise of an exclusionary mainstream in American literature that's faulty. So-called mainstream critics (a kind of self-determined genus of judges), scorning what they call ethnic; marginal, minor, or exotic writing, and claiming standardized "universal themes" as the proper realm of literature, can distort the question of archetypal human feelings and establish barriers of class and elitism and insider hegemony in the name of universality. That kind of standardized universality as established by presumed literary judges of what is right and what isn't is very suspect. It begets the painful process of self-censorship as writers block themselves from their specific material and try for mainstream and what has been described as "the flattest possible characters in the flattest possible landscape rendered in the flattest possible diction."

The reverse of universal is not ethnic, but parochial.

The false hurdle presented to so-called ethnic writers is the charge of not writing universally if they use their own material. Maxine Hong Kingston, asked by Bill Moyers in a television interview to account for the popularity of "exotic" books such as hers; replied, "They are not exotic, they are about human beings. When you take a raw, human event and put it through the process of art, then it speaks to all people." Just before that interview, at a writers' conference, Maxine Hong Kingston had identified herself with minority writers and said how they all had to fight against the term Universal. Margaret Atwood immediately rescued Kingston (and rankled some others) by exclaiming: "Oh, Maxine, no one would think of *you* as a minority writer!" (Echoes of Toni Morrison's comments how "they" decide who's bigger and better!)

Minority or ethnic or exotic writers explore a fundamental theme: how to create oneself anew in an alien world. It is a restatement of the dialectics of identity. And that is a quest that speaks to everyone.

Nonetheless, I came to a personal recognition that as a writer I would always bear a vexed identity—either I would deny the part of myself that my name signaled, or I would integrate it fully to find myself marginalized.

Yet to be a writer is enough. I agree with what I sensed long ago and what Gabriel Garcia Marquez put into words: "The duty of a writer—the revolutionary duty if you like, is simply to write well." We do not have to carry banners, sprout labels of identity. And yet as Isaac Bashevis Singer has said, when he looks in the mirror in the morning, who looks back at him is a man of Polish-Jewish origin in whose skin he lives and writes. And so I, too, live in my Italianate, female skin and write from it.

That was the approach of the Bordeaux panel: by focusing on literary works by writers from so-called *minority* or *ethnic* groups in the United States (their italics), they would be better able to appreciate writing that was not per se marginal, but "of difference." How, they asked, can these literatures provide a symbolic locus for the specific emergence of a new, conflictual, and multifaceted self? How does work produced in a context of intercultural conflict and exchange take on an additional degree of complexity with regard to the formation of a literary self caught between alienation and alterity? How does the narrative self come to terms with the threatening presence of the (cultural) "Other" through a dialectical process of rejection and integration? Such questioning gives a thoughtful status to much American writing called "ethnic" that has hitherto been ignored, forgotten, or thought unworthy of appraisal.

This panel gave me the opportunity to ask what, in fact, *is* ethnic in a nation which is wholly composed of a multiplicity of national origins including the Britannic one of the founding fathers who bequeathed not only their language but the power that goes with it.

Because of the past stigma of being identified "ethnic," earlier Italian American authors either anglicized their names or kept their names but used material that did not at all touch their background, as for example, Hamilton Basso and Don DeLillo. One wonders what would result if writers like DeLillo or Gilbert Sorrentino or Frederick Tuten did deal with their Italian Americanness; or if an esteemed literary critic like Matthew Bruccoli had examined the writings derived from the great Italian exodus to America as well as those of Scott Fitzgerald.

In my own question of Identity I think of Nobel laureate poet and immigrant Czeslaw Milosz who said for all of us: Language is the Homeland. I cannot ever doubt what I feel so deeply—that I was formed in the English language and its literature and that is my homeland.

I think of my letter exchange with John Ciardi, who asked me rhetorically why I do not write like Eudora Welty—why I am not Eudora Welty. I am still taken by surprise. With Black writers triumphant and cultural pluralism in writing creating a new dynamism in the national literature, Ciardi was implying that I was still supposed to be a facsimile Wasp! And of the Southern school!

The ring of his words (though Ciardi's ears were stopped against the sound) was of the old assimilationist mentality which would have us all cast off our particular shadings and voice and put on the covering cloak of Waspness. To cover Ciardi's regressive advice there is Jean Cocteau's: "Listen carefully to first criticisms of your work. Note just what it is about your work that critics don't like—then cultivate it. That's the part of your work that's individual and worth keeping."

If Ciardi's questions proved spurious, those worth answering were put to me by Professor Jean Béranger of the University of Bordeaux: What is it you want, he asked, meaning perhaps all Italian American writers collectively: to disappear into the mainstream? to keep your distinct identity and not be absorbed? to be coequal and as American as the Anglos, or dissident, a different voice?

I can only answer for myself. I want to be considered as what I am, a part of American writing undivided by the mainstream or minority rankings imposed not by literary standards but by ethnic origins. I will keep my material, my particular referencing and voice, confident that it can convey values from difference as well as from conformity.

As I left for the Bordeaux conference a welcome piece of news accompanied me: the announcement that the Nobel Prize in Literature had been awarded to Derek Walcott, the Black writer from the West Indies, citing his "multicultural vision and commitment." The validity and vitality of what was previously spurned as ethnic writing were being recognized.

Despite the nostalgic laments from apologists for the exclusivity of "mainstream" work as *the* literary canon, the widening and opening of American literature is happening. In the great republic of letters are writers of all sorts: each caught in the paradox of striving for the fixed sameness of Identity while claiming complexity, yet never achieving it until repose comes in the fixity of Saint Augustine's selfsame God.

Mary Cappello

Breakage and Beauty*

> *What makes them Italian is a politics, or really class is what makes them Italian, not any daily reincarnations at the altar of the discovery of pasta, though it is worth considering how being citizens of the United States makes them critically long for a different identity, how they want to stake claims on Mediterranean sunlight, soil, sensibility and history, language and face. They know who they are. They have habits.*[1]

"Keep it simple" was a directive bequeathed me by my mother and her father, both of whom were lovers of language and its transformative possibilities, both of whom were poets. My mother, Rosemary Cappello, is a master of Haiku and purity of line. My grandfather, John Petracca, plied aphorisms, cryptic one-liners in his shoe repair shop, where he jotted onto fragments a spare prose that illuminated basic truths. But I ask myself, how can I "keep it simple"? How can I speak simply to the ways their work with words has shaped my aesthetic as an Italian/American woman writer? How can I keep it simple given the complexities of their lives?

Perhaps I can work by way of distillation to share with you how aspects of those lives underline my poetry and prose. If I try to "picture"

---

*Used with permission of Mary Cappello, University of Rhode Island.
[1] I am quoting from a work-in-progress that I delivered at the Drexel University Conference on Italian American Women Writers. This excerpt, entitled "A Discursive Double Portrait," is from a chapter of a book of experimental portraits in which I explore the forms that friendship takes between gay men and lesbians.

in some sense the origins of my writerly impulses, I imagine three images placed alongside one another, surrounded by a double frame.

The first image to comprise the triptych is of an immigrant man, barely educated, but who loves language, is compelled to write—stories, poems, daily thoughts, at least one novel—in both English and Italian. At some point in the 1930s, this man musters the courage to take himself into Philadelphia to attend writing classes at The Franklin Annex. This immigrant man, this would-be writer, is discouraged by his teacher, who tells him that his work is "too racial," by which we might assume he means too ethnic, too indisputably Italian.

Alongside this image is the figure of a woman, the immigrant's daughter, my mother, who finds herself unable to sit at the center of a room; who finds, when she enters the social body, when she enters public spaces, that she can reside only on the fringe, the edge, the margin.

And the third image is of this same daughter, my mother, who finds, decades after the dismissal of her father's work by his teacher, that when she sleeps, she is unable to dream. Attached to this image for me is a line of my mother's poetry. The poem, called "Shall I Tell You How I Spend My Day," closes with the lines, "I must forget who I am / If I'm to remember who I am. / I return to sleep."

The three images—of the immigrant man whose writing is too racial, of the daughter who can sit only on the edges of a room, of the daughter whose access to dreams is blocked when she sleeps—are nestled into a double frame. Along one edge of the frame runs the image of a little American girl whom the immigrant teaches to play the mandolin. The girl, who is my eight-year-old self, receives the gift of handwritten musical scores, the ABC's of timing, the cry and joy of folk tunes and operatic arias. Between the man (a man of few words) and the girl (a loud little girl) arises a language apart, a duet, a share.

Bordering this image, the little girl appears again. In this instance, she is in love with the sound of her mother's voice, and with the sheer vitality that IS her mother, most especially when her mother is in her books—reading—or at her desk—writing.

This is the tableau (at least a portion of the influence) against which or out of which the formal concerns of my writing might emerge. I am interested, for example, in an aesthetic of the "too, too." In a prose that exceeds limits, perhaps by extending into poetry. My baroque style might be my way of reappropriating the too-ness that was ascribed to my grandfather's work with words.

With regard to the second image in my triptych, I am interested, in my writing, in reworking relations to space. Increasingly, I need to trust the reader to be willing to get lost with me so as not to be trapped either at a center or on a margin.

Third, my writing attempts to decolonize the imagination so that I might rewrite my mother's resonant line—"I must forget who I am / if I'm to remember who I am"—to read, "If I'm to remember who I am, I must forget whom I've been made to become."

The current formal imperatives of my work are dual. I'm aiming for breakage and beauty. Perhaps it goes without saying that the beauty I am after comes as the result of a concentrated looking and listening. In a separate essay, I describe it as the difficulty and desire to achieve beauty and grace in an ugly world, not a beauty that would allow us to escape the ugliness, I try to explain, but a disruptive beauty. An interruptive beauty. A beauty that requires confrontation.

The desire to achieve breakage in my work has to do with my conviction that my immigrant ancestors found no objective correlative for their passion, for their longing. It seems necessary to me, then, to break old forms and attempt to create new ones that can accommodate the unspoken.

The church and the family. The family and the church. Like a hiccup, these constraining figures are invoked to describe and represent Italian American "experience." I eschew the family and the church as institutions that have conserved, indeed cloistered, Italian/American energies, activisms, languages, and desires. I can't not acknowledge, on the other hand, that both church and family make up a dream space for my work. Each cultivated at the same time that it strategically quelled my imagination. What I learned from my mother and grandfather was the importance of the *extra*-familial.

Letter writing was an important feature of survival for them both: to reach, extend, cross, converse, open, bridge, embrace, venture, invite. An extra-familial interest drives my most recent project—an extended meditation on the forms that friendship takes between gay men and lesbians, and in particular the friendship between an Italian/American gay man and myself. The extended prose poem that opens this book I call "A Discursive Double Portrait." It's an attempt to picture our interarticulated selves in terms of some of the languages—familiar and arcane, embracing and alienating—that narrate who we are. The formal impetus of the piece was inspired by piano music that I'd been listening to, a performance by Glenn Gould. I was having an encounter with the obvious: I had made the simple observation to myself that certain compositions for piano exploited the dualness that the instrument makes possible: music in which left is not subordinated to right but in which two intricate lines of signification are spoken, heard, sung, *played* simultaneously. This led me to consider if one could achieve with language what was possible in the left-hand/right-hand double narrative of the piano music I was listening to. And thus the experiment that I call "A Discursive Double Portrait."

Collaboration. Conversation. Duet.

I have tried to bring incompatible modes of address together in my academic writing—for example, poetry and theory and oral history; working class knowledge and the knowledge of the academic. I began in such work to try to tempt the form of the scholarly essay into different permutations, which basically meant for me trying to create polyphonic rather than univocal texts. The synthesis that emerged for me was a newfound interest in what is now being called creative nonfiction. Ideally, in this kind of writing, the scholarly and the poetic voice are not antithetical (as they are imagined to be in an anti-intellectual culture such as ours). They enable one another, do battle with one another, and make possible a new voice in the space between.

Night Bloom, my memoir, tries to bring three voices into the same space. In the acknowledgements to *Night Bloom*, I say:

> The rhythms of my mother's poems, which I, from an early age, memorized, are the heartbeat of the sentences herein.

> I use the work of my grandfather and mother to orchestrate three generations of voices that are exquisitely in tune and horrifyingly dis-

sonant at the same time. Working with my grandfather's journals posed a special problem because they are bilingual and I don't read Italian. Reading them I was ever encountering this great cultural loss. But the positive upshot was that this forced me to share his work with others who could translate, and this led to a dialogue on the work with people not in the family. I use my grandfather's work in some ways to understand the conditions of my mother's life. The way that their words affect the telling of the story is in the timbre of the voices and in the nature of what they observe. I was struck by how some trying aspects of the life my grandfather describes haven't changed in four generations, but I was also trying to learn to see in the visions that both my mother and grandfather create. The voice of the book is maybe an amalgam of these voices: I'm trying to hear their voices with as much clarity as possible at the same time that I'm trying to create a new, unheard, unspoken voice. A voice of what generations could not say.

Polyvocality. Boundary crossing. The invitation to wander. These are the current impulses of my work. Always hoping to cast the net wider and into unpredictable waters.

I will close with a short excerpt from another meditation on my aesthetic choices, "Voices in the Outer Room." This essay is an argument (in the form of a demonstration) for the development of, in particular, a queer aesthetic. The essay asks whether it is our charge as lesbian writers to hold a mirror up to our experience, to "self-disclose" (so often such narratives change nothing but succeed in flattening our lives), or to find the form that will answer to queer habits of being, radical sensibilities, and ideologies. The essay takes three different liminal spaces as its ground—a sickroom, a conversation on an airplane, and a Catholic confessional—to explore my own aesthetic process, the role played by randomness and interruption in that process, the complex presence of external and internalized (dis)embodied voices in my self-writing, and the desire through my work to create disruptive beauty. Maybe any writer, I reflect, needs as a starting point to identify the voices that her work is in conversation with. The essay is multivocal and multigenre (it moves between cultural theory and poetry), and it is necessarily shot through with memories, dreams, and what I call cinematographs. Past narratives, remembered scenarios, current dreams tell us what we didn't know about the past and fail to know about the present. I conjure those in order to better speak their languages or more fully realize how their language speaks me . . .

I close this writing to begin again. I return to my writing desk beckoned by the voices in the outer room. Are the lights off or on? Is the body coiled or extended? Is the ground close at hand or a plummeting descent? Hushed or exuberant, their silences as real as their murmurs, the voices of other lives subsist in an outer room. It might be the voice of my mother trundling like a sewing machine across a textured surface. It might be the voice of my father, yelling, grunting, breaking. Or the cavernous voice of a newscaster, the high pitched laugh of a visiting friend, the repeated clucking of a child tongue against its palate. It might be one side of a long and winding story told into a telephone receiver, the climbing, the tremolo of the soprano who lives next door, the banal chuckle of the salesman at the door, "al-righty," you can sense the sweet smell of his aftershave. It is Aunt Francis' voice from whom everything was taken too soon, robbed, her voice was thin; it's grandmother Rose's robust cackle; the rise and fall to emphasis of Uncle Joe's latest joke. It might be Aunt Josephine's whose voice was sped up since the death of her daughter, or Sister Mary Conrad's stern command. The voices are even as when affect is flattened by dark news and the movement of acts that must be carried out. Arrangements. The voices are forgetful of themselves, loose-tongued, and gay, clanking of party-goers. The voices are desperate whispers punctuated by sighs, punctuated by sobs. The voices speak of a person in an inner room, with hope or care; the voices have forgotten the person in the inner room, without regret, unaware. The voices are inconsequential, and profoundly there. You only imagine the scent of rose water, or an encroaching blue light, when all that is real is these voices, their necessary but meaningless utterance. These voices can never go where you are going, or come to your calling. Their nature is to remain on the other side of the door.

You write to remember their comfort. You write to give them bodies. You write to understand how they suspend your body in solitude or pain. You write so they will hear you. You write to be among them, or in spite of them. You write because it is the tone of desire that is the salve. You write because the tone has not been struck, has not been heard, of this desire. And tone is everything. You write to coax your own voice, your own listening. You write because you must pretend to know what they were saying while you were gone. You write because you don't want to be afraid of saying what the voices would tell you if they could, or what you would tell them. You write to check the impulse to tell them to stop making so much noise, because their din is too much, you write in reply to their comforting discomfort. You write because there is always an absent one among the many whose voice you crane to hear. Because the sound of a voice is better than the sound of a second-hand ticking in an empty room. In the hour of my need, I know that I will want the voice of my lover to sing to me.[2]

Works Cited

Mary Cappello. "A Discursive Double Portrait." In *Appearances: Scenes from a Queer Friendship*. Forthcoming.

---

[2]"Voices in the Outer Room." In *Lesbian Self-Writing: The Embodiment of Experience*. Binghamton, New York: Haworth Press, 2000, 41–58. Copublished simultaneously in *The Journal of Lesbian Studies* 4.4 (2000), 41–58.

I contemplate the role that letter-writing played in my mother's and grandfather's survival in an essay entitled "My Mother Writes the Letter that I Dream," in *VIA: A Literary and Cultural Review* 7, no. 2 (Fall 1996), 125–134, a Special Issue on Italian/American Women Authors edited by Edvige Giunta. A portrait of music lessons with my grandfather appears in an essay that contemplates the relation between mourning and making, loss, and creativity entitled "Shadows in the Garden: Poetics of Loss, Italian/American Style," In *Beyond The Godfather: Italian/American Writers on the Real Italian/American Experience*. edited by A. Kenneth Ciongoli and Jay Parini. Fairfield, CT: The University Press of New England, 1997, 126–149.

Rita Ciresi

Toward a New Catholic Novel*

The Italian-American Woman Writer and the Church

When I first received an invitation to participate in a panel exploring how Italian American women's writing compares and contrasts to more mainstream narratives, I felt writer's block for the first time in my life. Perhaps I was afraid that what I claimed about my own writing would not hold true for other female authors who write about Little Italies. Maybe I was afraid to intellectualize, and thus stymie, what I loftily described (as a college sophomore) as my creative process. More than likely I just heard my mother's voice in my head saying, "Nobody wants to hear nothing about how you feel, so *stai zitta* already."

Gradually, it dawned upon me that although there may be many different ways of being Italian American, and writing about that experience, most Italian Americans would agree that our sense of ethnicity stems from ordinary aspects of our lives: the language we speak, the neighborhood we live in, the size and closeness of our family, and even the food that gets put on our dinner table. I thought: a lot of us may mourn the passing of our old neighborhoods, but we still call our

---

*Used with permission of Rita Ciresi.

brothers and sisters once a week and still say *salut* when we lift a wine glass. I thought: a lot of us still decline to eat meat on Fridays, but do we attend church with much regularity? Statistics suggest that Italian Americans have fallen away from the religion that once was such a vital part of our lives. Yet religion has continued to be a strong presence in Italian American storytelling.

So God gave me my subject matter; I decided to focus upon one facet of ethnicity—religion—in my presentation. I decided I would try to convince readers, mostly through my own storytelling, that the Italian American narrative is a natural continuation of a literary tradition known as the Catholic novel and that many Italian American women authors write about Catholicism as a way of discovering how the church has formed their characters' female identity.

In 1984, critic Richard Gilman published an article in the *New York Times Book Review*—"Salvation, Damnation, and the Religious Novel"—which proposed that the Catholic novel was a dying form. Readers and writers, he argued, no longer subscribed to the same concepts of sin and salvation put forth by Francois Mauriac, Georges Bernanos, and Graham Greene. The soul no longer was a viable fictional entity. The new Catholic novel, said Gilman, came from the pen of authors such as David Lodge and Mary Gordon, who grew up in the church but did not necessarily accept its dogma, or converts such as Muriel Spark (born of a Jewish father and a Presbyterian mother) who present a more dispassionate and Anglicized version of spirituality.

I'd like to argue that the Catholic novel is indeed very much alive, for the rise of the Italian American novel (and its close cousins the Irish American novel, the Polish American novel, the Mexican American novel, and so on) represents a new incarnation of this religious genre. American immigrant literature always has concerned family, food, work, money—and their relationship to faith. Because the vast majority of Italian American authors grew up in the Catholic church, their stories reflect their religious tradition. Whether or not Italian American authors choose to confirm or reject, celebrate or criticize their faith in their narratives is an open question. The church, and issues of moral choice, are plainly present in our fiction. Although some might argue that no Italian American novel is complete without a good, steaming plate of pasta appearing on the main character's table, others might legitimately claim it takes a stained-glass window, the smell of incense, or a ruler-tapping nun to make the narrative feel authentic to the Italian American experience.

When young, Catholic authors were taught to examine their conscience carefully. Although we may no longer make the sacrament of confession, through the act of writing, we make good confessions for our characters. We tell the stories of their transgressions and show their chances for redemption. Most importantly, we show them grappling with choices: between good and evil, and right and wrong.

I cannot claim to know the motivations and religious history of other Italian American authors whose work explores Catholicism—Tina de Rosa, Giovanna Capone, and Tony Ardizzone immediately come to mind. I can only confess why I myself write Catholic confessional tales. I'd like to begin with a memory from my own girlhood. When I was a child, the youngest of four daughters, my maternal grandmother presented to one of my sisters a porcelain doll dressed as a nun. Nun Doll, as she was reverently called, wore a full black robe and habit, and was outfitted with black rosary beads and a silver crucifix. In true nun style, her hands were hidden beneath her wide sleeves, and upon her nose, she wore silver spectacles rendered slightly less severe by the absence of glass or plastic lenses. Unlike the nuns I knew, who bore scowls and frowns and threatening names like Sister Paulinus and Sister Saint John of the Cross, she wore upon her bisque face a demure and understanding smile.

I really liked my sister's nun doll. No, let me be honest: I *lusted* after her. She seemed so petite, so content, and (as a bride of Christ) so *complete*. My sister, however, hardly seemed thrilled with the gift. "What am I supposed to *do* with this nun doll?" she asked me. It was a true moral dilemma. God knew we couldn't make new clothes for Nun Doll. And God forbid we should undress her, even though we did peek beneath her skirts and affirm that she wore a pair of lacy bloomers underneath. Would God forgive us if we made up stories about how Nun Doll, just like Maria van Trapp in *The Sound of Music*, got into trouble with Mother Superior for being late to meals and singing in the abbey?

Beyond pretending that Nun Doll could sing "The Hills Are Alive," my sister and I found her too fine, too pure, to play with. On the other hand, we had no trouble figuring out what to do with the other, normal dolls we were given that Christmas—cheap knock-off versions of Barbie and Midge. We shellacked their hair with Dippity-Do and used our Bic clics to draw green eyeliner and red lipstick on their pale faces. We colored their fingernails and toenails bizarre colors like black and purple before such urban grunge even became fashionable. We stripped these dolls naked on a regular basis and outfitted them with real mink coats fashioned from our worn-out mittens, and fabulous evening gowns made from dust cloths glued with glitter. In our imaginations, we took these trumped-up hussies to heathenish places: Manhattan, Atlantic City, Las Vegas. When my mother—who did not approve of these busty, tiptoed celluloid specimens of Womanhood—called us to put down our toys and finish our homework, we twisted the heads off our dolls and stuck them on the ends of our pencils, where they bobbed up and down as we practiced our Palmer penmanship and figured our long division.

Unlike Nun Doll, these beheaded gals exhibited every vice known to women. They stole, lied, wore diamonds, and cavorted with playboys and cowboys and bookies and other evil men. In the end though . . . in the end . . . they always woke up one morning and realized they could not keep up their sluttish ways forever. They repented, settled down, and agreed to marry their childhood sweetheart (usually called Jake or Chip). After an elaborate wedding (staged on top of an overturned shoe box, with a piece of cheesecloth functioning as the veil and train), the new bride moved into a split-level in the suburbs, and had many, many, many kids (even though Jake or Chip was not Italian).

Unbeknownst to me, the long, drawn-out stories I created about these bad, bad dolls already placed me, however precariously, in a literary tradition. In the typical Catholic novel declared dead by critic Richard Gilman, the main female character was tempted by (and succumbs to) sin, but was presented with some method of redemption. Conflict arose as she struggled to determine whether or not she would choose right or wrong—the path to perdition or the path to morality—the handsome, hunky-looking guy or the stern but forgiving God.

My dolls always chose God, but got the guy, too! This was hardly realistic—and years later, I realize, hardly very feminist—but all writers, whether they are four years old or forty, must follow the lead of their characters, and this was the way I saw the story unfolding.

I didn't plan on becoming a Catholic writer or writing about moral choice. In fact, I didn't plan on authoring books at all. I wanted, first and foremost, to break way from the teachings of the Church by leading a dissipated life. I thought I'd set up an easel on the banks of the Seine and paint great landscapes and portraits (while smoking *Gaulois* and wearing a black beret). After an art teacher pointed out that my sense of color and perspective were skewed, I thought I'd enter the next-best bohemian profession. I thought I'd be an actress until I realized how clammy my hands (and my armpits) became beneath the stage lights, and how pronounced my stutter became when I fished for a line that had failed to crystallize in my memory.

I couldn't paint. I couldn't act. And because my parents did not have money to send me to much-coveted lessons at the local hangout for would-be hussies, Miss Myra's School of Dance, what else could I do that was profane, or at least impious? I could lie. I could tell stories. My first inclinations toward storytelling came during mass, where hypnotized by the flickering vigil candles, I zoned out on the boring sermon and made up tales to amuse myself. Bowing my head, I considered all the bad things I (and my imaginary characters, no longer dolls) had done that week—and then my mind strayed onto all the bad things I (and they) still wanted to do.

The possibilities were infinite. Inspiration for much of the wild fiction I constructed in my head came from *The St. Joseph Baltimore Catechism*. This tome—printed in gray, black, white, and a sickening orange-red—pontificated (sometimes in coy and incomprehensible ways) against near occasions of sin. As if they were as entertaining as the Sunday funnies, I read and reread the catechism's crude drawings that cautioned against "immodesty in dress (especially in women)" or "bad companions" who could trick us into entering the local candy store and convince us to filch a Milky Way. I was equally intrigued by the drawings labeled THIS IS GOOD (which showed a bride at the altar modestly accepting a ring from her betrothed), and THIS IS BETTER (which showed a novitiate kneeling at the altar to accept her vows as a bride of Christ).

From the *Baltimore Catechism* to the infamous Index, the church always has strongly condemned indecent books, plays, and motion pictures. Yet it was easy to see that the seven deadly sins the *Catechism* warned us about—pride, covetousness, lust, anger, gluttony, envy, and sloth—formed the basis for the greatest stories ever told. Art, we were taught, was covert and dangerous. If we craved a good story, we were supposed to turn to the Bible. But unless these biblical stories starred Charleston Heston and other near-naked hunks in loincloths—and were accompanied by rousing Hollywood scores—they bored me. So the flood. So the ark. So the forty days and forty nights. Enough already. I liked characters who dared to do wrong, and do wrong, and do wrong—until they got into so much trouble they had to get down on their knees and pray for mercy.

Many writers who explore morality, Catholic or otherwise, have found their inspiration in children's literature, which—as critics Bruno Bettelheim and Alison Lurie have pointed out—represents the ultimate in transgression. Those of us who grew up within the constraints of Catholicism know just how early and how easily we were seduced by such naughty tales. Take, for example, Dr. Seuss's *Cat in the Hat*. How could a child so drilled in the Ten Commandments fail to fall in love with the cat—a very bad creature indeed, who unleashed pandemonium, dirt, chaos, and Thing One and Thing Two into the clean and orderly home of the innocent boy and girl left by their mother to play by themselves. Dr. Seuss's didacticism is lost on the average child reader. Although the author was careful to include the moral, scolding voice of the fish, who cautions the boy and girl against the wiles of the cat ("he should not be here while your mother is out!"), many a young and impressionable Catholic reader rooted for the naughty feline with his strange and sick machines to prevail (all the while feeling guilty for even contemplating the triumph of wrong over right).

I loved all these wayward literary characters: Curious George, who called the fire department when there was no emergency; Peter Rabbit, who, ignoring the counsel of his mother, lost his coat and ate himself ill in the lettuce patch; Peter's wayward cousin, Benjamin Bunny, who stole onions; and the consummate liar Pinocchio, who was a rotten son and a bad judge of human behavior. Mary Lennox in *The Secret Garden* thrilled me simply because she was "the most disagreeable-looking child ever seen . . . a sickly, fretful, ugly little baby" who became a "sickly, fretful, toddling thing." Finally, who could resist Jo March of *Little Women*, who climbed trees, whistled, cut off her hair, and wrote lurid prose?

I did not realize how important these tales of sin and ultimate redemption were to me until I started to write, and learned that misbehavior was the stuff of good stories. When I sat down to write my first novel, *Blue Italian*, which is about an interfaith marriage, I naturally found myself exploring the effects of Catholicism and Judaism on the main characters. But religion took even greater importance in the writing of my second novel, *Pink Slip*. The narrator of the novel is a twenty-five-year-old woman from a working-class, Italian American background. Lisa Diodetto is a would-be novelist who is at odds with her family, her employer, the God she isn't sure she believes in, and herself. The sources of Lisa's trouble are her mouthiness and her overactive imagination. She wants to have a good relationship with her sister and mother but ends up quarreling with them. She wants to climb the corporate ladder at Boorman Pharmaceuticals, where she works as an editor and writer, but she sabotages her success when she ends up in bed with her boss, the son of a Holocaust survivor. She wants to write a novel that will "press upon readers' chest so hard it made them hear their own heartbeat," yet her pen bleeds only potboilers. She wants to be a good friend to her cousin Dodie, who is the family outcast because he is gay, but ultimately she fails him.

Pink Slip is a coming-of-age story. At the end of the novel, Lisa has achieved a greater moral awareness. Not so, however, in my short-story collection *Sometimes I Dream in Italian* (Delacorte, 2000). These linked stories trace the youth and young adulthood of two sisters, Angel and Lina Lupo. Angel, the narrator, is less attractive than her older sister Lina. The wilder Lina gets—swearing, smoking, hanging out with boys—the more insular and resentful Angel becomes of the way Lina attracts attention. Angel wants to be pretty and vibrant, but as she attempts to emulate Lina, she only becomes more morally corrupt. Spiritually, she feels empty, but she has grown far beyond her family and can't return to the church she once so bitterly resented. The two sisters in this book long for something more meaningful in their lives, yet they have to turn continually to the past to find any significance in the present moment.

Readers often ask authors: How much of your story is true? I fabricate ninety-nine percent of what I write, but there is an essential one percent that comes through—and that one percent usually concerns the religious experience of my characters. Like everyone else on the planet, I've had a few "dark nights of the soul." These moments—and hours—in which I have questioned my faith in myself and in God have helped me write about Italian American women who live conflicted lives—who say prayers every night but who wake up in the morning and reach for a leopard-skin purse and high heels instead of a rosary and a habit.

Works Cited

Gilman, Richard. "Salvation, Damnation, and the Religious Novel." *New York Times Book Review* 1984.
Burnett, Frances Hodgson. *The Secret Garden.* HarperCollins, 1987.

Louise DeSalvo

Breaking the Jar/Mending the Jar*

It is 1983. I am on a very small airplane, flying from Boston to Maine, to give a series of talks at Colby College about my work on Virginia Woolf. I have published two books—one about how Virginia Woolf composed her first novel; another, an edition of an earlier, more radical and political draft of her first novel, *The Voyage Out*. I plan to write a book about Virginia Woolf's abusive childhood. I also have written a short memoir, "A Portrait of the *Puttana* as a Middle-Aged Woolf Scholar," for *Between Women*, a book I am coediting with Sara Ruddick and Carol Ascher.

Writing *"Puttana"* is the first time I have written about my own life, the first time I have spoken in a memoirist's voice, and the first time I have written the unlikely narrative of how an Italian American woman like myself, a daughter of working-class parents, has come to write about a privileged writer like Virginia Woolf. Writing this essay is the first time I define myself as an Italian American writer, the first time I contemplate how my ethnic identity and class of origin influence my life and work.

The unlikely story of my life's journey, of writing my life, is driven home on this flight, which has, so far, been thrilling. I am in a six-seater plane. The pilot has hugged the magnificent coast, has flown low

---

*DeSalvo, Louise. "Breaking the Jar/Mending the Jar." Copyright © 2003 Louise DeSalvo.

enough that we can see the waves pounding the rocks and the salt spray pluming the air.

Soon, the plane banks, heads inland, descends. "Below," the pilot announces, "are the tracks of the Maine Central Railroad." I burst into tears. For my maternal grandfather, Salvatore Calabrese, the one I write about in my memoir *Vertigo*, the one I write about now, worked on these tracks at the beginning of the century.

The richness and sorrow of this moment is evident to me immediately. For it is my grandfather's journey here, to the United States, that has made my work as a writer, as a thinker, possible. Without his emigrating, without his working on the railroad to support his family, without his devotion to a small girl who did not speak his language because her mother thought that speaking his language would impede her, I would surely not be here on this day, flying below the clouds, above the rails, on my way to giving a lecture about the life of this famous and privileged woman writer—a writer, I realize years later, who would never take tea with the likes of me, who would have been horrified that someone Italian American, someone formerly of the working class, would be writing her life. Without his emigrating, where would I be? In the South of Italy, somewhere, I imagine, poor as he was, uneducated in all likelihood, and working the fields.

* * *

In writing "*Puttana*," I have had no models. As I write, there are, to my knowledge, no memoirs written by Italian American women about their lives that can help me. That I know of no such works does not strike me, at the time, as unusual. That I have not read a single work written by an Italian American writer in high school college, or graduate school does not strike me, at the time, as unusual.

I feel very much a pioneer in doing this work, and this does not scare me. The style that I find myself using is not like anything I have read, not like anything I could have imagined myself writing. It is certainly not reticent, mannered, and highly inflected like the style of Virginia Woolf, my heroine.

If a model exists for "*Puttana*," it is Joyce Cary's *The Horse's Mouth*, a novel about creativity that I adore—that I read and reread. For creativity is a mystery to me and I want to fathom it, in myself, in others, in Virginia Woolf. The diabolical humor Cary uses, the over-the-top painting that the artist Gulley Jimson undertakes, the beautiful and painful musings of his psyche, make a profound impact on me. Although I admire Jimson, the artist, I do not like the way he treats women. I suspect that somewhere in his past, he has suffered a deep, unimaginable wound.

It is an arch, smart-assed, reflective, deeply personal voice that springs to the page as I write "*Puttana*," as if someone else is writing it. For until this moment, although the conclusions I reach in my academic work are considered radical, I have heretofore written a formal academic prose learned in the academy, one that involves an erasure of the self rather than its expression.

At the time, I believe that the plot of my life is that of the "American dream." Also, I think that I write about Virginia Woolf because our struggles are similar: we are both women and this erases the differences between us.

I discuss how my becoming a critic and a writer, though, given the fact of my gender and my heritage, is unusual. I do not realize that I write about Virginia Woolf because we are both incest survivors. Nor do I understand that I am writing about Woolf from the margins. For as an Italian American, I am an outsider to privileged culture, so that my critique of British imperialism in my work on Woolf is rooted in my personal history and in the fact that my people were colonized. Though Woolf herself condemned British imperialism in works like *Three Guineas*, the people of her class were nonetheless privileged and colonizers. The irony of my writing about Woolf, given my class background, escapes me.

Virginia Woolf had visited Italy. While I was writing "*Puttana*," I also was editing a diary she kept on a journey there. She described Italians as vaguely repellent creatures. She said she couldn't understand their emotionality and didn't connect works of art she saw in museums with the people she passed on the street. Still, when I am writing "*Puttana*," Woolf's portraits of Italians do not bother me. She is my heroine; she can do no wrong. I find her descriptions amusing; I do not understand that it is someone like me whom she is describing.

Writing this essay is a turning point in my life, for I can never approach my writing again without being aware that I am not just any writer, but that I am an Italian American writer. Glad as I am to discover this, this identification sits heavily upon me. To reclaim a history of privilege is one thing, but to claim a history of poverty is quite another. Although, in the year 2001, I still do not yet know the whole story, in writing "*Puttana*," I learn enough about my origins to cause me much pain.

Even as I am shifting my identity and realizing that I am not just any American, but a "hyphenated" American, like so many other Italian Americans of my generation (children of the children of immigrants), I am still only vaguely aware of why my forebears came to the United States. I am only vaguely aware of what being an Italian American really means. I believe, for example, that we are assimilated Americans. I do not yet know what being a Southern Italian American means, although I am one. I am completely unaware of the hidden history of persecution, racism, and exile that has shaped my people and my personal history. It is not something my parents told me, not something that we talked about at home.

What it meant that my grandparents were Southern Italian, I did not know when I wrote "*Puttana*." I did not learn about this meaning until I was in my fifties, and not from my family, but from conversations with the Italian American scholar Edvige Giunta, and from reading books she suggested to me like Richard Gambino's *Blood of My Blood: The Dilemma of the Italian Americans*. As a girl, the Italy my parents claimed was that of Dante, da Vinci, Puccini, and Caruso, and this was the Italy I was told about, not the poverty-stricken part of Italy that my grandparents left under desperate circumstances for the hope of a better life in the United States.

In the 1940s and 1950s, many Italian Americans, like my parents, buried the past, perhaps because it was shameful, and tried to assimilate, perhaps because it was necessary. It was, in part I think, because of the war. It was also the ethos of the times: racial and ethnic differences were not valued but condemned and ridiculed, the histories of grandparents buried. Still, I think, there was something about the past that my family considered shameful, and so they did not share it.

I knew my grandparents came from Italy, but I did not really know from where, nor did I ask. My grandfather's last name was Calabrese, and I knew there was a Calabria, somewhere, so when I was asked, that's where I said we were from. Nor did I know why they emigrated, what their lives had been like in Italy, nor anything much about their lives in the United States.

What I knew, I knew from firsthand experience: that none of my grandparents spoke English, that they (and we) lived in working-class Italian neighborhoods, and that they cooked foods that I didn't learn to like until I was a grown woman—which is to say I knew almost nothing about them at all.

I began to learn when I turned fifty, while writing *Vertigo*, which I undertook because Rosemary Ahern, then an editor at Dutton, suggested that I write it. She had read "*Puttana*," thought a book-length memoir about an Italian American life would be an important contribution to American letters, and contacted me. I am extremely grateful that Rosemary, an Irish American woman, insisted that this Italian American woman explore her ethnic past, for if she hadn't, I never would have.

In revisiting my past, while writing *Vertigo*, I learned much about myself and my parents' lives. My grandparents' pasts, our history as Southern Italian Americans, though, I wasn't quite ready to encounter.

But I am ready now. Had anyone predicted in the 1970s and 1980s, when I was writing about Virginia Woolf, that in the year 2001, I would be editing a collection written by Italian American women and writing about my Italian grandparents, I would have told them that they were crazy.

Then I wanted a subject of significance, and Virginia Woolf was, I thought, such a subject. My grandparents' lives weren't especially important, not even to me, though Virginia Woolf herself stated that the important lives to write were the lives of the obscure.

* * *

Why the change in my work? Why the shift into writing memoir? For one thing, the positive reception of my memoiristic writing by critics and general readers revealed that my story about my working-class Italian American past was significant to others. Also, reading the work of other Italian American women writers, most especially Carole Maso, inspired me to continue writing about my family and showed me how the writing could be accomplished.

When I read *Ghost Dance*, I had not yet begun writing my memoir *Vertigo*. However, Maso's portrayal of how Vanessa Turin describes her mother was extremely important to me, personally and, in time, artistically because of how she describes the impact of a "mad" mother upon her daughter, what she says about the character of the writer, and what she says about the potentially healing power of art. I admired, too, the density of meaning in her work, and it is an effect that I strive for in mine (though my prose is not evocative, poetic, and imagistic as Maso's is).

Maso's character, Vanessa Turin, struggles with what I also try to describe in *Vertigo*: the discovery of the reasons for a mother's depression, the problems an "unmothered" daughter faces, the attempt to use writing to heal the damage from emotional neglect. In *Ghost Dance*, Vanessa tries to discover her mother's history, and she realizes she must tell her mother's story so that she can cease being her mother's captive. This, I believe, is the quintessential woman's narrative: discovering the mother's story to understand the self, to embrace the mother, but also to be free of her.

* * *

Works of art are not single growths, Virginia Woolf stated. They emerge within a tradition. Knowing that there is a growing, sturdy tradition of Italian American women writers helps an emerging writer learn from the past, garner support from pioneers, and move on.

What has influenced my continuing to write memoir, too, is an important emerging grassroots movement, and a literary criticism, both spearheaded by the work of Edvige Giunta. Slowly, painstakingly, her work and that of other critics, writers, and scholars (like that of the editors and contributors involved in this project) is creating an audience for Italian American literature in the United States and in Italy, and a forum for its discussion and study in the academy, both here and abroad.

That works describing Italian American life are taken seriously and are not ridiculed or ignored impels the writer of such works (someone like me) to write such works again, and, yes, again. It takes someone with a skin considerably thicker than mine to write a kind of work, have it ignored, and return to the writing of this kind of work again. If *Vertigo* had been ignored or ridiculed (though the works of Italian American writers are largely ignored or written about disparagingly in, for example, *The New York Times*), I suspect that I would have gone back to writing the lives of famous, privileged women. I would have abandoned the continuing examination of my life and that of my grandparents. Such is the power of reviews and criticism. (Tillie Olsen has already said this in *Silences*.)

* * *

Once, when I was a child, after seeing pictures of Italy in the *National Geographic*, I asked my maternal grandfather why he left Italy, and he told me, "You can't eat beauty." He says this in an Italian that I have never really learned, never really spoken, and that my mother has to translate for me.

"You can't eat beauty?" I ask my mother what this means. She tells me it means that her father was poor—that he came to the United States so that he could earn a better living, and that, when he came here, he worked on the railroad, like many other Italians.

She does not say (perhaps she herself does not know) that in Italy people like my grandfather lived through periods of semistarvation punctuated by famine; that there were few sources of employment for men; that cheaper sources of wheat were making its cultivation increasingly unprofitable in Italy; and that peasants like my grandfather, whose family had worked as laborers in the wheat fields of the South for generations, suddenly found themselves without work. This period coincided with the need for cheap labor in the United States; hence, his emigration.

I did not know these things then because no one in my family told me, because no one in my family talked about *la miseria*, for it was far too shameful a history to claim, as if being unable to work was your fault, your problem, not a problem over which you had no control.

Until the time that I write *Vertigo*, I have lived under the guise of being an assimilated American. In writing *Vertigo*, I learn just how unassimilated I am, just how unassimilated my people are. These insights empower me and infuriate me. I realize that I can never write the same way again. After this moment, there is a ferociousness to my work that scares even me, for though I am routinely afraid of small things (going to the market, making a shopping list), I am not afraid of difficult things (like taking on a powerful literary establishment, like writing against the grain, like writing about abuse and violence).

* * *

I am the first person in my father's family to complete grammar school, to complete high school, the first person in my mother's or my father's family to go to college, to get an advanced degree. Salvatore Calabrese, my maternal grandfather, who worked on the railroad, emigrated to the United States from a small village near Bari on the Adriatic coast in the south of Italy. He came from a peasant family, and as a small boy, he worked the fields with his father and mother.

Recently, my father told me the story of how, on a particularly difficult day, when my grandfather's small hands were covered with cuts from the stalks he was binding after his parents cut the wheat, he looked up to the road that was high above the field and saw a small boy about his age, walking along the road, carrying a book bag.

This was at the end of the nineteenth century, well after 1860, that year that is the great divide in Southern Italian history, when the peasantry became increasingly poor, increasingly despised, increasingly unable to extricate themselves from debt—a time when there was never money enough or food enough, though families toiled from before dawn until after dusk and they lived lives of virtual indentured servitude.

"Papa, where is that boy going?" my grandfather asked, looking at the boy walking alone on the road, for a boy walking alone on a road in this part of Italy was an unusual and wondrous thing.

"That boy," his father said, "is going to school."

"Papa," my grandfather said, "I would like to do that. I would like to go to school."

"Figlio mio," his father said, "you cannot do that, you cannot go to school."

"But why can't I go to school Papa?" my grandfather asked.

"You cannot go to school," his father answered, "because you are a peasant and your lot in life is to work the fields."

"But Papa," my grandfather said, "what about my children?"

"Your children," his father answered, "cannot go to school, for they, too, will be peasants. They, too, will work in the fields like you."

As my father tells the story, my grandfather paused for a moment, looked again at the boy on the road, and said, "But papa, my children's children. My children's children, they will go to school."

According to my father, though poverty was an impelling cause for my grandfather's emigration, wanting his descendents to be able to go to school, like that boy on the road, was the major reason why my grandfather emigrated to the United States—so that his children's children could go to school.

I am the eldest daughter of his only child, a daughter, and I have gone to school, and I have become a teacher and a writer. Though I am certain that my grandfather would have been very proud of my having become a teacher, and though I am fairly certain that my grandfather would have been proud of the fact that I have become a writer, I am quite certain that my grandfather would not have liked that I have written about my family. For there were always secrets in my family (that my mother's mother had died; that the grandmother I knew was her stepmother; that after her birth mother's death, she had been abused by her caregivers; that she had been institutionalized; that my grandfather drank too much; that my father was violent; that my sister killed herself; that I was sexually abused by someone known to the family). Things were not talked about, much less written about.

Still, schooling was always encouraged in my family. My mother went to high school and stopped only because the family needed her income to remain afloat. From when I was very small, as I write in *Vertigo*, everyone took great pride in my academic accomplishments, the men in my family as well as the women. That I would become educated was assumed. That I would become a writer was never imagined. Or was it?

* * *

My father, who fixed the house we moved to in Ridgefield, New Jersey, made me a special desk that fit into a small, triangular space at the top of a flight of stairs. He took time and trouble with this desk, though it was made of plywood because it was the only wood he could afford. He sanded, stained, buffed, and polished; he bought a special handle for its one small drawer.

"This is where you can write your homework assignments," my parents announced when the desk was finished and installed in its place. My mother had bought an expensive desk lamp secondhand so that I could work at night, too.

My retreat to my desk in my troubled household was encouraged, even sanctioned. Often, I would make up fake homework so I could stay there and escape chores.

Most of the writing I did at this desk was schoolwork. It included essays like "Safety in the Home, Street, and School" that I describe in *Vertigo* and that won me a prize, and research projects like "The Shakespeare Controversy" in which I concluded that Christopher Marlowe had written Shakespeare's works.

There were times when I wrote elaborate schemes for a club a friend and I had organized. It was a club of two, she and me, the only members, and we called it "The Elms Club," a name that combined our initials.

That it was a club of two, that it was a club of two because no one else would have us, and that it was a club of two Italian Americans because no other groups would include us, I was not altogether aware of at the time. That we were only two seemed fitting and right: it meant that we were never excluded from any of the activities that we planned; it meant that we could lead often, and follow nearly never.

Our club activities (which, as I recall, consisted of doing things with dolls, with the old clothes in my friend's attic, with the rubble that we collected on the street, and having luscious snacks prepared for us by my clubmate's mother) didn't interest us as much as being together interested us.

It was at that desk that my father made that I first invented a realm that did not heretofore exist—a place where two girls could do things that enriched their lives and make them exciting. It was at that desk that I learned the power of the imagination, and the power of language to create the world, and the power of language to create a bond between people. It was at that desk that I did my first important writing.

That I might become a writer, I never dreamed. I was destined for more practical matters: a career in teaching, or, perhaps, in the law (because I had a "big mouth" my father said).

* * *

Actually, I would not have written *"Puttana,"* would not have started writing memoir, if Sara Ruddick, editor of the landmark *Working It Out*, hadn't invited me to write it (two women: two homework assignments; one life, changed thereby).

It was her dream to have biographers and critics write about their work in relationship to their lives. So, one day, she called to invite me to write about my work on Woolf in relationship to my life. This call was unexpected, but welcomed. For I respected Sally, loved *Working It Out*, and very much wanted to contribute to this project.

Through writing *"Puttana,"* I was forced to confront how ethnic identity figures in the creation of a writing persona. So I explored what it meant for me to work on Virginia Woolf; I explored how my work was informed by my outsider position in relation to privileged culture.

Writing my own story in my own voice was not difficult for me: I enjoyed it. Contemplating its publication, though, was terrifying. So terrifying that I tore up the only copy of the piece when I reread it (and this was before computers, so tearing up the only copy meant that I had destroyed my own work). For how could I publish a work that spoke of my father's violence, my husband's adultery, my son's deafness, my depression? How could I tell these things to the world?

* * *

When I tell my husband that I have ripped up my work, he tells me to dig the essay out of the garbage. He knows that I have written about him, how he betrayed me, how he almost left me and our small child.

Even so, this man has become such a man that he tells me that what we have on our hands is a jigsaw puzzle situation, and that, although I detest puzzles, I had better get to work and piece the damn thing together. Which I do, while he makes dinner.

I publish "A Portrait of the *Puttana* as a Middle-Aged Woolf Scholar" to great acclaim. I choose the title because James Joyce's *Portrait of the Artist as a Young Man* sitting on my bookshelf catches my eye. The arrogance, I think, and mock his title in my own.

Because of the piece's reception, I think that someday I might write my life as an Italian American woman, but I have no definite plans. For who, I think, would want to read a full-length work about a life like mine? So, for years, I write about other people, famous people, British people.

* * *

My entire writing life (indeed my entire adult life) has been a series of breakings and mendings, a shattering of the writing self that was, a repairing, through writing, of something in my life that needed fixing. I found an image to describe what I do in Luigi Pirandello's *La Giara*. In that work, a pottery mender climbs into a broken olive oil jar to glue it together, only to discover that to get out, he must break it and begin the process again.

I like this metaphor, for I see it as a very Italian way of describing the creative process, and, though in Pirandello's work the mender gets the padrone to smash the jar into irreparable pieces, I have appropriated the image and changed it, and have recently begun describing the writing work that I do in these terms—as a continuous breaking and mending. I especially like that it is an oil jar that is being repaired, for like others of my kind, I consider olive oil sacred, and the inside of the vessel that holds the oil, a sacral space, one in which I rather like imagining myself.

Because my father was a handyman, and because my mother was a mender—of clothes, of pottery—a woman who never threw away a dish or a plate, but rather repaired it for everyday use, and because my sister, the one I describe in "My Sister's Suicide," was a very fine potter, and because my grandfather repaired railroad lines, and because my grandmother was a "super" in the tenement where we lived and was responsible for making small repairs, seeing my writing work as that of fixing a broken piece of pottery has important personal meaning for me.

At first I was a textual scholar, devoted to discovering how works of art came into being, using extant manuscripts, journals, letters, diaries.

Then I became a feminist literary historian, then a biographer, increasingly aware of issues of class, ethnicity, sexual violence, and the creative process. Then I began writing memoir, and I began to identify myself as a writer who was Italian American. Finally, here I am, a Southern Italian American writer. But not finally, I hope, for I am sure that there will be new breakings, new mendings, before this writing life is over.

* * *

Learning that my grandparents came from an oppressed people, a despised people, now fuels my writing desire, more than anything else has, except, perhaps, when I discovered that I was an abuse survivor. I want to write, now, to understand what this means, to unravel the conundrum of my past, to honor those people who came before me. I want to assert, in my work, something that has heretofore not often been acknowledged: that the Southern Italian American experience is the human experience.

Breaking the jar. Mending the jar. Then breaking the jar and mending it again. That's what I do. That's what I will continue to do until my writing days are over.

Rachel Guido deVries

Until the Voices Came*

> **Until the Voices Came**
> She had no name
> no name of her own
> until the voices came . . .
>   Denise Nico Leto

I am like my mother, I am like my father. I am warm and funny and easy to like. I am moody and brooding and deeply suspicious. I have the nose of my mother's side, the jutting nose with what everyone on her side calls the Guido bump in the middle. I have the eyes of the Rappises, hot and intense and sometimes furtive. I am Calabrese like the Guidos, peasants and farmers and stubborn with life. I am Sicilian like the Rappises, peasants and farmers and angry with life. I work hard. I am lazy, I am a dreamer. I love solitude. I am lonely and long for a yelling crowd of family to sit at my table each night. I love to cook, to fill the house with sauce and meatballs and beer and wine. I love the smell of cigars, the idea of poker games all night around a smoky table, with the kids sleeping everywhere in the small houses we lived in—three kids to a bed, kids on the couch, on blankets on the floor. I love the arguments that jumped around the game. I

---

*Used with permission of Rachel Guido deVries.
[1]Parts of this essay, in different forms, originally appeared in *Fuori, Essays by Lesbian and Gay Italian Americans*; *Voices in Italian Americana*; *Belles Lettres*; and *Paterson Literary Review*.

hate discord and want only silence. I live alone. I want family. I love independence. I long for someone to be waiting for me. I am a lesbian. I was married to a man for seven years. I have no children. I am a notmother, a *malafemmina*. I simmer with dreams and frustrations and rage and joy. *Malafemmina*. It makes me laugh, it makes me cry. I am tired. I bristle with energy. I want to sleep. I wake at 3 A.M. night after night and rise and worry and cry. I wake at 3 A.M. full of energy, rushing to my desk to write a poem, a story, to get it down, to remember the ways that are dying. They live in me, always. I hate them. I love them. I shape them with words, with clay, with color. My mind dances. I do the tarantella all night long. My mind rages. I storm and fume and get lost in its fury. I make a world of books and artists and poems and confusion and freedom. I crave the world of family and rules and values that have lived for centuries. I want money and CD players and good clothes. I love to dress and look flashy and hot. I avoid money, its taint, the way it drives everyone away from their dreams. My dreams. My dreams are lately of going away, of staying home. Of making home out of words and clay and color and love. When I dream of going away I see only the sea, a harsh and gray rocking sea. A calm and blue and soothing sea. I want language. I want the words in Italian, in Sicilian, in Calabrese, in English, in poems. I dream in Italian, messages I understand only in my sleep. Pigeons fly in and out of my head. Homing pigeons. Gray and simple like my mother. Intent, focused, mad like my father. This is what I am like, now, at midlife.

The above passage is from a book I am working on—part memoir, part fiction—called *How It Was*. In it, I explore what I think of as vanished or vanishing cultures and the contexts that allowed them to exist for a while, and how the influences of family and story and class and gender are embedded in my understanding. When I look at my work, beginning in 1978—the year *An Arc of Light*, my first book of poems, was published—I find a long history of exploring silence and voice, family and those beyond the family. Here is "Martyr," an early poem of mine in *An Arc of Light*, dedicated to my mother:

Martyr
I resent the years
you spent alone.
Your hair and you
in disarray
the cardboard in your shoes
worn through.

The years
you polished his shoes
fed his dandyism
his socks rolled neat
his handkerchiefs pressed
and you, gray as a pigeon
cooing, billing,
asking for more.

The years
you waited
pulled pennies like wishbones
from your pockets
spent them on him
or me.

I resent
and love
the martyr in you
the taste of blood
between your teeth
your eyes, still gleaming,
and even
your silent
bitten tongue.

Today, more than 25 years since the poem was written, I would change only the word *resent*, for I have come to see that my mother's silence was a silence borne of need, a need to be safe, and she communicated that need to me, as she communicated so much else. My mother, and all of our mothers, with their "silent/bitten tongue(s)," gave us another language—the language in which we discover our truths, and so too, our voices.

From this midlife view, I see well how ambivalence and change and silence and voice serve me, providing a kind of useful tension that infuses every line of poetry I write, every story I create. I see there has always been an urgency to name myself and my world, to see and to be seen. The urgency to name myself, to name my world, to find community, exists right alongside the desire for privacy and silence. I found all of that in Denise Nico Leto's poem "What's in a Name":

> She had no name
> no name of her own
> and so moved through
> the world with all
> edges exposed.
> She could be just
> about *anybody*.
>
> It is dangerous
> not knowing who I am,
> she thought,
> because then
> they take
> my blood
> for their own.
>
> They called her
>   simple
>   simply white
> they called her
>   dirty
>   dirty good for nothin'

Until the Voices Came

they called her
  bright
  bright for an Italian
they called her
  olive
  olive oil
they called her
  whatever they wanted
  because somebody somewhere
  couldn't pronounce her real name.

She had no name
no name of her own
and so she looked everywhere
in libraries
old photo albums
on back street walls
tree trunks
between newborn toes
something somewhere
essential was lost
and so she moved
through the world
with her *who*
entangled in their *what*.

WHAT DO YOU THINK
YOU'RE DOING

WHAT'S THE POINT

WHAT'S IN A NAME?
She had no name
no name of her own
until the voices came
at first a whisper

    a tiny sound in the distance
    she could barely hear it
       Oliverio
    the sound became louder and clearer
       Oliverio
    and sweeter
       Oliverio
       Cavacini
       Spizzioni
    a chorus of names
       Andolina
       Pettini
       DeLorenzo
    a waterfall of names
       Lafatta
       Sacco
       D'Angelo
    a delicious lyrical
    feast of names
       Benfante
       Cicalo
       Oliverio
         Oliverio
           Oliverio

    She had many names
    she called them
    all her own
    and as her own
    they called.

  Oh, how that waterfall of names comforts me, soothes me like the familiar bell-like laughter of my aunts. And how much the "she" in the poem is like all of us Italian American women writers, those of us who ". . . had no name / no name of her own / until the voices came / at first a whisper / a tiny sound in the distance / she could barely hear it . . ."

Our early whispers have evolved into full-throated voices singing a myriad of songs, exploring our many identities and singing our poems and our stories. In *How To Sing to a Dago*, published 18 years after my first book, my voice has expanded to include lesbian love poems and family love poems; ethnic slurs like *dago* become phrases in songs of acceptance and resistance and love again. These notions of identity, I have come to understand, are complicated, sometimes stony. Other times, they are more like rivers, weaving and changing and unafraid of motion.

I am a southern Italian American and a lesbian and a poet: dago-wop-guinea-greaseball-gangster-mafioso-dyke-lezzie-lesbo-dagger-butch-femme-bulldyke-bull-headed-woman. *Malafemmina*-notmother-spaghetti bending-ginzo. Egghead and used-to-be pothead. Bilingual and cunnilingual. I've crossed classes, continents, genders, and ages. I make poems and stories, biscotti and clam sauce, and love. Every time I go to the dry cleaner, the supermarket, the classrooms where I teach, I am all of those things, and I am partially unrecognized and unrecognizable. What am I seen as when I stand in the front of the room in my dyke guinea teacher clothes, wearing various rainbow pins and necklaces, the gold horn around my neck, the "100 percent Italian" charm dangling next to it? I imagine myself charging up the atmosphere by my nature, by my just being there. In a newspaper article on my teaching, I was described like this: "Guido deVries is a small, energetic woman . . ." I found that interesting. Great headline too: small, energetic woman writes a poem, takes a walk, makes love, eats a Hershey bar, mows the lawn. In this reporter's description, I have size, albeit a small one, and I have energy: I am, therefore, a force. I am recognized for it. I like that. There is a picture of me to go along with it. I look Italian, Spanish, Native, Puerto Rican, Indian. I look white. It depends on how you look. I am a small, energetic woman who is other.

Yet, part of my identity is as white skinned and privileged. It seems to me a responsibility to say that, to acknowledge the way the dominant culture responds to me: I am not afraid, for example, or uncomfortable, or self-conscious, about walking into a restaurant or coffee shop in any small town in mostly white rural and suburban America, an experience not all of my friends of color share. I have always known I was Southern Italian American, Sicilian on my father's side, Calabrese on my mother's, and never part of white, dominant culture. Some of my friends on the west coast claim themselves as olive, making the distinction more clear. Giovanna Capone, a Southern Italian American writer and a founder of Bay Area Sicilian and Italian Lesbians (BASIL), has a great deal to say about this, and she told me a story about her sister. When her sister was a little girl, she would take the salt and pepper, pour a little of the black pepper and say, "This is Black people," then a little of the white and say, "This is white people." Then she'd pour olive oil on top and say, "here come the Italians." Another friend, the African American poet Kate Rushin, told me her father used to say, "You know, an I-talian is just a Negro turned inside out."

When I trace my own history, these are the facts: I grew up in a working-class, Southern Italian American family, in and just outside of Paterson, New Jersey. From fifth grade and on through high school, my classmates were almost exclusively white. There were a few Puerto Ricans, one native American boy, a couple of Jews, and no African Americans.

The neighborhood I grew up in was white, working class, and populated by factory workers and truck drivers, like my father, who was also a small-fry bookie. He was a physically and emotionally abusive man, although growing up in the fifties, no one considered him that. He was just, as was his job description, a Southern Italian father and husband, keeping his family together, and trying to make us all adhere to the old ways through any means possible. He had a fierce loyalty to all underdogs, befriended gay men and women, and black men and women, yet otherwise hated all outsiders.

So many memories of my father are tied up in fear—his step up the back stairs into the kitchen in the middle of the night, his car pulling into the driveway, that certain tone to his voice when I knew we were all in danger, the whine of the belt. There are other sounds and memories, too: his laughter, the way he excited a room, his beautiful voice when he sang. His voice then was full of melancholy, lost love, of an intelligence so keen it only deepened his sadness: he understood it.

The last time I heard my father sing, we were on a gambling boat in Florida. In the karaoke lounge of the ship, he sang the tune Dean Martin made famous, "Everybody Loves Somebody Sometime." My father had already been diagnosed with dementia and could no longer drive or remember what he had said five minutes ago. I stood behind him at the microphone, afraid he might lose his balance or forget what he was doing there. Instead, he closed his eyes, made love to the mic, and sang that song so full of pathos and beauty. When the song ended, the people in the lounge exploded into shouts and applause. That scared my father, and I saw a glimpse, so late in his life, of the fear he must have carried with him always. For the few minutes he sang that song though, he had no fear, no confusion. He had only a clarity of sensation, emotion, and intelligence that for those few minutes came together in a blaze so illuminative that everyone felt it. He was a poet.

This is one of the qualities I identify as Italian American: the clarity of insight fused with sensation. That clarity is sometimes painful, if one moves ". . . through / the world with all / edges exposed" (Leto, "What's in a Name"), but it can also be as knowledgeable and changeable and self-identified as Loba, the magnificent she-wolf of Diane di Prima's work. This is what the image—in poem or story, song, painting, or sculpture—reveals. I think we are a sad people, full of loss and grief and beauty; it is in the making of art, perhaps, that our sadness is best translated. I don't mean that Italian American artists go around moping or feeling grief struck, but that sadness and grief are part of the foundation on which we balance. I see that in Diane di Prima's early book of poems, *Dinners and Nightmares*, and in so much of the work of Maria Mazziotti Gillan. In *The Dream Book*, edited by Helen Barolini, I discovered writers sharing a familiar bridge—family on one side, their fingers to their lips telling us to be silent, and the rest of the world on the other side, a world we somehow want to reach. Rosemarie Caruso's piece in that anthology shared words that could have been my own mother's: "Roe—don't write about it. It's going to start trouble, then I can't go there next Christmas." This bridge between silence and story or poem is why, I think, so many of us turn to art—the poem, the painting, the movie, the sculpture—to reveal our ways. Long before I heard the word *omertà*, I had been taught it. When I wrote *Tender Warriors*, my novel, I had an image of wearing rearview mirror glasses, so that always at the sides of my vision, I saw a long line of Sicilian women, dressed in black and bowing toward the earth. My father stood to the side, and all of them were gesturing, warning me to be quiet. I also had a dream during that time of that same group of old Italian crones in a circle—only the women now—holding their cupped hands to me, offering me the secrets and stories they held there.

I think of those women as my grandmother, my mother, and her five sisters. I was named for my Calabrese grandmother, Rachel Guido. I never knew her, never even saw a picture of her. She died when my own mother was only eight years old. Through the years, I heard over and over again that this first Rachel Guido was a storyteller. She would gather her eight children around her and say, "You want to hear a story?"

"Yes, yes," they would say.

"All right," the first Rachel Guido would say. "What do you want to hear, fact or fiction?"

This same storytelling is passed on from the women to the children in Maria Mazziotti Gillan's collection of poems *Things My Mother Told Me*. In her poem "You Were Always Escaping," the mother stands with her arms around her kids, "and her bruised eyes / Her voice quivering, she'd say, / 'Can't you stay home tonight?' / staring at the empty doorway, / then she'd sigh, lift her shoulders, / and begin some project with us." This coming together of the women and children makes the children part of the history of women. Alone with the children, the mother becomes storyteller: ". . . she'd tell us stories about San Mauro, the town where she grew up."

We are full of those stories. My mother and her sisters, the Guido girls, were always together talking or talking on the telephone. As kids, my cousins and I slept over at each other's houses, sharing beds and each other's clothes regardless of gender, listening to late night poker games and the fights that so often erupted. Yet the gatherings and the poker games went on. Every holiday or birthday, the aunts and their husbands and kids would gather at one of their houses and we would eat and talk for hours, the women in the kitchen around a yellow Formica table, smoking cigarettes and telling stories. Their laughter is always in my ear—throaty and bell-like, sexy and smart-assed, rueful, resigned, and somehow hopeful. I hear it all the time.

* * *

I was into my late teens before I remember there being non-Italians in our house or at the table on Sundays. My mother was less Italian identified in an outward sense. She resisted the label Italian American insisting she was an American with no interest in seeing the old country, as she and my father called it. He, of course, wanted to go and see his one remaining cousin, Luigi, a baker in Palermo. My mother was and is a typical Southern Italian American wife and mother. She deferred in all things to my father, put up with his adulteries, and tried to shush the spirit out of me and my brother and sister as we grew up. She also had a fierce devotion to the son and ignored all of his bad traits, caring for him until his sudden death in his forties. I had boyfriends in grammar school and high school, but sometime in my early adolescence, I made a conscious choice to avoid all Italian boys, though they were, in my opinion, the best looking and the sharpest dressed. That may have been my first experience with internalized anti-Italian sentiments. Perhaps it was a wise move, based on experience. In any event, I dated boys, had a mad crush on an Italian American girl in my junior year, and had feelings in kindergarten for my teacher, a woman who, through a coincidence, I met again when I was eight in a whole new neighborhood. I was at a friend's house and experienced the same wash of heat I had felt as a five year old on Trenton Avenue in Paterson, my first school. In my early teens, I went out with Native American and Puerto Rican boys, and then had a rush of effeminate boys, as my mother called them—not "real" men. I see clearly now that during this whole period, I was identifying with the "other," while simultaneously denying my ethnic and my lesbian self. Then I met the boy I grew up with and married. He was WASP, and through the lens of history, I see how desperately I was trying to be normal.

This was by now the late sixties, and he and I became active in the antiwar movement. I had gone to nursing school, where I had the chance to form close relationships with other women, one of whom I was seriously in love with, though I wasn't calling it that then, and my then husband was at Harvard on a scholarship.

It was in Cambridge, finally away from my family, that the world began to change for me. The six months we lived there was a time of enormous growth and deep sadness. I was mute around the people he knew there, blonde girls who spoke perfect English and who knew things about Freud and classical music (about which I then knew so little). So, of course, they grew in importance in my mind. I felt stupid, "too" Italian—this was long before I had the work of Denise Nico Leto and Maria Mazziotti Gillan and others to give words to my feelings. To this day, many white people provoke this response in me.

I begin to feel that my nose is enormous, that I reek of garlic, that I must lower my voice to pass. Passing for white, and I see now, passing for straight, as well—for what I thought of as normal—was in those days important to me. I wanted away from my family with their loud fights and hysterics, from the police or the ambulance in the night for one of my father's outbursts, from the whine of the leather belt, from the mocking of each of us my father specialized in, always the putdown of one's talents or loves or desires or dreams. I wanted away from my mother, who was alone night after night and who coped with all the vagaries of my father's behavior and my sister's pregnancy out of wedlock and her later heroin addiction, and from the fear of being killed one night when my father pulled out his gun or gathered my throat in his hands. When I saw "Jungle Fever" and the scene when Annabelle Sciorra is beaten by her father flashed on the screen, I burst into tears, and although I have serious issues with much of what Spike Lee has to say about relationships between African Americans and Italian Americans, in that scene I saw my life.

I saw and continue to see my life reflected, and much more fully, in the work of Diane di Prima. Her use of language is at once idiomatic working-class Italian speech, yet full of the passion of revolution and change and of her identity as an Italian American, as a woman, and as a woman with the courage and the intelligence to break free of the constraints on young and older women in our culture—this courage to break free and break boundaries, to create for herself a politics *and* a poetics, to make art. *Dinners and Nightmares*, an early and powerful collection of di Prima's, set something off in me that continues to move me to this day. Even the title awakened me, recalling how many dinners at home had turned into nightmares with my father forcing meatballs down my little brother's resisting throat. That theme, longing for the perfect communion no matter how many times it goes unfulfilled, came early and goes on in my work. It seems that so many of our women and our men lean into this desire to surround themselves with family and food, a kind of shield and familiarity that only we understand, without footnotes.

In *Dinners and Nightmares*, I found a language I felt lived somewhere not yet quite accessible within me, in the cadences and voices of family and traffic and bird and wind. Years later, I carried another book of di Prima's, *The Calculus of Variation*, around with me wherever I traveled, reading only a few paragraphs, sometimes even just a few lines, before I was transported to a place of translation within me, so that my own pen would now rush along the pages of my journal and later become poems of my own. In Renee Hansen's novel *Take Me to the Underground*, about obsessive love, I saw myself again reflected in the passionate and intense way we often turn to the loved one, in the style of dressing, through our own defined identities. Dodici Azpadu's *Saturday Night in the Prime of Life*, and later the lovely and stirring work of Maria Mazziotti Gillan, filled me with recognition.

* * *

In Cambridge, I became politicized in a way I never would have been had I stayed close to my family. I had been writing poems since my early teens, though I showed them to no one. Now, I began to read more and more poetry and to write more seriously, though still privately. After Cambridge, we moved to Rochester, New York, where my then husband went to medical school. I found a community of poets and began to share my work and to think of myself as a writer. I went to women's liberation meetings, where I met many women, some of whom were lesbians, and I watched them with a longing given language when I read Adrienne Rich's line about ". . . this homesickness for a woman." I also became a nurse practitioner in pediatrics and took a position at a migrant farm workers' clinic. At that time, in the early seventies, the migrant workers were primarily African American, and my work in that clinic further politicized me.

I will never forget my visits to the camps, where workers were shoved and crammed into tiny rooms, often with only the most basic plumbing and cooking facilities. I saw several camps where workers had to dig pit latrines because the farmer had disconnected the plumbing for punishment. It was in the camps, in conversations with the women, that I heard from them some of the same superstitions I'd heard from my mother: don't wash your hair when you're pregnant or the baby will be marked; a bird that flies in the house brings bad luck. I heard those, and other familiar superstitions, again when I lived in Kenya, East Africa.

In Rochester, I kept attending women's liberation and anarchist meetings and was extremely preoccupied by being a good wife: a wife out of what I now call the Granola Set—baking bread and cooking exotic meals, and trying to fit in with the other med students, their partners, and the mostly male doctors and their wives. In a way, I can now see that though I thought I had broken with my Southern Italian American family, and their values, I had not—not at all. I was into the new ways. I pursued an education, wrote poems, attended meetings. I was also fiercely devoted to home, to making home, to keeping home. Sauce every Sunday—and I still like to do that, but with some consciousness and choice.

In 1974, my then husband took a year out of med school to do a research project in child development in Kenya, East Africa. For a year, we worked together on a study there, and some of the results were published in a pediatrics journal. For me though, my real life began. We lived in a small village called Mwaembe (Mango Tree) in the Msambweni district, about sixty kilometers south of Mombasa, right on the Indian Ocean, with the Digo tribe.

It was in Kenya that my identity emerged. I like to say that 1974 is the year Rachel Guido deVries was born, although it took me until 1985, when I read and reviewed *The Dream Book*, to claim my Italian self with my name. In Mwaembe, I spent most of my time with the Digo women and children. At night, the women would gather under the palm trees and begin the familiar ritual of storytelling. It felt just like home. In a neighboring village, Shimoni, I met an mganga—a healer—and through an elaborate ritual, found the nerve at last to tell myself, out loud, and written on paper blessed by the healer, and which I wore encased in a silver amulet for many years after returning to the states, that I was a poet and a lesbian. Amidst the color and the women in a small village in Kenya, I came out, long before I'd published a poem or slept with a woman, and about a year before I would leave my husband and embrace simultaneously my desires: writing and women.

From that point, from the moment I spoke my desire out loud, there was no turning back, and I suppose, had I not been in East Africa, I might never have gathered the courage. It hardly seems courageous to me now, twenty-five years after the fact, but then I was aware of giving up heterosexual privilege and the life I thought was normal for something I thought I'd had no experience with at all.

In Kenya, I was rarely taken for white, or for *mzungu*, foreigner. Kenya had a large East Asian population, and as I darkened in the sun, I was assumed to be from India, and not infrequently to be African. In a way, it was in East Africa that the otherness I'd so often felt in the States made sense. In Kenya, where I had expected to feel different, to be outside the norm, I did not feel that way at all. Yet I was white in the sense that many Africans who knew I was from the United States saw me as privileged—which I was, after all. I traveled a large distance at considerable cost; I was well fed and comfortably dressed; I could take a year out of my working life to live in another culture. If that doesn't constitute the benefits of privilege, I don't know what does. Distinctions afforded by education and economic class switching, and by global heterosexism, were contributing elements of privilege, but I believe the primary privilege was skin. Paradoxically, it was an understanding of white skin privilege that illuminated my own sense of color and other. My emotional vision sharpened, and I began to come to grips with the notion of skin privilege at the same time I was preparing to give up my heterosexual privilege.

Back in the United States, I took writing classes and workshops. At one, I met Marge Piercy, a fierce writer, full of politics and poetry, her own ethnicity and class background so much a part of her language. She wrote the introduction to *An Arc of Light*, and she encouraged me to carve out a place for myself, a place in which to write and to live. For me, this was a struggle—it meant abandoning many ideas I had been lugging around for decades; it meant fighting for myself.

* * *

One of my father's most memorable fist fights was with a white guy who called him a Wop over a beer in my father's *compare's* joint. My father hauled off and whacked him good, came home with a blackened eye himself and all full of pride. I was about ten years old, and today, forty-three years later, my whole body fills up with pride too, remembering. Perhaps it was this incident of my father's that led me to stand on third base in fifth grade, playing kickball and defending myself against the anti-Italian taunts of "guinea" that my classmates aimed at me. Until fourth grade, I'd gone to Catholic school, first at St. Anthony's in Paterson, New Jersey, a school run by Italian nuns. I recall them as nice; they were nice to me, I recognized them, and they recognized me. Of course I didn't have the language for that then, but that is how I remember it.

When I was in second grade, we moved to a neighboring town where I stayed until I graduated from high school. At St. Paul's, the Catholic school I attended through fourth grade, the nuns were Polish. From my rather cloistered world view, I hated them for being Polish, or, more specifically, for not being Italian, and I know that is a feeling I had then. I know they despised me, and all the other Italian kids as well, pulling our hair, pinching us, walloping us on the knuckles with those brutal, thick wooden rulers. The Italian kids at this school were my friends: Tommy Pengitore, Joey Citro, Diane Perrotti, Raye Ann Corsetto. Of course there were many non-Italians, too, but, I can't remember the name of a single one of them. But by fifth grade, my parents could no longer afford Catholic school tuition, and so my sister, brother, and I went off to public school. The kids were mostly white, and most came from Dutch and German backgrounds. When the Italian name calling began, I would scream on the playground: "You think Italians are bad? Read the obituary page in the paper. Italians are the only ones who remember their dead." I was fascinated by that phenomenon, or what I thought was phenomenal. As a serious ten year old, I pored over the obituary pages, struck by the fact that all the "In Memoria" were to Italians who had died. This made sense to me then, and it still does. In *Tender Warriors*, Josephine, the deceased mother and wife of the De Marco clan, is omnipresent in the story, and is a force in each of the character's minds and actions. So many poems and stories written by Italian American writers today are full of references to family, past and present. They are bearers of cautionary tales, and keepers of tradition and history, too. They remind us of who we have been and of who we are now.

Coming out as a lesbian and as a poet challenged my family in ways they had never been challenged before. All of their prior challenges fit, somehow, into a context: the cheating husband–abusive father–small time gangster–ex-con; the heroin-addicted–unwed mother sister; the long-suffering–completely loyal wife/mother; the years of Sicilian grudges on my father's side that kept us from seeing his relatives until I was in my late teens. All of that was considered somehow within the range of normal. When I came out, my late kid brother, nine years younger than I am, articulated exactly that: "Everything in this family," he said, in the learned voice of Italian male authority, "has to go on the back burner now. This is the worst thing that's happened to us." My mother would frequently ask me why I didn't just write as a hobby and go back to nursing, something familiar and female and safe to her.

So how does all of this fit into my work as a poet and fiction writer? As a Dago dyke poet? When I read and reviewed *The Dream Book*, I wept. I felt I was meeting my lost family, a family of women. In her poem, "Naturally, Mother," Janine Veto says: "Freud aside, all our fathers / do not matter / A woman bleeds through her mother / . . . We are buoyed by our own messy faith / we love." I read Sandra M. Gilbert's words about her name: "I always felt oddly falsified with this Waspish-sounding American name, which I adopted as a 20 year old bride who had never considered the consequences of her actions!" I had done the same thing. Finally, it was the words of Fran Claro to her mother, again in *The Dream Book*, that moved me to action: "After all these years," Fran Claro tells her mother, "she was ready to be Italian." So was I. It was then that I claimed the name of Rachel Guido, the long-gone and original storyteller. To reveal my name meant revealing myself. In that decision, the weeping was joined by power and joy and lustiness. Until the voices came, I was alone. Now, I have a "name of my own," a voice of my own, and a community of voices, where I can speak, and where I listen.

Works Cited

Azpadu, Dodici. *Saturday Night in the Prime of Life*. Iowa City, Iowa: Aunt Lute's Books, 1983.
Barolini, Helen, ed. Introduction to *The Dream Book*. New York: Schocken Books, 1985.
deVries, Rachel Guido. *An Arc of Light*. Cazenovia, New York: Wild Goose Press, 1978.
———. *Tender Warriors*. Ithaca, New York: Firebrand Books, 1986.
———. *How to Sing to a Dago*. Toronto and New York: Guernica Editions, 1996.
di Prima, Diane. *Loba*. New York: Penguin Books, 1998.
———. *Dinners and Nightmares*. New York: Corinth Press, 1961.
———. *The Calculus of Variation*. San Francisco, California: Di Prima, 1972.
Gillan, Maria Mazziotti. *Things My Mother Told Me*. Toronto and New York: Guernica Editions, 1999.
Hansen, Renee. *Take Me to the Underground*. Freedom, California: Crossing Press, 1990.
Leto, Denise Nico. "What's in a Name." *Voices in Italian America* 2, no. 2 (1991).
Claro, Fran. "South Brooklyn, 1947." In *The Dream Book*. Edited and with an introduction by Helen Barolini. New York: Schocken Books, 1985.
Veto, Janine. "Naturally, Mother." In *The Dream Book*. Edited and with an introduction by Helen Barolini. New York: Schocken Books, 1985.

DIANE DI PRIMA

Recollections of My Life As a Woman*

My earliest sense of what it means to be a woman was learned from my grandmother; Antoinette Mallozzi, and at her knee. It was a house of dark and mellow light, almost as if there were fire and kerosene lamps, but to my recollection there was electric light, the same as everywhere else. It is just that the rooms were so very dark, light filtering as it did through paper shades and lace curtains, and falling then on dark heavy furniture (mahogany and walnut) and onto floors and surfaces yellowed with many layers of wax, layers of lemon oil. The light fell as if on old oil paintings, those glazes, that veneer. Sepia Portraits: Dante, Emma Goldman. There was a subtle air of mystery. The light fell on my grandmother's hands as she sat rocking, saying her rosary. She smelled of lemons and olive oil, garlic and waxes and mysterious herbs. I loved to touch her skin.

There was this mystery: she sat, saying her beads, but the beads and her hand never completely left her apron pocket. My grandfather was an atheist, and if she heard his step on the stair she would slip the beads out of sight and take up some work. They had lived thus for forty years, and the mystery was how much they loved each other. To my child's senses, already sharpened to conflict, there was no conflict in that house. He was an atheist, she a devout Catholic, and for all intents

---

*"Chapter One", from *Recollections of My Life As a Woman* by Diane di Prima, copyright © 1999 by Diane di Prima. Used by permission of Viking Penguin, a division of Penguin Putnam Inc.

and purposes they were one. It would never do to argue with him about God, and so when he came into the room she slipped the beads away.

As for him, he never seemed to inquire. Though those clear blue eyes saw everywhere. The I Ching has the phrase: "He let many things pass without being duped."

My grandmother's Catholicism was of the distinctive Mediterranean variety: tolerant and full of humor. When I was a little older, I would frequently hear her remark, at some tale of transgression, sins of the flesh reported by a neighbor in hushed Neapolitan—"Eh!" (an exclamation whose inflection communicated humor and seriousness, and a peculiar, almost French, irony—"Eh!" my grandmother would say, "The Virgin Mary is a woman, she'll explain it to God.'

This response to the vagaries of human existence, the weakness of the flesh, especially female flesh, gave me pause for thought. It indicated on the one hand, that the Virgin Mary knew much better than God the ins and outs so to speak of human nature, what we were up to, and that she had a tolerance and intelligence and humor that was perhaps missing from the male godhead.

* * *

It was at my grandmother's side, in that scrubbed and waxed apartment, that I received my first communications about the specialness and the relative uselessness of men, in this case my grandfather. There was no doubt that he was the excitement of our days, the fire and light of our lives, and that one of his most endearing qualities was that we had no idea what he was going to do next. But it was the women, and there were many of them, who attended on all the practical aspects of life. In the view that Antoinette Mallozzi transmitted, there was nothing wrong or strange about this. We women had the babies, after all, and it was enormously more interesting to us than to any man to know that there would be food on the table.

Not that I wish in any way to denigrate my grandfather: he worked enormously hard for his family—*but he would at any time throw everything over for an ideal.* There were many stories of his quitting an otherwise okay job to protest some injustice to a fellow worker. At which point he would arrive home with the fellow worker and his entire family, at the very least for dinner. Often they stayed for weeks. My grandmother would set the table for that many more, and if a solution was not rapidly forthcoming she and the six girls would take in crochet beadwork to keep cash coming in until my grandfather found another, less unjust employer.

Now, this sort of thing was not still going on when I was little—by then my grandfather was no longer working for others as a custom tailor—but the stories and the memory of it were in the air. My grandfather was regarded somewhat as the family treasure: a powerful and erratic kind of lightning generator, a kind of Tesla experiment, we for some reason kept in the house.

It was clear to me that he was as good as it got. My father, a sullen man with a smoldering temper, was easily as demanding as Grandpa, but did not bring these endearing qualities of excitement and idealism, this demand for something more than we already had or knew, into our lives. It was like tending a furnace in which the fire had gone out.

Antoinette was always busy, but there was a way in which she communicated the basic all-rightness of things. I loved to watch her hands. As I think about it now, I realize that as a little person I was not separated from the old: the sight and feel of soft, dry wrinkled skin was associated with the sight and feel of love. Of those who had the time to listen, to tell a story. I learned to love the smells and feel of old flesh—I loved to put my round child's cheek up against her wrinkled one.

Her hands always smelled of garlic and onions, beeswax and lemons and a thousand herbs. There was that sense of cleanness and the good smells of the world. A sense of the things that went on. In the turbulent 1930s into which I was born, my grandmother taught me that the things of woman go on: that they are the very basis and ground of human life. Babies are born and raised, the food is cooked. The world is cleaned and mended and kept in order. Kept sane. That one could live with dignity and joy even in poverty. That even tragedy and shock and loss require this basis of loving attendance.

And that men were peripheral to all this. They were dear, they brought excitement, they sought to bring change. Printed newspapers, made speeches, tried to bring that taste of sanity and order into the larger world. But they were fragile somehow. In their excitement they would forget to watch the clock and turn the oven off. I grew up thinking them a luxury.

* * *

Antoinette Rossi and Domenico Mallozzi met in their hometown in Italy, a town whose name translates as Saints Cosimo and Damiano. Antoinette's family was the aristocracy of the town (hence, perhaps, her French first name—French was still to some extent the language of the upper classes) though how aristocratic or wealthy the aristocracy of this small town was, I can only guess. I do know that later in my life, when Antoinette undertook to improve my education, she taught me the fine arts of embroidery and hemstitching in linen—a delicate process in which you pull out the threads of the linen weft and rework the warp into intricate geometric patterns. Though I remember her hands endlessly darning old clothes and making practical pieces of clothing—skirts, aprons—when it came time to teach sewing to her granddaughter she went back to the work she'd been taught, and no doubt the only work it had been expected she would ever do: fine embroidery, working in linen, and crocheting lace.

I am not sure how, or under what circumstances, Antoinette met Domenico: he was of a much poorer family I imagine, though, that in a town the size of Saints Cosimo and Damiano, everyone more or less knew everyone else. One of the things we grandchildren were frequently told about Domenico was that he had had to quit school in the third grade to help support his family. He had learned the trade of custom tailoring and become a fine tailor, and it was with this profession that he supported his numerous family later in America. Domenico was of a fierce and fiery disposition, and seems to have had a certain difficulty in getting along with folks in his native part of the world. He was for one thing, then as later, an atheist, and—fairly common in the Italy of that period, and not at all as far out as it sounds to us now—an anarchist. The combination, together with a burning curiosity and intellectual zeal, and a love of argument for its own sake and as a tool to uncover Truth, whatever that might be, didn't make him a popular guy. Or that's the impression I get.

At some point, he and Antoinette encountered each other and fell in love. For all her wealth, she was in a state of serious servitude. Seems my grandmother had six brothers and a father, and her mother had died, and nobody in the family had any intention of letting her marry at all—she was living, it was quite apparent to the men of the household, solely to keep house for them and provide the womanly comforts, however they might have been conceived back then. (We are talking the last decades of the nineteenth century here.) Keeping house in her situation didn't have the onerous overtones it has for us—she mostly had to oversee the servants and make sure things were done right. Probably plan the menus and things like that. Though she was a very skilled cook and may well have done a bunch of the work herself, I don't have the sense that she had to. Or that any really grubby or depressing tasks fell her way.

Still, servitude isn't in the quality or quantity of the work, but simply in performing tasks that your heart isn't in. Where the True Will, to use a magickal term, isn't engaged.

I am not sure how many servants the Rossi household employed, but there were enough so that Antoinette had her own personal maid. This is crucial to the tale. When her brothers (and presumably her father though my mother and aunts never mentioned him) found out that she was being courted—and by such a low-class type as Domenico—they locked her up in her room. She was their property, clearly, and they weren't about to let the only woman in the house go anywhere. If there were going to be a marriage at all—which was unlikely—it would have been "arranged" for the family convenience. In any case, Antoinette's maid, who remains nameless in these stories, smuggled letters from Domenico to Antoinette and back again for some time, while Antoinette remained behind a locked door, refusing to yield. The maid eventually helped her escape. She eloped with Domenico, and for a time the couple lived at Domenico's house—probably quite a change for her. It must have been crowded there, and clearly uncomfortable to remain in the town after such an outré move. Eventually they emigrated to America.

I'm sure this was no fun either, though Grandma never complained, and to my knowledge never regretted her move and her choice. When I knew them after some forty years of marriage they were still in love, with all the fierce clinging to their differences that creates such beautiful sparks in a long-term love. That struggle for truth that lay between them.

* * *

As I went into the kitchen this morning to make some tea, I saw through the (intentionally?) open crack in her door, my beautiful young daughter in the arms of a beautiful young Black skateboarder, who had evidently spent the night (skateboard propped against the wall in front of her door, like an insignia). As I went tranquilly into the kitchen and called out to ask them if they wanted tea or coffee, I thought with deep gratitude of some of the women I met when I first left home at the age of eighteen: those beautiful, soft and strong women of middle age with their young daughters who made me welcome in their various homes, where I could observe on a given morning mom coming out of her bedroom with a lover, male or female, and joining daughter and *her* lover at the table for breakfast in naturalness and camaraderie. These women, by now mostly dead I suppose, were great pioneers. They are nameless to me, nameless and brief friends I encountered along the way who showed me something else was possible besides what I had seen at home. Some trust and mutual joy in transient or long-term mates possible between parents and kids. (So that a mom myself, I have always felt the house is blessed by young love: the bliss and softness it radiates to all corners of my flat: discovery and tenderness, like a new spring morning. Trust.)

I think, too, of those other women who taught me other ways, when I was much younger. They had the same strength but not always the same softness. They were the "art teachers" and music teachers I encountered in school, or the women of the arts who sometimes found their way into my parents' home, to be spoken unkindly of later. They usually wore what my mother considered too much make-up. They mostly had sad eyes, but they were sensitive and alert to—well, to me among other things. They were single women and that in itself was considered an anomaly. Single women who had given themselves to the arts—though in fact none of them had achieved great recognition in her loved field. They taught, and wore large jewelry, did not hide behind aprons, were considered more than slightly non-respectable. They showed me a way, and I loved the lines under their eyes their make-up accented rather than hid.

As I loved my cousin Liz, who would show up sometimes, cutting classes. Her cropped hair, and soft, slightly chunky figure. Her intelligence, and spirit. There was a rare day I was home from school when she came by, and we sat together; I was eight, she almost ten years my senior, and she recited poetry to me. "If" by Rudyard Kipling was her favorite, and I soon got it by heart. Liz was unique in my world. No one sat with me, in that way, simply to share feeling. Some early communion of spirit I had found with my grandparents, but with no one else. Years later, my mother hinted that Liz might be gay. She was gone by then, far from family judgments, living in Florida. And I had grown my own agenda, my own ideas of human freedom, so that news made her something of a Hero.

These styles, these possibilities of being, and being a woman, being alive as a woman, have stayed with me. As I write now I see how each is still with me, in the form I make for myself, my way of being in the world.

* * *

My grandfather and I had our secrets—as when we listened to Italian opera together. Opera was forbidden Domenico because he had a bad heart—and so moved was he by the vicissitudes and sorrows of Verdi's heroes and heroines that the doctor felt it to be a danger. We would slip away together to listen—I was three or four—and he would explain all the events extraordinaire that filled that world. All that madness seemed natural as anything else to my young mind. The madness in the air around me, I felt, was no different.

We would share forbidden cups of espresso, heavily sweetened. Drops of the substance, like an elixir of life, were slipped into my small mouth on a tiny silver spoon, while the eggshell china with its blue and gold border gleamed iridescent in the lamplight. I remember that his hand shook slightly. It was the world of the child-full of struggles larger than life, huge shadows cast by the lamp, circumventing the grownups. It was a world of enchantment, and passion.

But then, he told me stories. Terrifying stories, fables whose morals seemed to point to the horror of social custom, of emulation. Or he read me Dante, or we would practice my bit of Italian together. Italian which was forbidden me in my parents' house, and which I quickly forgot when we were finally separated. Italy was a part of that world of enchantment. Domenico would describe the olive groves of the south, till I saw them blowing silver-green in the wind. When I was seven he promised to take me there "after the war", but he died before the war was over. I grew up nostalgic for a land I'd never seen.

* * *

He read me Dante. Told me the book had gone around the world. A world I saw much like the Bronx: tall apartment houses side by side. Marble and potted plants in the lobbies. Linked hands of housewives, passing my grandfather's book from window to window. They would read that one copy and pass it along. That's why it looked so worn: crumbling cover, thumbprints, and dog-eared corners.

* * *

Struggle for truth bonded Domenico and Antoinette. Her rosary, his Giordano Bruno. Fierce, luminous, and coexistent. As how much else my child's heart could only guess at. And in that struggle for truth my grandmother had the last word.

Domenico died when I was eleven, of that sane great heart they had tried to protect him from. Antoinette survived him by eleven years. During that time she lived with her various daughters: my aunts and my mother, and much to their annoyance she conversed nightly with her husband. I still remember her in her room at our Brooklyn brownstone, in her cotton and lace nightgown, her luxuriant grey hair brushed and ready for bed, talking to my grandfather's picture, telling him all the varied events of the day in the dim light. Her soft voice would go from indignation to laughter or grief, as the story changed. She told him everything.

Those years must have been hard and sad for her, but I don't remember that she ever complained. She threw herself into the life of whatever household: mending our clothes, teaching me embroidery and linen working, rolling our endless batches of egg noodles.

When Antoinette was on her deathbed, I was no longer living at home, and hence barred from family life. The story of her passing came to me secondhand from one of my aunts—one of the few who didn't consider me too much of an outlaw to speak to:

> When Antoinette knew she was dying, she had a last request. She had all these eleven years worn only black, worn mourning for Domenico, though he himself "didn't believe in" wearing mourning. But now she was dying, and she wanted to make sure that she was buried in a bright-colored dress. It was a matter of deep concern; she was restless and distressed till she was certain it was understood, and promises were extracted. "Because," she said, "when I meet your father in the next world" (which world, of course, Domenico the atheist adamantly insisted did not exist) "I don't want him to scold me for wearing mourning."
>
> Certain she was right—how could there not be an afterlife?—and fierce in her love and her right to mourn her husband to the end, but not wanting him to scold her. Like the rosary she slipped in and out of her apron all those years. She was buried in light blue.

He told me stories. There were many, and I remember that there were some that made me joyous, but the one that stayed with me all these years went something like this:

> Once in a village far away, there was to be a feast. The people of the town picked out a very fine animal, and led it to the center of the square. And they decked it out with a wreath of flowers around its neck, and praised it highly. And they played music, and danced around it and killed it with great rejoicing. And the next day the children of the village got together to play. They picked one of their number, and put a wreath of flowers around his neck and another wreath on his head. And they played their flutes, and danced around him and killed him, rejoicing.

It's hard to say now what I made of this then. Only that a sense of foreboding, and of a huge responsibility of knowledge lay on me, age four or five. *That this was the nature of the world, and we shared this knowledge*. If that was how it was I was willing to accept it, only I wanted him not to suffer for it. How often I wanted to comfort him—old man and child sharing an existential bewilderment. A willingness to peer into darkness. Struggle for Truth.

* * *

I stood beside him as he sat at his desk. He only half-looked at me as he spoke. This was unusual, in the story times I always sat on his lap. Sat in a bentwood chair, sometimes facing the wall together as if to shut out distractions. A Zen austerity. Or were there only certain corners we could go to for these exchanges, where the grownups would not see us and swoop down—"Leave the child alone. . . . Come on, Diane, your mother (or whoever) wants you. . . . Pop is a little crazy" (an aside, an undertone). If Pop was crazy, I well knew by then that I was crazy with him. They were too late, with their attempts to save me for themselves. The conspiracy between us ran too deep.

I stood beside him at his desk, and his eyes were not on me. Only, I could feel the stuff of his shirtsleeve against my cheek, the smell of bluing, of starch. He said, "Someday you are going to go out at night and look at the stars and you will wonder how they got there. Then you'll study like I studied, and you'll suffer like I suffered, and in the end you'll find nothing". I was not very old but I didn't flinch at that "nothing". Only I knew with my full child's certitude that it wasn't true. Or anyway the despair that accompanied the word had no truth, however much he felt it. I had no words to argue, only the desire to comfort. I may have put my hand on his starched shirtsleeve.

I was being recruited, initiated, and I knew it. With my full consent, entering a world larger than life. I knew there was no turning back, and in fact, yearned only to go forward. To go forward, with him, into the darkness. The struggle for Truth. Only, for me, the darkness held no despair. *Not nothing, Grandpa*. It was someone other than a child who longed to say that.

Not nothing, Grandpa. It was a promise, a vow. I, Diane, age four or five, would make meaning in the world. Make meaning for him, for myself. The dark was luminous, of that I was certain. That much I *knew*.

With that exchange we achieved the full status of lovers. Without further touch or words, we shaped the prototype, the pattern for all my deepest loves to come. Always this despair, this hope, this luminous dark. The conspiracy between us was complete.

Complete, a world in itself, but it couldn't protect me from my parents.

"Pull up your skirt and pull down your pants." This was a little me, five and under. This was mom, and she would send me for the hairbrush first, myself and then, make me get myself ready for the beating. In some ways she was much harder to take than my dad because there was a crazy meanness to her, she hurt you even when she wasn't mad: dressing, washing, everything was painful. *She* was a methodical hurter, *he* was driven by rage and weird perversion.

Being sent to my room by my mother, to wait for my father to come home to beat me for something. (This person was a teenager, or close to teens. After dad beat me he was sexually aroused. Would sit me on his lap with a hard-on to "comfort" me—or worse, I don't remember, only sense.)

He would always say "Be-Jesus," before he swung at me with his hand (this was different from formal beatings with the belt. He would just lash out and start slapping you across the face, and if you tried to protect yourself you were "raising your hand to him" and your nose would usually start bleeding, and if you fell down he would keep hitting across your shoulders, and neck, and in some ways it was scarier than formal beatings, because you didn't know what part of you would be hurt, and with the belt it was usually, but not always, your ass, or your back and ass, or your legs—thighs, where it wouldn't show, and the front of you was mostly protected).

"Be-Jesus, I'll kill you," he would say and you believed him, and then mom or Aunt Ella would come when it was over and try to stop the nosebleed, and sometimes it would go on for a couple of hours, and my mother would say over and over to me, "Your father is a very gentle man, (or a very patient man), but when he loses his temper he has a heavy hand." Or "but when you try him, he loses his temper." And I would be only half-conscious really, it seems now, looking back, as they put ice on the back of my neck to stop the nosebleed, and I would wonder what "try him" meant. And after a while I knew just how long his arms were, and never got that close if I could help it.

My grandparents' house, my parents' house—the two worlds parallel, but never meeting.

* * *

I don't remember my father's mother at all. In the few pictures I have she is a very young bride—almost a child—weighed down by the requisite elaborate lace, or she is holding my father, her firstborn, a round, large-headed baby in a long white dress. She has the soft face and large, round eyes of an Arab woman.

Rosa di Prima died when I was two, quite suddenly, from what I always heard at home was "diabetes". It hit and carried her off in two or three weeks, whatever it was. There was no diagnosis (no doctor?) and certainly no autopsy. My mother always described her as a "saint"—which seemed to mean she had endless patience for menial tasks and the rudeness of her children.

It was 1975, six years after my father died, when my mother came to visit me in a northern California country town, and told me with great trepidation a story of those early days, a story which filled in the picture of my father's family somewhat. It seems that in the first years of my life, during the Depression, my father's father was not earning enough to support his wife and his other five children who were still at home. He was a baker by trade and had had his own store in Brooklyn at some point, but perhaps he had lost it. In any case, my mother and father, who had been married just a few years, felt it incumbent on them to help out, and did so by the simple expediency of giving Rosa their grocery money, or most of it. We all three ate at her table every night. I suppose my mother would take me and meet my father there when he came home from work.

Now this sane and eminently practical solution to hard times was told me amidst the cedar and wild hollyhock, the free clams and leopard shark, the wild pot and wilder music, of that 1970s north country culture, in hushed and shameful tones. My mother had never told anyone in her family. I am not sure if even her sister Ella knew. She read it as a disgrace, somehow, that she, a married woman, had not been able to keep her own table. That my father, a beginning lawyer making seven to fifteen dollars a week, had not been able to support the two households separately.

I remember nothing of those early dinners, and though my father's family lived there for some years, I remember almost nothing of their house on Butler Street. I know that my mother would say in such a tone as to indicate that what we were doing wasn't quite desirable, "We're going over to Butler Street." It meant we were slumming, were going to visit the poorer side of the family. Although I am sure she never said anything that my father could quite pin down.

What is a puzzle to me still is who would have found those dinners disgraceful. Certainly not Domenico, who brought home entire squalling families of would-be union organizers; nor Antoinette, with her welcoming frugal abundance. I can only think that some imagination of my father's as to the status and parameters of the provider-role; or some projection of my mother's as to what a husband is, or should be— some preconceived idea about what it meant to be American, perhaps— hung over the simple problem, and kept all ten of us from the enjoyment of its solution.

MEMORY SHARDS

We are in my grandmother's apartment, and she is standing at the sink. The sink is a slate grey, made of grey slate in fact, with flat, slanting sides, and the dishwater is greasy from Sunday dinner: tomato sauce and roast. My mother and one of her sisters are arguing with my grandmother. She is small, soft, the skin on her arms hangs loose, her grey hair is drawn back into a bun. My grandmother is soft-spoken, but she stands her ground. I am on her side, I stand at her side, wordless. Children are not to speak at times like this. They are persistent, angry, my mother and the aunts. I know only that my grandmother holds her ground and I am afraid for her.

* * *

I am in the park with my grandfather, and it is night. I have almost never been out of the house at night, and I love it. I love the city at night, the lights, the noises. It smells of mystery. In the park, Bronx River Park, the stars come clear. They are very bright, they burn. There is some kind of meeting. A "rally" is the word. My grandfather has taken me with him, and I know somehow it is without my parents' permission. They are anyway not there to object, I have been visiting my grandparents without them.

There is a rally in the park—I am not sure now what sort of rally. Was there in fact a particular occasion—perhaps a protest against the coming war? (This would have been the late 1930s.) Was it routine, an anarchist meeting? I don't know that word then, of course, only that there are many people, most of them men, and most of them are not young. Grey hair and white predominates. The smell of the old men of my childhood: cigars, and a particular kind of soap. The low, hoarse voices of Italian men, gravelly, the pitch set by tobacco and wine. There are women, too, in the crowd, not as many, but they are fierce and earnest. Perhaps I am the only child. I do not at any rate remember any other children.

At one point my grandfather begins to speak. Everyone is still to listen. This has been going on for some time, people speak and the others listen, but this time I listen too—it is my Grandpa. I am not sure what he is saying, and then, at the end I am sure. At the end he is talking about love. He talks for long time about love. He is saying that we must love each other or die. I understand this part, I seem to know it in my bones. He means that we'll all die, the people of the world. He is saying that we must love, and it seems it is more than we must love one another. There is a love to learn that is generic, that is just love, and it doesn't need an object. I know this then, I understand it as he speaks, though there is no way I could find the words for it. It is as if he is saying we must learn HOW to love. And it is very clear: if we do not, we will die: all the people of the world will die.

This time I don't want to comfort him, he doesn't need comfort. This time there is no answer to his "nothing," it is not nothing, it is an invitation to love. The stars shine down on us, the leaves glow in the electric lights of the park. I am proud of him, and afraid, but mostly amazed. His words have awakened my full acknowledgment, consent. I hear what he says as truth, and it seems I have always known it. I feel old, self-contained, passionate with the pure passion of a child. In my child's way I remember this kind of love.

Perhaps he is the last speaker, or perhaps we leave after he speaks. Perhaps not, but this is all I remember. And the rough cloth of his coat under my cheek as he carried me home.

* * *

I have been out with my Aunt Evelyn, whom I love best of all my mother's sisters, because she always sings. Heart full of joy, like a bird. We are in Bronx River Park, and Aunt Evelyn has introduced me to rolling down hills. It's a sport I deeply love, the first joyful physical activity I remember. No joy in walking or running in my mother's house. I never tire of rolling down hills, in spite of stones and dog shit, but after a while my aunt tires of following me, and she sits down on a bench. I have a pail and shovel and I start to dig. I know better than to dig up the grass, so I'm digging on the dirt path, the ground is hard, but I am making headway. I am busy, and quite determined. A man in a uniform approaches my aunt, and whatever he says makes her very angry. And it is later endlessly discussed at home. Aunt Evelyn was "given a ticket", "fined" because I was digging a hole. She is furious, seems to think the ground was made for kids to dig in. Says so. But at home when my mother talks I am not so sure. Is it the ground was made for kids to dig holes in, or is it I've somehow gotten my aunt in trouble?

After this when we go to the park with pail and shovel, Aunt Evelyn spreads her skirts, and I somehow squunch behind them, behind the park benches, and dig. It is still fun, but scary. Especially scary remembering how mad she could get.

* * *

I am older, maybe six, and we are outside. It is night again, stars over the apartment houses of the Bronx, paler because of the lights. My parents and grandparents are walking a little ahead. I am looking up at the buildings, and the sky and I am very sad. Knowing this is the last time I'll see this street, my grandparents are moving. It is the first time I know that "this is the last time" for something and I can hardly bear it. (I'm not much better at it today.) I have somehow some paper with me is how I remember it, but maybe I make it up then and write it down later. For years I had the copy in my first-grade Catholic-school hand: the poem I made to comfort myself that night, to "remember forever" the stars over those tall white apartment houses. My first poem and it worked, still works, I still remember that sky. Poem as the gift of memory. Mnemosyne. Mother.

My grandparents are moving, and I walk behind them torn by the knowledge that this is the last time for something. Beginnings of dying, for me, for them. I am sad too because I sense that they don't want to go. This is a defeat for them, some kind of defeat. Their children want them to move, their place is too far away. No more the river, Bronx River Park, no more this particular light. As we return I passionately love their building, its lobby, huge and white marble. The polished stone, the urns in the entry hall. Brass work over the elevator. The cool space and the silence.

DREAM (AUTUMN 1987)

I am in an ancient church in Sicily. In the dream I think that it is "like a mosque"—it is actually bare stone, hung with incredibly rich cloths: deep colors of red, gold, green-satins and brocades. The light is the light of sun on grey stone, but filtered through all these colors. There are pews without seats—we can stand or kneel only, and I am jammed in with members of the family, to attend a funeral. My Uncle Joe has died, and my Aunt Mary is up in front with the coffin, more or less conducting the event.

The funeral service is going on, and it is mainly music, incredibly beautiful vocal music, Arabic in its modulations, but polyphonic, with one voice joining another. In the dream, it is very important for me to understand how "Arabic" my people are (the Sicilian side of the family). It will help me to understand my life.

People are crowding in beside me, there is a lot of jockeying for position by various (female) relatives—the aunts and my oldest daughter and I am pushed to the outside of the pew, close to the aisle. I decide to move up one row: closer to the altar, which is just the coffin and these incredible hangings. There is more room there, for some reason the next "pew" is half empty.

I start to move, and then out of nowhere my father comes and stands beside me, blocking the way out. I feel as I always felt when confronted with my father's physical presence—claustrophobic and repelled. But I am mostly taken by the ambiance: the music, and the light of that place. Intensity of grief, the melody line of a dirge. Without looking at me, or otherwise acknowledging my presence, my father puts a hand of the back of my neck, just where my neck joins my shoulders. The gesture is humble in a way—even apologetic—and yet it presses on me. It is heavy, demanding: "You're going to have to deal with me somehow". I am aware of the nexus of nerves in that place in my body, the chronic pain of my shoulders and arms.

I don't turn or look at him, but in the light and the passion of the "Arabic" music, I begin to pray. I am not used to praying and I reach for the words, forming them very slowly in the dream-time:

"LET ME FIND IT IN ME
TO FORGIVE THIS MAN."

In my dream I repeat this over and over. And I wake forming the words with my lips, an enormous sense of physical release in my body, and a real sense that the work is to find it in me—in my very flesh, the release point for this past.

Maria Fama

La Carta Parla*

As a writer, as a woman, and as an Italian American, I believe I stand on the shoulders of my foremothers. As a poet, of course, I must begin with a poem. This poem, "Tablecloth," is a true story of continuity and solidarity with an ancestor, my great-great grandmother.

> **Tablecloth**
> Nonna Angela speaks to me in May
>
> She returns with May roses
> She comes with May sunshine
>
> My great-great grandmother speaks to me in May
>
> > when I cover the dining room table
> > with the tablecloth she wove
> > over one hundred years ago,
> > I set a vase on the dazzling center
> > and a voice scented with roses
> > whispers into a shaft of sun.

---

*Used with permission of Maria Fama.

Nonna Angela grew cotton from a seed
She spun and wove the fabric on a rickety loom
She washed and rinsed it in a mountain stream

Nonna Angela pounded the cloth on rocks
and let the hot Sicilian sun bleach
the tablecloth a glistening white
for her daughter's wedding day.

Nonna Angela speaks to me in May

    I know her still young and twice-widowed
    her sun-struck face hopeful
    for five children to find a good life.

Nonna Angela embroidered with field-roughened hands
tiny May flowers, pea pods and blossoms
on the tablecloth's borders
long-life and fertility, embroidered wishes,
for her oldest girl.

    The tablecloth has come down to me
    over a century of Mays and mothers
    across an ocean
    to grace my city table every Spring

Nonna Angela speaks to me in May

    I answer in gratitude
    for her long-ago labor of love
            and of hope.

    Domenica Formica Famà, Maria Certo Adamo, Francesca Sgrò Guaetta, and Mattia Sgrò Bongiovanni—these are the names of my great grandmothers. They all were born in a small town in Sicily, San

Pier Niceto, in the Province of Messina. All were illiterate. They all knew oppression, injustice, and poverty, yet they all were part of a rich, oral culture filled with folktales, family stories, ghost stories, religious stories, poems, proverbs, and songs, which were committed to memory and passed down orally.

I know that Nonna Domenica lived in a haunted house filled with the ghosts of people and animals; that Nonna Maria was a wet nurse for the rich because all her babies, except for my grandmother, died; and that Nonna Francesca made beautiful *biancheria* (linens), that were burned when she died because they thought she had something contagious. I know these great grandmothers only from the snatches of stories told about them. However, I had the great good fortune to know from birth until I was in my mid-twenties my Nonna Mattia, my mother's maternal grandmother. She, too, was illiterate. She, like all my ancestors, came from the little Sicilian mountain village of San Pier Niceto, called *Samperi* by its natives. She, like all my great grandmothers, sent her children, the girls as well as the boys, to school even if only for a year or two.

Yet, unlike my other great grandmothers, my Nonna Mattia made the ocean crossing. She came to America. She was the vibrant link to the oral culture that all my ancestors possessed. My Nonna Mattia was a kind of griot, who told family stories, tales of the village, folktales, ghost stories, and religious stories. She had memorized proverbs, long poems, prayers, and songs, and she performed them all with great flare and drama. She was delighted to say some of them into my tape recorder when I was in high school, so her voice is ever vivid, ever present for me.

Nonna Mattia was the oldest daughter of Nonna Angela of the Tablecloth poem. The Tablecloth was her wedding present. This is my poem about Nonna Mattia.

Nonna Mattia
Nonna Mattia,
great grandmother
large and generous
I ask for your strength
I found your hand made apron

in an old chest of drawers
I shook it out
Neat cross hatched stitches of repairs
rise like sailboats
across the billowing white

I think of the storms
of your ocean crossings
first with your new husband
traveling from sun baked mountains
to an Ohio mining town
Then, having lost your first child
you sailed alone and pregnant
to deliver your second in Sicily

with your mother at your side

You crossed again the ocean expanse
with a year old daughter

returning to your husband's American home

I wrap the apron around me twice
and there is room left over
as I look for cover
in your largeness of body and heart

You wore this apron in Ohio
across Pennsylvania into Philadelphia
In Jersey fields as you picked crops
in the city as you prepared meals
scrubbed laundry, took in boarders

nursed the sick and dying

La Carta Parla

Nonna Mattia,

I remember you elderly and brave
caring for me with smiles and laughter
your coal black eyes watching the world
as you sang in clear Sicilian cadence

Nonna Mattia,

I wrap your apron around me twice
as I look for cover in your
largeness of body and heart

Grant me a portion of your
robustness of spirit, great grandmother

Let this apron be my shield
Let this apron transfer your strong faith
your compassion and your courage
to me, your great grand daughter

I view Nonna Mattia as a powerful woman, a true heroine. When I was a child, we lived across the street from Nonna Mattia; therefore, I often was in her company. I remember that one day she told me that I could do something she could not—read and write. I recall being so surprised. Everyone could read and write. My mother read to me, took me to the library, and bought me books with leftover grocery money. My parents, grandparents, aunts, and uncles could read and write in English and Italian. In my family, someone was always scribbling cards, letters, and journals, especially my parents. In fact, my father kept a journal during World War II when he was a soldier; and one of my earliest memories is of me imitating my mother writing and wanting my scribbles to mean something, too.

Nonna Mattia was the first to tell me a little story, which was often repeated by my parents and grandparents. It is the story of a man in

Sicily who was going to a nearby town. A woman told him, "Please bring these cheeses to my sister who lives there." She gave him three fresh cheeses in a bag for her sister. On the way, the man got hungry and ate one of the cheeses. "What harm could it be?" he thought. When he arrived, he gave the woman's sister the two remaining cheeses. She opened the bag, looked at a scrap of paper that was in the bag, and demanded to know where the other cheese was. The man was shocked and admitted that he'd eaten one of the cheeses. He asked the sister how she had known that there had been three cheeses. The angry women said, "It says it right here on this piece of paper!"

"Ah," the illiterate man said, "*la carta parla.*" The paper speaks.

Paper talks. It can tell us things. "*La carta parla*" (paper speaks). Here was a magical power. My ancestors, my peasant foremothers, were aware of the power of the written word. They all knew what Nonna Mattia had told me: that paper speaks. And I wanted this. I know that I am a writer today because I wanted to continue talking with paper, telling my stories and my family's stories. One of my greatest influences is the glory of the words and music of that oral culture—the prayers, the proverbs, the tales, and the songs—which Nonna Mattia had known by heart.

In our fast-paced society, there is no longer time to memorize and pass down the culture orally, but I can preserve some small part through writing. I can do one small, but powerful thing that Nonna Mattia could not do: I can write a poem on talking paper.

A Conversation with Mary Bucci Bush
They are in the kitchen
those shades of the grandfathers
    sitting at our sides
    at the table

we are two friends
writers   women
    talking
about our grandfathers
who learned to read by oil lamp and candlelight

each packed a favorite book
for the journey across the sea
her grandfather carried THE ARABIAN NIGHTS
mine THE BRIDGE OF SIGHS

They are in the kitchen
those shades of the grandmothers
   standing over our shoulders
    by the stove
as we stir the soup, cut the bread
tell each other about
my only child grandmother, sent to school
by her illiterate wet nurse mother
who sold a pair of earrings so her son
could study the trumpet
my father traveled Sicily in a symphonic band
   because of her

Mary speaks to me of her grandmother
who urged her daughter
to go to school, become a teacher
buy a car
be the first Italian, let alone a woman,
to drive a car in a little New York state town

We talk over the pasta and the *insalata mista*
the shades of the aunts and uncles
   stand by the door
   attentive that we speak their stories
the Aunt who taught Math
the Aunt who learned to read and write
   in one year from on old, neighbor lady

the Uncle who left the coalmines
   injured and cursing Christ
   to become a master chef

The shades of poetry reciting onion farmers
the shades of opera singing coalminers
squeeze into the kitchen
as we chat, swapping what we know
   of their stories
the snatches we heard growing up
   around the kitchen table
     eating pasta e piselli, fagioli,
     pastina in brodo, ceci, pesce spada
     pane and biscotti

The shades of the relatives
and the comari and compari
   crowd us at the table
they want us to get it right

They whisper for us to drink our wine
   sip our espresso and remember
when we speak of them

that their struggle for bread was fierce
they wept because
they could not afford school or books
music filled their lives
prayers, proverbs, memorized poems comforted them

The shades are with us
around the table
they want us to tell
   of their great desire to learn
   of their great desire to better their lives.

Unlike my great grandmothers, I went to school, although elementary school, in my working-class neighborhood of South Philadelphia, was not always a pleasant place to be. I have written poems about my grade school experiences, and one of them is called "The Captain of the Safeties."

The Captain of the Safeties
Sister Euphrasia, the eighth grade teacher,
said Italians were irresponsible
    but I was an exception

She counted on me
    to run errands
    tabulate grades
    do her roll book
    handle money

Sister Euphrasia said I was
different than most Italians
    who were dishonest
different than my Italian classmates
    who were lazy

I was smart, responsible
I was the Captain of the Safeties

I had a red book
with all the safety patrol members' names
I put a mark against their names
    if they were not at their posts
    if they did not have their badges on straight
    if they forgot an item of the regulation uniforms
    white shirts, blue ties, blue pants for boys
    white blouse, blue jumper, blue beanie for girls

Sister Euphrasia said
the beanie symbolized a girl's modesty
the safeties must set an example

most of the marks against the girl safeties
were for beanie violations

I secured my beanie tight with bobby pins
so even the strongest winds did not blow it off the head
of the Captain of the Safeties

One day my beanie disappeared
maybe it was stolen
maybe it was lost
but it was a disaster

at home I cried and cried
my mother gave me money for another
I cried harder
I would have to buy a new beanie
from Sister Euphrasia
who then would know that
even the Captain of the Safeties
was an irresponsible Italian

My grandmother, a seamstress,
told me not to cry
she knew how to make a beanie
my grandfather gave her
his best blue workpants for material
she worked all night
fashioning a hat
that fit me perfectly and
looked exactly like a regulation beanie
except for the inside where
my grandmother placed a thick cloth hatband
not the regulation leather band

The next day and everyday
until the end of the school year
I wore my imposter beanie

The Captain of the Safeties
was determined
that nobody
would ever see the inside of the beanie

Sister Euphrasia
would never know
that I, too, was an irresponsible Italian.

In high school and college, I read widely. I still do. I studied Latin, Italian, and English literatures. I read and still read Asian, Latin American, Middle Eastern, African, African American, and Native American writers. In my senior year of university, I went to Italy to study. There I made the connections to family, made friends, and created the bonds that tie me to that land and people. I visited Sicily and stayed with relatives in San Pier Niceto. I have often returned and have written several poems about my Italian and Sicilian experiences. Here are two.

Sicilia
The Volcano's creature are you,
Land of the sea and mountain face
How many sought to have you in your fragrance?
How many did you tempt with your honeysuckle bloom?
Your beauty lavish with orange fruit and jasmine air
Who could resist you bathed ever in rainbowed seas?

Land, to you they came to take from you their fill
        turbaned or armored
        black or blonde
        togaed, striped, or wooled

They came to take you, but your anger sucked their blood
You shook their bones with quakes
You cracked their boats on your sharpened sides
Your wind breath blew away their homes
              threw their crops into sparkling seas.

As your beauty smiled they roasted and they froze
Hypnotized they stayed
Drugged by beauty they stayed
Exhausted by sweat they stayed,
And your mountain face has carved your image on these
  people
              too wise to trust
              too old to change
              too bitter to regret

The sameness of all centuries they know, your children,
They know hot winds come and the sun burns,
The tempests freeze, the land slides,
ships sink, blood spills and is wet.

They, like you, smile
They, like you, are harsh.

Picking Apricots with *Zia* Antonia
Late afternoon   in June
when the sun was less intense
my aunt and I picked apricots
   in a terraced field
   on a mountainside

We picked buckets of apricots
from a sturdy tree
I on a ladder
she below

her everyday life
special for me
fresh from a city
an ocean away

From the ladder
I saw the dusty roads
snaking through the town
the laundry waving on balconies
I heard goat bells and bleats
    a motorcycle buzz, a Fiat horn
I breathed sweet apricots and sun

I slowed and swayed
my aunt called up to me
    that apricot fragrance
    was making me drunk
she said I was not used
    to the power of Sicilian apricots

we switched places

at sunset   we carried the buckets home
some to sell, some to trade, some to eat ourselves
at twilight   I sat in the kitchen
a little dizzy
my aunt was right
her everyday life
my ancestors' lives

Sicilian apricots had made me drunk.

    I consider myself both American and Sicilian. I belong to both cultures. I am, however, aware that culture, like language, is flexible and ever changing. I am also aware that much has been and is being lost in the continuous quest for assimilation into U.S. culture, despite obstacles.

I Am Not White
The dentist says my teeth tell of invasions
    mixed blood
the tale of a proud, mongrel people
    I am Sicilian
    I am not white
I will not check the box for white
    on any form

In Sicily
my ancestors recognized white
to be the color of sparkling linens
    towels, tablecloths, sheets
    the color of clouds, seafoam, and bones
not family faces with their
    African, Greek, Arabic, Norman casts

North Italians call us Africans
a Milanese told me that in Sicily
    He heard Africa's drums
I hear them, too,
    especially when
    from across the little stretch of gleaming sea
    North African winds
    blow through our homes

Sicilians left for other lands
trying to escape poverty   injustice
    they prayed to their
    Black Madonna of Tindari
    miraculous advocate for the poor
    for guidance
    packing her image with their clothes

In America at first
they called us colored
Sicilians lynched in the South
   along with Africans
   in the fields, the railroads, the mines
   the children and grandchildren of slaves
   worked at our sides
   taught us American life
   were thought good people, even friends

In America over the years
Sicilians stayed quiet spoke English
   learned to stand apart
   from those darker sisters and brothers
Sicilians passed to that lighter
   opportunity side of the color line

In America now
some of the Black Madonna's children
   have forgotten her
   ignorant of their roots
   they check the box for white on every form
   no longer aware
   that they are of mixed blood
   the mongrel heirs
   to a proud people of every feature

I cannot forget
when even my teeth tell our story

I will not forget
I have prayed at the Black Madonna's
   ancient, wind-swept shrine at Tindari

I am Sicilian
I am not white.

In recent years, I have been writing a series of poems about our fellow creatures, the animals, who share this planet with us. Here are two examples.

Horses
Horses
    hats on their heads
    bows on their tails
    bags below their rumps

sweat and pull
tourist packed carts
through hot city streets

    slow steps and pull
    slow steps and turn
    bus fumes
    car exhaust
    everyday the load
    waiting for a break in the shade
    some oats an apple
    till home and sleep

I sweat and look for a job
on hot city streets
    slow steps I turn a corner
    slow steps I interview with a man
    who wants to know
    if I'll be a good horse
    wear a suit
    carry the workload
    from nine to five
    plus overtime

Horses,
   the man says
   I must work hard
   pull my weight

Horses,
   I dread the harness
   fear the bit

Horses on asphalt,
dreaming of meadows,
teach me patience.

The Rooster: For Lina Insana

"Cicciu" he called me
a diminutive of his own name, Francesco,
we lived in a cave   in North Italy
he fed me
during those dark, confusing days
of the Second World War

I crowed and strutted while he worked
I got used to his Sicilian tongue
though I was a proud *Alt'Italia* rooster

we were males   without women
firelight   oil light
it was dim as he worked
he practiced his craft
making shoes for the partisans
   so they could fight sure-footed
making fake seals for the partisans
   so they could stamp the discharge and identification papers
   for all in need

He was an honorable man   creative   energetic

    he left the Italian army in disgust
    over fascism's false promises

a Sicilian man and a Northern rooster
    we kept each other company
    till the partisans won
    the war ended
    the farmer returned and
    I ruled a harem once again

The grape vines told me
Francesco returned to Sicily
then traveled to a faraway land
he took a beautiful bride
fathered beautiful children

I kept the name Cicciu
because I was a proud *Alt'Italia* rooster
who wished to honor Francesco Insana
my human companion
of long ago.

I currently have been trying to integrate my love for music, including jazz, and writing by doing performance pieces. The next poem, called "Watching Dizzy Gillespie on TV," is a jazz piece, where I have tried to combine jazz elements, such as scat and bebop, with Catholicism and a personal story.

Watching Dizzy Gillespie on TV
Dizzy Dizzy
Chipmunk sweet Chipmunk blow sweet notes
Notes blue and hot and cool and bop do what

La Carta Parla

Do scat with Hendricks just hands
hands and mouth
hand to microphone to mouth to phone
phone do phone do phone do saxophone

Due Due due duewhat
What dues are due due due we we we
Try to be so cool together
paying dues be dues

Bop Do Bop Do Bop do Bop Do We

We when we when we when
We saw each other last
it felt right right oh right alright
nothing holding back do back, do back, do back due
We you we you we you
You called me back, do back, due show
do show it was a shadow a shadow
in your voice I thought trouble trouble
Trouble and oooh and oooh ooh ooh

sweetheart sweetheart
I can't can't can't
get through through through
I told you you you you
love love love I love love love
you be do you be do
but you but you oooh you
said yes, oh yes, yes, yes
and what I thought and what
the hell does that mean?
you said it sweet yes and yes and yes
But Bay Be Bay Be Babe Be Bay you
Wha wha wha what can it mean?

Za Za Za Za
Max Roach is on the High Hat Cymbal
High Hat HI HI High High Hat
Za Za Za MMMMNNNN Zim Zim
Zimma Zimmma Zimma Zimma
Za Za ZA ZA
Simmer Simmer Simmmerrr
I'm scared and mad and mad
and scared and wha wha wha why
Zim Zim do zim do zim do zim do do
do do do you just say yes
and not I love you, too, too, toooeeee
Zimm who's there Zimm who's there Zim with you
Do zista do zista do zista

Dissa Dissa Zimma Diss Diss Diss
Disappeared you went and disappeared
off the line
Behind the dip do dip do dipzim zim
and I can't say love oh love oh love
and now I say yeah baby yeah baby
yeah baby do dit do dik do dik you
zim bad zim bad another sister hey sister
like in grade school all I could say was
yes sister yes sister yes sister
scared and mad yes sister

Gerry Mulligan is playing hothot hot hot
The Hot Society Hot Society
old clips of Charlie Parker
The Birds flying flying flying
flying and he's dead on the videotape
To To To Toooh Bad la la la la
Zim do zim sweet sweet sweet

La Carta Parla

I try to write right write right
write right oh do do do you you
are you scared some people
will say you go with a nut
Tut Tut Tut Sax Saxo Saxo
Saxophone oh that phone phone
phone the last phone call and then
you diss diss diss disappeared

Frank Foster and Dizzy on the special
Dizzy on the special on the horn
horn horn that special special horn
oooh oooh oooh a phone
The Night in Tunisia
wind blow hot wind blow hot
wind in the phone sax oh sex oh phone
wind wind wind and win win win
win a song from the des from the des
from the desert the desert the des the des
desk win a pub pub pub do zim
do zim publishing contracts tracts
on track do sim do zim do
tract tract tract tract

Ter ter ter ter teres teres teres teresa
Teresa was a sa sa sa saint
Saint Teresa Saint Teresa Saint Teresa of Avila
wrote she wrote she wrote a lot
lot lot lot lot do zim do tracts do wha
about she wrote about
an angel piercing her heart heart heart
witha witha with a
flaming flaming flaming arrow
whoa whoa whoa whoa
They made her a saint.

Dizzy play Dizzy play St. Dizzy
play Charlie Bird Charlie Bird
Charlie Bird Parker is a saint
is a saint do phone do phone do saxophone
whoa whoa oh woe woe woe
Dizzy'll be Dizzy'll be
A Saint
Trumpet cool trumpet hot
do what do what flaming arrow trumpet
hot do hot be bop be bop cool
cool coolie oh coolie oh
could could could
They make me a saint?

Do saint do saint 'cause I write
about your yes oh yes oh yes and the pain
and the hot do hot of hurt and
chest heart of chest heart hurt
do hot hurt do hot
Zimm and the Zimm and the Zim
when the phone hangs up and the
line is cold and you're gone
and gone and gone and cool cool
cool and cold and cold and
the words words words are all
brok brok brok en en en
oh do you do you broken and the heart
and the heart is pow is pow pow pow
do what do what
is power and be oh be oh
love love love lovely lovely
and zim crash zim crash and Zim

The comets come round they
come round and around and around

and around and get famous
do I do I do I do I do I
wa wa wa want to
be famous yes famous and
no no no no no no no
noticed and walk and write
and walk and do bop do bop
do bop and be read and oh read
oh ready yes ready and read.

Dizzy, oh St. Dizzy oh
St. Dizzy we working all
the same and saying and playing
and swinging and singing
Do Dizzy St. Dizzy oh
and it's all be do be do be do be
do be bop oh bop do zim
about love and love and yes.

As a poet, I believe that I have taken Nonna Mattia's words that *la carta parla* to heart. I try to fuse continents and cultures by writing the words and then performing the works aloud. I would like to conclude with a poem, "Comari," where I have attempted to take an oral family story with the cadences of American language and infuse it with rhythm and some Italian words and cadences. I wrote "Comari" specifically for the 1998 American Italian Historical Association's Conference in New York, where I was on a panel, The Politics of Mary, with Mary Jo Bona, Mary Bucci Bush, and Mary Russo Demetrick, all wonderful writers and dear friends and my *comari*.

Comari

My *comari*, my co-marys, my co-marias
Comari, Comari, Comari, Comari
we are rich   we are strong
   in *comari* tradition
comari, comari, comari, comari

My *comari*, my co-marys, my co-marias
   I tell you now
   a story of my Aunt
the story of *Zia* Angelina
   proud and regal   with burning black eyes
she had a *comare*
a dear *comare*
a beautiful *comare*   a loving comare
Comare Comare Comare Comare Maria
they lived   they lived two
they lived two doors away
   from each other
these *comari comari comari comari*
   Angelina *e* Maria
   Maria *e* Angelina
   They passed   they passed
   they passed
they have since passed
but when   but when
   but when
they were alive
alive alive alive alive
when they were alive
they passed flowered china dishes
   filled with delicacies
   to each other
they passed dishes of
   tortellini in *brodo*
   merluzzo in *bianco*
   insalata d'arugula
these *comari comari comari comari*
Comare Angelina   *Comare* Maria
late afternoons they sipped
   they sipped and dipped
   they sipped espresso
   they dipped biscotti

La Carta Parla

in late afternoons they sipped and dipped
before   before   before
   the husbands
before   before   before
   the suppers
they sipped and dipped
before the suppers and husbands
filled their homes
these *comari comari comari comari*
They remembered these *comari*
   each name day
   each birthday
always a greeting card these *comari*
comari comari comari comari
inside and outside
dishes   coffee   greeting cards
through South Philadelphia streets
far from their Sicilian town
   they made do
they had to
   they made do
     with dishes   coffee   greeting cards

Once once once
Comare Comare Comare Maria's birthday
her birthday was coming
Comare Comare Comare Angelina
made *spumetti*
she made *spumetti* from eggwhites and nuts
eggwhites and nuts and sugar
sweets for her *Comare Comare Comare* Maria
then Angelina went
Comare Angelina went she went
Comare Angelina went to the Avenue to buy a card
a beautiful card   a beautiful birthday card
for her *Comare Comare Comare* Maria

Angelina read cards that said Happy Birthday
No good   no good   no good
    too plain   too plain
for the beautiful beautiful *Comare Comare Comare* Maria
Angelina read cards that said Happy Birthday Friend
No good   no good   no good
    no words to describe
the dear, the dearer, the dearest
Comare Comare Comare Maria
Angelina read cards that said Happy Birthday Sister
No good   no good   no good   no good
    too boring, too boring
    not love enough
for the lovely and loving and loved
Comare Comare Comare Maria

Angelina read cards that said Happy Birthday Husband
and there and there and there
    was the perfect card
there was the perfect card
for the beautiful, the dear, the loving
Comare Comare Comare Maria

Angelina bought that card
she bought the To My Dear Husband card
she bought it and loved it
and took it home
where she took a pen   a black pen
she took a black pen
she crossed out HUSBAND
she crossed that word right out
she crossed out Husband   and wrote COMARE
    in her Italian script
TO MY DEAR COMARE

the words all fit
the words inside and outside
the card   her heart
inside and outside
the words all fit
they fit   she knew they fit
inside and outside
she knew they fit her
Comare Comare Comare Maria
Angelina's *Comare* Maria.

Works Cited

Fama, Maria. "Tablecloth." In *La Bella Figura: A Choice*. Edited by Rose Romano. San Francisco: Malafemmina Press, 1993, p. 127.

Fama, Maria. "Nonna Mattia." *Paterson Literary Review* 24–25 (1995): p. 194.

Fama, Maria. "A Conversation with Mary Bucci Bush." *Phati'tude Literary Magazine* 1:1 (1997): pp. 92–93.

Fama, Maria. "Captain of the Safeties." In *Identity Lessons*. Edited by Maria Mazziotti Gillan and Jennifer Gillan. New York: Penguin Books, 1999, pp. 268–269.

Fama, Maria. "Sicilia." In *La Bella Figura: A Choice*. Edited by Rose Romano. San Francisco: Malafemmina Press, 1993, p. 123.

Fama, Maria. "Picking Apricots with Zia Antonia." In *Italian Notebook*. Syracuse, New York: Hale Mary Press, 1995, pp. 10–11.

Fama, Maria. "I Am Not White." *Paterson Literary Review* 30 (2001): pp. 70–71.

Fama, Maria. "Horses." *Mad Poets Review* 14 (1999): p. 25.

Fama, Maria. "Watching Dizzy Gillespie on TV." *VIA: Voices in Italian Americana* 12:2 (2001): pp. 72–75.

Fama, Maria. "Comari." *VIA: Voices in Italian Americana* 12:2 (2001): pp. 69–71.

Sandra M. Gilbert

Adventures on the Hyphen*

Poetry, Pasta, and Identity Politics

> "I think the notion of a hyphenated American is un-American. I believe there are only *Americans*. Polish-Americans, Italian-Americans or African-Americans are an emphasis that is not fertile."—Daniel Boorstin

L ast summer a friend and I spent a week cruising the waters of the Mediterranean off southern Turkey—sailing in Byzantium, as a matter of fact—with an Italian couple, a Turkish couple, and a Turkish crew of three. We were (obviously) a lucky and elite little band: our boat, a traditional wooden *gulet* of the sort that has plied these seas for centuries, was fitted out with spacious cabins, a cosy galley, and a shaded deck where we spent long, sybaritic mealtimes engaged in absorbing cross-cultural discussions of books, ideas, music, food, computers—the substance of contemporary lives. Our "seminars," we began to call them.

---

*First appeared as "Mysteries of the Hyphen: Poetry, Pasta, and Identity Politics," in *Beyond the Godfather: Italian American Writers on the Real Italian American Experience*, ed. A. Kenneth Ciongoli and Jay Parini (University Press of New England, 1997). Poems appeared in *Kissing the Bread: New and Selected Poems 1969–1999* (W.W. Norton & Co., 2000).

The other passengers were mostly mathematical economists (my traveling companion is a retired mathematics professor, and the Turkish economist who chartered our boat had been a student of his some years ago) fortified by a businessman (one of the Italians was CEO of a computer company based in Milan), but our conversations were so wide-ranging that I usually felt quite at ease, even though I was the only humanist on board.

I was at ease, that is, until strange tensions began to develop between me and the rather elegant Italian couple. I'd told them, of course, that I'm an "Italian-American." More precisely, I'd said "My mother is Sicilian, she was *born* in Sicily and went to the States when she was seven. And my father's father was French—Nicois—but *his* parents were probably from Liguria, originally. From a town called *Ruta*, near Genoa." My maiden name, I'd added, was Mortola, and, just outside Ruta, near the church of San Rocco, there was even a little Via *Mortola*.

I meant these disclosures as a gesture of warmth, one that might inspire bonding of some sort, or at least trust. I had intended, indeed, a hands-across-the sea overture ("My people are *your* people") of a kind that one can only rarely make.

But the Italians responded with curious indifference, even coolness. The handsome, forty-something Milanese CEO, who liked to regale us with information about the opera CDs he often played while we sipped our aperitifs (yes, the boat was very well equipped!), seemed not to hear when I not only waxed enthusiastic about some of the performances but ventured knowledgeable comments on them. His companion—a Roman woman who taught economics in Brussels and was also handsome, also forty-something—appeared, if anything, even more oblivious of my remarks, although she herself talked with considerable animation about her current efforts to educate herself in music, especially opera.

I finally realized that there was something peculiar happening when we had an odd exchange about, of all things, *pasta*. Although the Turkish crew unfailingly produced extraordinary meals, Pietro and Lucia (not their real names) had shopped assiduously for Italian delicacies in the port from which we'd embarked, and I thought there was something winsome in their determination to instruct our cook in the ways of an Italian kitchen. One night, after much discussion, they oversaw the assembly of a splendid *pasta*—a sort of spaghetti *primavera*, with lots of garlic and zucchini, that we had for a starter at dinner.

Of course I complimented all concerned profusely, congratulated the cook, praised the recipe, etc. But why was there a puzzling silence when I added that my mother makes a very similar *pasta primavera*, as did, I am told, my grandmother before her? Mooning over garlic, zucchini, basil, and freshly grated parmesan cheese as the *gulet* rocked in a glassy inlet known as Cleopatra Bay, I confessed I was nostalgic for the lively Italian odors and flavors of home—of, that is, my mother's shoebox of a kitchen in Queens along with the big, practically floor-through dining room/kitchen over which my Aunt Francesca used to preside, many years ago, in Brooklyn. Sipping wine and enthusiastically twirling spaghetti, I celebrated the flavorful familiarity of this dish on which Pietro, Lucia, and the Turkish cook had, I thought, so delightfully collaborated. But although Pietro and Lucia nodded and smiled politely, their smiles seemed forced, and they contrived to nod a bit censoriously, as if I had been, somehow, impertinent.

Impertinent familiarity! *That*, I realized later, had been the social solecism I committed. I had professed familiarity with the ways of a culture that, from the perspective of "real" Italians, is not my own. My Italian is dreadful, practically non-existent (my French-born father and my Sicilian-born mother could only speak *English* to each other, so that's the language we talked at home when I was growing up), but I could grasp a few of the words I overheard Pietro and Lucia exchanging as we all lay on deck sun-bathing the next morning. They spoke rapid, intimate Italian sentences that they assumed I'd never understand, and no, I can't reproduce their words accurately, but I caught their meaning. *She's just an American, what does* she *know about Italian cooking, about opera, about being Italian?*

And truly, after all, the answer is *almost nothing*. The easy cosmopolitanism of Pietro and Lucia was clearly grounded in an unproblematic ethnic sureness to which they had been born. The culture of which and for which they spoke was fully, seamlessly, *theirs* in a way in which it can never be mine—a way in which, as a matter of fact, it had probably ceased even to be my mother's within a year of her landing on

Ellis Island. Thus, whether they saw my eagerness to show familiarity with things Italian as a competitive striving toward sophistication or as a sentimental gesture of recuperation the (really) Roman woman and the (really) Milanese man must have at best ascribed a kind of pathos to me. Rather than supplying me with an engaging internationalism, my insistence that I was an *Italian*-American meant not that I was more than an American but that I was less than an Italian.

"Less" than an Italian: perhaps it is the sense of lessening or dilution that I associate with Italy, the *lack* that the Italian language especially signifies in my personal history, which gives special poignancy to my experience of a cultural selfhood that is (yet is also somehow not) my own. I am an Italian-American who doesn't speak Italian just the way I'm a French-American whose French ranges from dreadful to abysmal to non-existent, as well as a Russian-American who barely recognizes the sound of Russian and has never seen a street in Russia. Because of all these complex combinations, moreover, I am an American-American who spent years denying *being* American. In other words, I inhabit a country (or perhaps countries) of hyphenation—maybe even a hyphen-nation. Indeed, in a confused and tentative fashion that Pietro and Lucia might never be able to understand, I don't just live on a hyphen in some abstract theoretical sense, I eat hyphenated food, sleep and dream among hyphens, and in a sense am a walking, talking hyphen. But because the Italian part of my hyphen-nation looms so grandly, tragically, glamorously and persistently over the politics of my identity, it is to Italy as a country and a concept, as a lost land and a sometimes lost, sometimes found history that I have turned again and again in poetry and more generally in that struggle toward self-discovery of which poetry is a crucial element for me.

Fifty percent of me, through my maternal lineage, is one hundred percent Sicilian, and behind my French-born paternal grandfather, who represents another twenty-five percent of me, there is a heritage that is also somewhere in the not so distant past one hundred percent Ligurian. So at least for the last three decades, my poetry has dwelt at various times on the mysteries of Italy as they appear to an outsider who is also in a vexed and vexing sense an insider.

My poetry has dwelt on and been *fed* by these mysteries, literally as well as figuratively. For as a number of commentators have observed, today in the United States we "know" our ethnicity through knowing our ancestral food. Thus for me the stuff and staff of Italian life—for example, *pasta*—has a kind of poetry, indeed *is* a staple of poetry, a sometimes delicious, sometimes poisonous food I cook obsessively on page after written page, now and then, like so many other women writers, even scribbling about its symbolic significance while the real thing bubbles in the oven.

But culinary idealizations are not the only ways, of course, in which my hyphenated Italian-nation manifests itself to me, though they may be the least problematic. As I meditate on the ways in which my heritage has haunted both my poems and my thoughts, it begins to seem to me that Italy has had at least four or five kinds of meaning for me as a person and an artist. To begin with, I've long—and for obvious reasons—associated the country of my forebears with family secrets and more generally with the mystery of origins. At times, too, because of the way Italians, and in particular Italian-Americans, have been depicted in films and on television, I've expressed ironic ambivalence toward painful stereotypes with which my heritage links me. At the same time, I've idealized Italy as a lost Eden or dreamed of this simultaneously foreign and ancestral land as a center of otherness, a kind of anti-nation or place of alienation where I might find what William Butler Yeats would have called an "anti-self". Maybe finally, therefore, Italy has often become for me, as it has for many artists—including a number who were *not* fortunate enough to have Italian roots—a symbol of something eternally desired but therefore perpetually remote, deferred, even inaccessible.

When I've represented Italy as a locus of mysterious origins, I've drawn on both my Italian "sides," the Ligurian and the Sicilian. Here are two poems that seem to me to have arisen out of an effort to dramatize what I'll never really know about my ancestors. The first is about my Nicoise/Genovese grandfather, the second about my Sicilian-born mother and *her* mother, a midwife trained in Palermo who continued to practice her profession when the family emigrated to New York.

Grandpa
Garlic and cigars recall you, stuffed mushrooms,
spinach ravioli, Genoa haunting your kitchen,

and you with your dragging foot—
bad circulation, maybe a stroke—

5'/3", bald, gray forehead, gray mustache, failed
restaurateur, failed painter, thinning as you cooked,

thinning to the one you were in the bottle-green
Hotel Negresco uniform in Nice,

only now in Queens, pining for the old farm,
the hills above the sea. . . .

When they paced the cobbled wharf at Genoa
planning their moves five centuries ago,

what did they imagine? The men
must have been seamen: leaning landward like old walls,

they must have dreamed you as a wave
breaking on some far island. You must

have been their intention for the future. When the great
ship set sail, heeling and running free,

you lay in the hold, naked of uniforms,
painter of frescoes, master of promised spices,

rosy, perfect. What accident
of the mid-Atlantic

turned you into a scrap of cargo
lost by the civilization of the wind—

the calm sea, the prosperous voyage—
that left you and your dragging foot behind?

Kissing the Bread
1.
and the fields inside it.
The winter of the crumb, the iron
hoe hacking the furrow,
the hiss of grain in the wind.

The priest in the crust
says *kiss*, says
In nomine Domine,
bless, kiss.

2.
My mother in the four by seven
yellow kitchen in Queens,
pressing her lips to half a
loaf of day-old challah, the food
of someone else's sabbath,
before dropping it into the red and white
step-on can:
her mother the Sicilian midwife
taught her, taught all nine,
to kiss the bread before you
throw it away.

                Why?
Non so. You kiss it, like
crossing yourself before a crisis, before
the train leaves the station,
before the baby falls,
startled, into a sudden
scorch of air.

3.
No. No doubt
no that. But instead
Dickinson's "the Instead."
They were full of terrible
accurate sentiment,
        those old Italian ladies in the kitchen—
        crones, with witch hairs haloing
        their chins, with humps and staggers
        and nodes of bone ringing their fingers.

        Kissing the bread was kissing
        the carrion that was the body
        of every body, the wrist

        of daughter and husband, the crook'd
        arm of the mother, the stone
        fist of the father.

Kissing *goodbye*,
saying the daily
goodbye, the skeptical
god be with you
as the long loaf sank into ashes,
as the oven sputtered its
merciless complaint.

4.
They were kissing the corn god, you say?
Kissing the host, the guest,
the handsome one who grows
so tall and naked
in the August grove?

But what if they were mocking him,
mocking the crust that stiffened, the crumbs
that staled and scattered?

> *You thought,*
> *bread, that your magic*
> *salts were eternal, that your holy*
> *taste was your final shape,*
> *but see, you were wrong:*
> *I bid you goodbye, my tongue*
> *gives you a last touch, my teeth*
> *renounce you.*

5.
But no again: my mother's kiss
was humble, the mortified
kiss of guilt—*I can use you
no longer*—and the kiss
of dread: *what will I do, challah,
pumpernickel, rye, baguette, sweet white,
thick black, when you
are gone?*

                    And the kiss, I think
I thought she meant,
of sorrow, as if kissing
the bread is kissing
the crows that fly low over
fields we never saw in Queens,
the blurry footprints
between long rows of wheat,
the blank sun roaring overhead.

We stood in the Jackson Heights kitchen.
The white 1940s Kelvinator
whirred, no comment, and strips of
city snow crisscrossed the window.

I was eight and baffled.

*If an angel should be flying by
when you make that face, she said,
you'll be stuck with it forever.*

    As the following two poems will probably demonstrate, my ambivalence toward my Italian origins was culturally "constructed," as we say today in literature departments, by stereotypes with which I grew up, images of Italians that made me both anxious and angry.

Mafioso

Frank Costello eating spaghetti in a cell at San Quentin,
Lucky Luciano mixing up a mess of bullets and
calling for parmesan cheese,
Al Capone baking a sawed-off shotgun into a
huge lasagna—
                    are you my uncles, my
only uncles?

               O Mafiosi,
bad uncles of the barren
cliffs of Sicily–was it only you
that they transported in barrels
like pure olive oil
across the Atlantic?

                     Was it only you
who got out at Ellis Island with
black scarves on your heads and cheap cigars
and no English and a dozen children?

No carts were waiting, gallant with paint,
no little donkeys plumed like the dreams of peacocks.
Only the evil eyes of a thousand buildings
stared across at the echoing debarkation center,
making it seem so much smaller than a piazza,

only a half dozen Puritan millionaires stood on the wharf,
in the wind colder than the impossible snows of the Abruzzi,
ready with country clubs and dynamos

to grind the organs out of you.

The Leeks
fatten like marsh weeds, silvery pipes
exhaling the mild onion smell
of Vermont April.

They tell me I want to be an American,
I want a name that ends in a Protestant consonant
instead of a Catholic vowel!

Stooping above the cool
New England fronds,
I become a red-haired freckled

Presbyterian girl: I've inherited
a farmhouse (cracked panes, splintery
porch) outside Brattleboro.

Once town clerk, my steely grandma
squints behind smoky glass in the parlor.
Her mother's samplers sag in the upstairs hall.

The kitchen floor's the color of
store-bought cheese; the kitchen stove
has garlands of cast-iron daisies.

On an April Sunday I journey
over the fields, down to the murmuring swamp:
going to pick leeks and lilies, mint and camomile.

Humming *Rock of Ages*, I inhale
the damp New England spring: America's
my dooryard, my quilt, my rag rug!

I've never eaten *potage parisienne*,
never drunk red wine,
never tasted olive oil,

but I've a skinny aunt beyond the hill
who makes Presbyterian love-drinks
from lilies and camomile and leeks!

Yearning for Italy as a lost Eden no doubt became inevitable for a writer like me, whose parents and grandparents usually spoke glowingly of their native places. At the same time, seeing the country as a paradigm of otherness, a kind of alien-nation, was probably also inevitable for a writer raised thousands of miles away from what ultimately seemed to become as much a dream land as a land of dreams. The first of the poems below, focused on a virtual myth of Sicily, translates a ruined *palazzo* where my maternal grandmother once held court into an earthly paradise; the second, inspired at least in part by thoughts of Ligurian cuisine, meditates on estrangement.

In the Golden *Sala*
Sun of Sicilian hillsides,
heat of poppies opening like fierce
boutonnieres of Apollo,
light of Agrigento, fretting the sea and the seaside cliffs–
light of the golden *sala*,
the great *sala* of the ruined *palazzo*
where my Sicilian grandmother and her nine children
camped in Sambuca Zabut.

Gold leaf, gold moldings,
shredding tapestries with gold threads.

"Once it belonged to a prince.
Mama kept chickens on the terrace
but they came in sometimes, and the donkey too."
Gold chairs, gilt around the windows,
angels with shining hair and empty eyes
staring from the ceiling.

"Mama made our beds in the corners:
the big room scared us, we thought
the prince's ghost was there."
Gold railings where her laundry hung,
gold curtains, new eggs under them.
Her cooking fire in a corner,
the center of the *sala* a cave of gold
for spankings and scoldings.

"Mama was a midwife, knew
everything about herbs and births.
The peasant women came from farms around Sambucca
so she could help them."
On floors still streaked with gold
she made them spaces
in the dazzling spaces where the prince once walked.
Gold of forgotten dances, tattered rugs.

When a new baby slid out in a splash of water
he must have looked up, dazed,
toward the prince's Apollonian light,
and the black eyes of the midwife
and the black eyes of the midwife's nine black-haired
    children
would have looked quizzically down,
as if from a high cliff by the sea
hot and yellow with new poppies.

Basil
A question the box of earth
still asks the kitchen,

as in green blades
of Liguria, green

spears of the watery
forests of Thailand,

peppery keen
airs of August

as in wise king
do not fade,

as in a pot of,
where the lover's head

explodes into new
ideas, *as in*

chop the loss finely,
add salt and stew

and halo the old charred
grandmother stove,

as in what to do
with the last

three stained tomatoes
hung on the vine.

And what of Italy as a place eternally desired but therefore perpetually remote, deferred, even inaccessible? As I noted earlier, this riveting trope of my ancestral land isn't limited to Italian-Americans, so I want to pay tribute to the visionary tradition in which Italy plays such a part by giving the last word here to the great American poet Emily Dickinson. Here is one of her most powerful musings on the subject, a work in which she voices the thoughts of many who live on—and off—the hyphen.

> Our lives are Swiss—
> So still—so Cool—
> Till some odd afternoon
> The Alps neglect their Curtains
> And we look farther on!
>
> *Italy* stands the other side!
> While like a guard between—
> The solemn Alps—
> The siren Alps
> Forever intervene!

Maria Mazziotti Gillan

Shame and Silence in My Work*

When I was asked to give this presentation, I knew I needed to think about my own work in a more objective and scholarly way. The first thing I realized is that my work springs from shame and silence, the shame I felt growing up as an Italian American, a shame so strong, so overwhelming that I spent the first twenty-five years of my life unable to speak. Of course, that is the ultimate hyperbole, but it is a hyperbole that best exemplifies the twin themes of shame and silence that have so influenced my writing.

Before I went to school, I spoke a southern Italian dialect inside my home, but as soon as I stepped outside the old brown doors, I was in America, and I soon learned that I had to speak English in school and on the streets. In school, I was always terrified that the Italian word would come flying out of my mouth before I could prevent it from happening. I was intimidated by the teachers, and I learned from them how to be silent, how to sit with my hands folded neatly on my desk, how to be a good girl. In truth, I was afraid to be anything else.

My poem "Public School No. 18: Paterson, New Jersey," expresses my feelings of fear and shame. It also describes my search for words to

---

*Used with permission of Maria Mazziotti Gillan.

express my sense of outsiderness and invisibility, and the feelings of courage and empowerment that came when I was able to find the words to express my anger.

Public School No. 18, Paterson, New Jersey

Miss Wilson's eyes, opaque
as blue glass, fix on me:
"We must speak English.
We're in America now."
I want to say, "I am American,"
but the evidence is stacked against me.

My mother scrubs my scalp raw, wraps
my shining hair in white rags
to make it curl. Miss Wilson
drags me to the window, checks my hair
for lice. My face wants to hide.

At home, my words smooth in my mouth,
I chatter and am proud. In school,
I am silent, grope for the right English
words, fear the Italian word
will sprout from my mouth like a rose,

fear the progression of teachers
in their sprigged dresses,
their Anglo-Saxon faces.

Without words, they tell me
to be ashamed.
I am.
I deny that booted country
even from myself,
want to be still
and untouchable

as these women
who teach me to hate myself.

Years later, in a white
Kansas City house,
the Psychology professor tells me
I remind him of the Mafia leader
on the cover of Time magazine.

My anger spits
venomous from my mouth:
I am proud of my mother,
dressed all in black,

proud of my father
with his broken tongue,
proud of the laughter
and noise of our house.

Remember me, Ladies,
the silent one?
I have found my voice
and my rage will blow
your house down.

 Another facet of my shame and silence came to me through the books we were given that were intended to teach us how to read. While I loved the "Dick and Jane" books that we read because they opened a door into a life totally different from my own, I also knew that I did not fit into the world of those bright primary colors, their perfect house, their perfect dog, their perfect doghouse, their perfect lawn, their perfect father, their perfect American faces, their big white colonial house. I knew their world was so far removed from mine, it might just as well have been on Mars; yet it filled me with longing to be those people, to be blonde and cute and middle class. Those books told me that I was all wrong and that I didn't fit in to the world I wanted to inhabit. I think when I started to read those books and look at the pictures, I began my journey toward trying to erase what I was—a working-class Italian American. Of course, my family wasn't even fully working class. Because of my father's health, our position was always precarious; we were always hanging on to the edge economically, and my shame at my parents, their inability to speak English, to be anything but what they were, was a way of accepting a negation of myself, of accepting that I was not worthy of being validated. It filled me with the desire to pretend to myself and everyone else that I was American and middle class, even against all evidence to the contrary.

I learned to pretend in school through the unintentional lessons teachers taught me. In fact, school taught me a great deal about identity, and in doing so, it shaped my self-image. One of the most important lessons I learned was how to be silent as a way of hiding, of not calling attention to myself. My poem "Learning Silence" clearly illustrates the way I internalized that lesson.

> **Learning Silence**
> By the time I am in first grade, I know enough
> to be frightened, to keep my hands folded
> on my desk and try to be quiet "as a mouse."
> I am nervous most of the time,
> feel sick to my stomach.
> I am afraid to raise my hand, afraid
> to ask for the bathroom pass, afraid
> of the bigger children, but most of all,
> afraid of Miss Barton who does not like me.
>
> We read the DICK AND JANE books. The world of
>   these books,
> painted in bright primary colors, seems so free and perfect.
> When I open the pages, I feel I can walk through them,
> like Alice stepping through the looking glass,
> into that clean world,

those children with their wide open faces,
their blonde curls, their cute, skipping legs,
their black and white dog with its perky tail,
their big, white house with its huge lawn of manicured grass.
In those books, I can forget Miss Barton and her icy
eyes and the grimy, shopworn classrooms of PS 18,
with their scarred wooden desks,
their dark green blackout shades,
reminders of the war that has just ended.
In that house, where even the doghouse is perfect,
there would be no reason to be afraid.

I try to be good. I try to be quiet.
I hope Miss Barton will not curl her lip
when she looks at me.
I would gladly turn into Jane
if some magic could transform me,
make me blonde and cute, instead of sad
and serious and scared, with my sausage curls
my huge, terrified eyes,
my long nose, my dark, olive-toned skin,
the harsh cheap cotton of my clothes.

Although these experiences in school were painful, there was a more positive dimension to my school experiences. In school, I learned to love poetry and the sound of the language through poems read aloud by my teachers, who seemed to me to be immensely educated. I would have forgiven them anything to have them recite poems or to hear them read stories aloud. Of course, my mother told us stories, but she couldn't read them to us. She couldn't read English because my father believed that women didn't need to go to school. Though she cried and pleaded, he would not permit her to attend night school. Her one big regret was that she never learned to read in English. In light of this repression of her voice, I learned to see reading as a rebellious and revolutionary act.

At first, however, I did not learn to speak in my own voice in my writing, but rather to imitate the established literary figures whose words captivated me. Most of my attempts at poetry from the time I was quite young until I was about forty were very much in imitation of the poets I read in school. I thought I was part of the English literary tradition, and I learned about craft from studying these poems. I wanted to be Keats or Shelley or Amy Lowell; it took me a long time to realize that this yearning was part of my attempt to erase myself.

I tried hard to do just that. I had my mass of curly, wiry hair thinned constantly, trying to shape it into order. I even made up stories to tell my friends about my family and where we lived, and I seldom invited anyone home. The truth is I could have called myself anything I wanted, but I still looked dark and foreign. I did everything I could to transform myself into a real American. I bought preppy clothes; plain wool skirts and soft, lambskin sweaters; pastel-colored, oxford cloth shirts and crewneck sweaters. I bought makeup to lighten my skin and erase the dark circles under my eyes, and I eventually went to a plastic surgeon to have my big Italian nose altered to look smaller, less obtrusive, less foreign. Still, I could not stop being shy around anyone who was not Italian, could not make myself forget the high school English teacher who looked at me and said, "Anyone who speaks another language at home and thinks in that language will score 100 points lower on the SAT tests than people who do not." I constantly practiced speaking in English, practiced erasing those Italian words that filled my mind.

When I married, I chose a man with blond hair and blue eyes, a handsome man who lived in a white colonial house in an upper-middle-class town. His parents went to college and his father was an executive with a shipping company; he had an Irish last name. To me, these people, four generations removed from Ireland, were American. Marrying into that family, I thought I was being transformed, lifting up and away from my own Italian self. My husband seemed to be everything I was not. In marrying him, I could deny my past and forget my name with all its awkward, pointy *z*s and *t*s. With my new name, I thought I could forget that my parents couldn't speak English correctly and were poor. In my poem "Growing Up Italian," I give voice to that period of self-denial, and I also mark a turning point in my own life, the point at which I decided to take back my own name.

Growing up Italian
When I was a little girl,
I thought everyone was Italian,
and that was good. We visited
our aunts and uncles,
and they visited us.
The Italian language smooth
and sweet in my mouth.

In kindergarten, English words fell on me,
thick and sharp as hail. I grew silent,
the Italian word balanced on the edge
of my tongue and the English word, lost
during the first moment
of every question.

It did not take me long to learn
that olive-skinned people were greasy
and dirty. Poor children were even dirtier.
To be olive-skinned and poor was to be dirtiest of all.

Almost every day
Mr. Landgraf called Joey
a "spaghetti bender:"
I knew that was bad.
I tried to hide
by folding my hands neatly
on my desk and
being a good girl.

Judy, one of the girls in my class,
had honey-blonde hair and blue eyes.

All the boys liked her. Her parents and
grandparents were born in America.
They owned a local tavern.
When Judy's mother went downtown
she brought back coloring books and candy.
When my mother went downtown, she brought back
one small brown bag with a towel or a sheet in it.

The first day I wore my sister's hand-me-down coat,
Isabelle said "That coat looks familiar. Don't
I recognize that coat?" I looked at the ground.

When the other children brought presents
for the teacher at Christmas, embroidered silk
handkerchiefs and "Evening in Paris" perfume,
I brought dishcloths made into a doll.

I read all the magazines that told me
why blonds have more fun,
described girls whose favorite color was blue.
I hoped for a miracle that would turn my dark skin light,
that would make me pale and blond and beautiful.

So I looked for a man
with blond hair and blue eyes
who would blend right in,
and who'd give me blond, blue-eyed children
who would blend right in
and a name that could blend right in
and I would be melted down
to a shape and a color
that would blend right in,
till one day, I guess I was 40 by then,
I woke up cursing
all those who taught me
to hate my dark, foreign self,

and I said, "Here I am—
with my olive-toned skin
and my Italian parents,
and my old poverty,
real as a scar on my forehead,"

and all the toys we couldn't buy
and all the words I didn't say,
all the downcast eyes
and folded hands
and remarks I didn't make
rise up in me and explode.

onto paper like firecrackers
                like meteors
and I celebrate
                my Italian American self,
rooted in this, my country, where
all those black/brown/red/yellow
olive-skinned people
soon will raise their voices
and sing this new anthem:

Here I am
       and I'm strong
       and my skin is warm in the sun
       and my dark hair shines,

and today, I take back my name
and wave it in their faces

In 1985, when Helen Barolini's *The Dream Book: An Anthology of Writing by Italian-American Women* came out, I saw my name, Maria Mazziotti Gillan spelled, out above my poem and saw it in a *New York Times* review where they quoted from it. I was, for the first time, incredibly proud of that name and all the lineage it embodied. Then a man with whom I had gone to college called me and asked me if I was the same Maria Mazziotti who went to Seton Hall University, and I said yes. In that moment the idea of taking back my maiden name surfaced. I used the name tentatively at first, fearing that people would be confused because I had been using my married name for so long; but with the encouragement of my publisher, Stanley Barkan of Cross-Cultural Communications, I started placing that name on everything that I published, including my third book, *The Weather of Old Seasons*. Later I wrote a chapbook published by Malafemmina Press called *Taking Back My Name*, which placed together the poems I had written over the last twenty-five years about my ethnicity. It included my poem "Betrayals," which was published first in 1972 but was originally written in 1969 and worked on between 1969 and 1972. It also included new poems from 1990 and 1991, and many poems from the early 1980s.

My consciousness of the necessity to take back my name, however, grew as I began to be ashamed of my own attempts to erase myself, to deny what I was, and to try to be white. Because my married name was Irish, I had made only a small step up the ladder to Americanness; I had thought myself more American when I had light-haired children who could pass as fully American. In yearning for this ability to pass, I see that I am similar to people from many ethnic and racial groups where individuals yearn to take on the trappings of a typical American and to be received by others as such—to blend into the mainstream of a society where all differences would be magically erased. Of course, in passing, in allowing the erasure, we risk losing ourselves. Nevertheless, I wanted so desperately to be accepted that I was willing to endure erasure.

I felt desperate because I felt doubly cursed with dark skin and a poor family. After all, how ethnic one is considered usually has a lot to do with class. Because my father was a janitor and not a lawyer, because we lived in the ghetto and not the suburbs, my outsiderness was doubly insured. I did not have the class training to cover over the markers of my ethnicity. Even with such training though, my frizzy hair and olive skin would have given me away. Only gradually did I realize that no matter what my name, I still looked too Italian, too foreign, to pass. I learned that it didn't matter if I changed my name or not. I didn't ever have the luxury of passing because other people always picked me out as foreign, as un-American. "What are you?" people asked me, and when asked I always said, "Italian." Of course, when I went to Italy in June 1977, I discovered I was not Italian but American. Yet, back in the United States, I found I was not American either, but some hybrid creature, neither fully American nor fully Italian. In recognizing this truth, I began to embrace what I had always denied, and I did so with a vengeance. If you look like an Italian and sound like one and think like one, you are one, and no amount of pretending is going to change that.

At an early age, I knew that how others marked me was significant. I remember in grammar school two teachers standing in front of the room and saying, "Look at her. She's such a scared little rabbit. I bet her father beats her!" At the time, I was just humiliated by their words. When I became a writer, I knew that I could use words to reshape the way others saw my family because I had the power to tell our side of the story. I think my poem "Arturo" explains most clearly how we learned shame and silence.

Arturo
I told everyone
your name was Arthur,
tried to turn you
into the imaginary father
in the three-piece suit
that I wanted instead of my own.
I changed my name to Marie,
hoping no one would notice
my face with its dark Italian eyes.

Arturo, I send you this message
from my younger self, that fool
who needed to deny
the words
(Wop! Guinea! Greaseball!)

slung like curved spears,
the anguish of sandwiches
made from spinach and oil;
the roasted peppers on homemade bread,
the rice pies of Easter.

Today, I watch you,
clean as a cherub,
your ruddy face shining,
closed by your growing deafness
in a world where my words
cannot touch you.

At 80, you still worship
Roosevelt and JFK,
read the newspaper carefully,
know with a quick shrewdness
the details of revolutions and dictators,
the cause and effect of all wars,
no matter how small.
Only your legs betray you
as you limp from pillar to pillar,

yet your convictions remain
as strong now as they were at 20.
For the children, you carry chocolates
wrapped in gold foil
and find for them always
your crooked grin and a $5 bill.

I smile when I think of you.
Listen, America,
this is my father, Arturo,
and I am his daughter, Maria.
Do not call me Marie.

Marie was the name I adopted in my assimilationist phase. During this time, my first book came out, and the poems in it were mostly imitative of all the poets I read, though a professor in graduate school said to me, "It's in this poem about your father that you find what you have to say." That professor gave me courage to write about my life. Maybe I'll never be Keats, I thought, but I have to write about what I know. This choice has its consequences, especially because some critics label narrative, personal poetry as confessional poetry and wrinkle up their noses at it. I would not call my poems confessional, but I do try to convey the emotional truths of my life in my work. It is not always easy to do, though, because I still am that shy, inarticulate child on the inside. When I stand up in front of an audience to read my poems, I feel vulnerable. The more I've written, however, the more I have moved toward simplicity and clarity. I want there to be no separation between my poems and what I am.

This truth policy has not been easy on my family. My mother, like many Italians, didn't want her secrets revealed. She was horrified by my poems. She wanted me to convey an idealized version of our lives, even lie about them, if possible. She really wanted me to write poems like the kind she memorized in Italy, the kind found on the backs of Mass Cards. Like my mother, my son also was horrified by me and by my poetry. As my poem, "My Son Tells Me Not to Wear My Poet's Clothes" suggests, he is the product of my assimilationist period. He would like me to continue to try to blend inconspicuously into the background.

My Son Tells Me Not to Wear My Poet's Clothes
My son tells me not to wear my poet's clothes. "They're weird," he says. He wants me to look like an old-fashioned grandmother, someone out of an L. L. Bean catalog in a preppy sweater and a corduroy skirt, the kind of clothes that would have been all wrong for me even when I was 20 years old and 104 pounds. I love thin flowery dresses that float around me when I walk, long colorful scarves with fringe on them. My son does not say it out loud, but I know he thinks I'm the wrong kind of mother and that I

should act my age and give up my poetry because it is strange for me to be running off to all those poetry readings and giving workshops and working so many hours a week at my job. Sometimes I think we should trade places. He could be the staid, conservative mother and I the recalcitrant son. When we talk on the phone, I hear how he shoulders the responsibilities of his life: wife, children, job, house, yard. "John," I say "You're only 31. Give yourself a break." I hear him sigh, that expelled breath fraught with meaning that is the sound I make when I am anxious or bored, and I am saddened when I hear it coming from him over the wires across all that distance, not only the landscape that separates us but the language that fails us. I cannot find a way to make him understand that I love him, this son who needs to be far away from me so that it's as though I am chasing him down a path but he's always faster than me. I see him sitting with his son Jackson in his arms, Jackson who looks just like John did at two, and I see the way they lean together, Jackson so relaxed and trusting, his ear pressed to his father's heart.

I never could have imagined as I was growing up Italian, writing poems about shame, that my own children would someday be ashamed of me. My son always tells me I'm too loud, and I say, "Well, we worked to send you to those private schools so you could be soft-spoken."

For myself, I stayed silent too long to be quiet now. Lately, I am trying to speak about the way death and illness have touched my life recently. I have been profoundly affected by the deaths of my mother and father, nine years and one year ago, respectively. I feel, however, that they are still part of my life and my poetic voice as I suggest in the following poem.

Last Night My Mother Came Back
Last night my mother came back.
I saw her in the distance, her body
draped in wisps of fog, ethereal

as she never was in life, my sturdy
mother, her feet always planted
on the ground, practical
and no-nonsense and scolding.
Why doesn't she move toward me
instead of moving away?

My sister tells me my mother visited
her the night she ended up
in the hospital again. In that room,
in that North Carolina hospital,
my mother, who never traveled,
who in her life had only been to Italy
and New Jersey, came to my sister
and my father came too. My sister woke
up and they were there, sitting
in straight-backed chairs near
her bed. They tell my sister
to be careful, and then they talk

for a long time about her children
and the family and what she can do
to save herself. "It was so nice
to see them," my sister says,
I am hurt that they do not visit me.
When she was dying, my mother
said she couldn't wait until I arrived
every day. My sister who has always
run away from things she could not face,
had to be forced to visit, but I knew
my mother needed me. I had to be there
with her, that swollen belly,
the cancer turning her skin
as yellow as a legal pad, her small hand
soft in mine. Now I watch my mother

move away from me, see the white light
she said she saw when she was dying,
watch her turn one last time to look at me,
her smile almost a hand on my face,
her love, as always, delivered in gestures
rather than words. I mention her

every day, remembering
the things she said, the way
she taught us to be women
who have the grace to find
the nugget of gold
hidden in the center
of our ordinary days.

In examining this poem and my other work closely, I see that women are the central driving force of my books, that it is my connection to women that makes me strong, and it is this strength that I pass on to my daughter. I try to clarify these feelings in "I Dream of My Grandmother and Great-Grandmother."

I Dream of My Grandmother and Great-Grandmother
I imagine them walking down rocky paths
toward me, strong, Italian women returning
at dusk from fields where they worked all day
on farms built like steps up the sides
of steep mountains, graceful women carrying water
in terra cotta jugs on their heads.

What I know of these women, whom I never met,
I know from my mother, a few pictures
of my grandmother, standing at the doorway
of the fieldstone house in Santo Mauro,
the stories my mother told of them,

but I know them most of all from watching
my mother, her strong arms lifting sheets
out of the cold water in the wringer washer,
from the way she stepped back,
wiping her hands on her homemade floursack apron,
and admired her jars of canned peaches
that glowed like amber in the dim cellar light.

I see those women in my mother
as she worked, grinning and happy,
her garden spilling its bounty into her arms.
She gave away baskets of peppers,
lettuce, eggplant, bowls of pasta,
meatballs, zeppoli, loaves of homemade bread.
"It was a miracle," she said.
"The more I gave away, the more I had to give."

Now I see her in my daughter,
that same unending energy,
that quick mind,
that hand, open and extended to the world.
When I watch my daughter clean the kitchen counter,
watch her turn, laughing,

I remember my mother as she lay dying,
how she said of my daughter, "that Jennifer,
she's all the treasure you'll ever need."

I turn now, as my daughter turns,
and see my mother walking toward us
down crooked mountain paths,
behind her, all those women
dressed in black.

In this poem, as in many others, it is the men who are distant. As Joe E. Weil wrote in his review of *Things My Mother Told Me* in *The Connecticut Poetry Review*:

> The men are distant. They come in and out of doors, sleep, eat, involve themselves in pursuits. The poet loves her father, loves her son, but feels a constant separateness in their presence, a love far more dream than earth-bound, far more likely to bear the sting of the unrequited.

For me, that passage contains an essential quality in my work that is best illustrated in this passage from "Papa Where Were You."

> In pictures of myself when I was growing up,
> I cannot find you. I search through a catalog
> Of memories, old pictures, frayed and yellowed.
> You are not there. Papa, where were you
> While mama kept our kitchen warm, covered up
> Your absence so it was years before we realized
> That you were rarely home.

The one presence I never imagined becoming slowly absent was my husband. Although he was always a healthy person, his body has been ravaged by early onset Parkinson's disease. To watch these changes in his once-strong body is unsettling. In "The Ghosts in Our Bed," I suggest how the shadow image of his younger self is always present to me:

The Ghosts in Our Bed

To My Husband Who Has Early Onset Parkinson's Disease
The mahogany four-poster bed your mother left us
is high up off the floor. It folds us into
the smell of lavender in sheets sprinkled with violets
the thick blue and green comforter.

> For years we are happy in it,
> lusty and young and so alive together,
> this safe place to which we return each night
> to lie in each other's arms, warm and exactly
> where we want to be.
>
> Now, when we climb into our bed, those people
> who for so many years were ourselves, the ghosts
> that we live with, sleep between us.
>
> You have become so fragile. You are always
> cold and need extra blankets, and you sleep
> so quietly, your arms folded across your chest,
> that when I wake up in the night, I have to reach out
> to find you because I'm not certain you're there.
>
> You used to take up so much space, with your energy
> and strength, the big bones of your body,
> I pile blankets on you, now,
> your face rigid and frozen even in sleep.
> The ghosts of the future hover over us, reminding us
> every night of how much more we have to lose,
> even as out old ghosts whisper, "Remember, remember."
> I fall asleep with my hand on your shoulder,
> to keep you with me as long as I can.

This idea of keeping loved ones with you as long as you can is certainly a product of the closeness of my own Italian family. I felt lucky that my father lived into his nineties, especially after we lost my mother to cancer so quickly. Each night during the last years of his life, I would go to his house and sit with him. He would tell me stories of his family and his life. He would reveal secrets I had never known. He even still did his bills and our taxes. I finally fully understood what an amazing man he was. Although he always had jobs such as janitor or night watchman and my mother worked in a factory sewing sleeves into coats, they managed to buy a two-family house. I realized that there was so much to admire in this man and his outlook on life. I felt ashamed that I had betrayed and denied him during my life because I took on the attitudes of other Americans about class and ethnicity. Through these last years with him, I fully re-envisioned myself and my heritage, and finally could speak about my shame and voice my pride in my family as I do in the poem "Daddy, We Called You."

Daddy, We Called You
Daddy, We Called You

"Daddy" we called you, "Daddy"
when we talked to each other in the street,
pulling on our American faces,
shaping our lives in Paterson slang.

Inside our house, we spoke
a Southern Italian dialect
mixed with English
and we called you "Papa"

but outside again, you became Daddy
and we spoke of you to our friends
as "my father"
imagining we were speaking
of that "Father Knows Best"
T.V. character
in his dark business suit,
carrying his briefcase into his house,
retreating to his paneled den,
his big living room and dining room,
his frilly-aproned wife
who greeted him at the door
with a kiss. Such space

Shame and Silence in My Work

and silence in that house.
We lived in one big room—
living room, dining room, kitchen, bedroom,
all in one, dominated by the gray oak dining table
around which we sat, talking and laughing,
listening to your stories,
your political arguments with your friends,

Papa, how you glowed in company light,
happy when the other immigrants
came to you for help with their taxes
or legal papers.

It was only outside that glowing circle
that I denied you, denied your long hours
as night watchman in Royal Machine Shop.
One night, riding home from a date,
my middle class, American boyfriend
kissed me at the light; I looked up
and met your eyes as you stood at the corner
near Royal Machine. It was nearly midnight.
January. Cold and Windy. You were waiting
for the bus, the streetlight illuminating
your face. I pretended I did not see you,
let my boyfriend pull away, leaving you
on the empty corner waiting for the bus
to take you home. You never mentioned it,

never said that you knew
how often I lied about what you did for a living
or that I was ashamed to have my boyfriend see you,
find out about your second shift work, your broken English.

Today, remembering that moment,
still illuminated in my mind

by the streetlamp's gray light,
I think of my own son
and the distance between us,
greater than miles.

Papa,
silk worker,
janitor,
night watchman,
immigrant Italian,
I honor the years you spent in menial work

while your mind, so quick and sharp,
longed to escape,
honor the times you got out of bed
after sleeping only an hour,
to take me to school or pick me up;
the warm bakery rolls you bought for me
on the way home from the night shift.

the letters
you wrote
to the editors
of local newspapers.

Papa,
silk worker,
janitor,
night watchman,
immigrant Italian,
better than any "Father Knows Best" father,
bland as white rice,
with your wine press in the cellar,
with the newspapers you collected
out of garbage piles to turn into money

you banked for us,
with your mouse traps,
with your cracked and calloused hands,
with your yellowed teeth.

Papa,
dragging your dead leg
through the factories of Paterson,
I am outside the house now,
shouting your name.

Works Cited

Gillan, Maria Mazziotti. *Winter Light*. Midland Park, NJ: 1985.
———. *Where I Come From: New and Selected Poems*. Toronto, Canada: Guernica Editions, 1995, 1998.
———. *Things My Mother Told Me*. Toronto, Canada: Guernica Editions, 1999.

Daniela Gioseffi

Forging into the American Mainstream since the 1960s*

On Being a Woman Writer with an Italian Name

Forging into the mainstream of American poetry with the Italian name Daniela Gioseffi was not an easy thing to do in the 1960s. I realize I was a bit like a tarantella dancer trying to perform a classical ballet, but that fact hardly occurred to me—naive and blithe spirit that I was then! My Italian-born father's deeply passionate nature, his ability to empathize with others' sorrow, joy, and longing—even when they were characters in poetic dramas and romantic novels—much inspired my writing. His histrionic sensibility was not in the stereotypic style of all-American educated culture. Perhaps, as an immigrant daughter, I felt among the misfits whose family manner or mode of expression was frowned upon, or completely misunderstood in literary circles dominated by T.S. Eliot recitations and modes of understated angst.

Dr. Robertiello, well-known Harvard psychiatrist, in his 1986 analytical text on the subject, *The WASP Mystique*, demonstrates that Latino, Italian, African and Jewish American styles of communicating—modes

---

*Used with permission of Daniela Gioseffi.

with passionate displays, talk with gesticulation, animated body language, folksy warmth and informality—were misunderstood by the all-American style of social behavior. Robertiello concludes that this emotional restraint has caused much neurosis in ethnic peoples, and sometimes in white Anglo-Saxon protestants themselves. These polite inhibitions seemed to dominate literary styles, in particular, during my college years, making a display of passion in poetry unacceptable.

At the same time, it seemed there was a kind of passion envy afoot in all-American life and art, the sort of fascination that had made Hollywood characters like Valentino fascinating in my father's generation, and that would make Al Pacinco, Robert DeNiro, and John Travolta fascinating in later decades. I recall that a student-poet named Frances Vanderbilt Whyatt—in workshop sessions, which I attended early on at The Poetry Project at St. Mark's Church in the Bowery—wrote a poem titled "The Passion Through Daniela's Window" in response to my work. I was embarrassed by a quality I had not so much realized others saw in my writing. In any case, the Italian operatic style in which my father read literature to me as a child motivated me to write poetry and caused much of my work to have an ornate emotionalism and dramatic content.

My identification with the drama of my father's immigrant struggle against prejudice and discrimination was strong because of the feeling with which he related the painful stories of his youth. His family, like many others in southern Italy in the early part of the century, came here to escape poverty and hunger, only to be met with bigotry. His father, Galileo, sought his fortune, as so many men of his *Mezzogiorno* village did then, in the New World, later sending for his family via steerage passage. My father and his family were to be met with much prejudice and snobbery in their attempt to Americanize themselves and assimilate.

I inherited my love of literature from a poor, hardworking, immigrant father who had struggled to achieve an education. His dramatic quoting of Shakespeare to me as I grew is an important influence on my themes and style. He'd memorized the Bard's plays while tending a parking lot nights, working his way through Union College with an ambition to learn the English language better than his American tormentors. Felix Stefanile, a fine Italian American poet, has told me he deliberately portrays working men's themes in classical, formalist style.

Like my immigrant father, he wanted to use perfect English and metric form to portray ordinary lives.

My father's first American teachers and his classmates had cruelly mocked his immigrant speech when he'd first arrived through Ellis Island in 1910. With hard work and study, he amassed an extensive English vocabulary and spoke with eloquence. He wanted to use language better than his American classmates. He admired Abraham Lincoln and believed in the log-cabin mythos of Lincoln's life—the American Dream. That dream forged my ambition as he read to me such authors as Cervantes when I was ten years old, and Shakespeare's *Romeo and Juliet*—weeping with me at the finale. He loved Italian Renaissance painters, whose work he would show me with pride in color-illustrated and much-treasured books he'd labored to buy. He was proud of being an Italian and always told me anecdotal narratives of the lives of Leonardo da Vinci, Michelangelo, Fermi, Caruso—those whom he considered to be the great Italian *men*. However, he never mentioned a woman to admire in his stories of Italian accomplishment!

Because my father had always dreamed of becoming a writer, my writing has been an attempt to fulfill his dream for him. I can still picture him sitting with his back to us, hunched over his typewriter, forgoing the glories of a sunny afternoon, trying when he could between the duties of his full-time job as a chemical engineer, to become a writer. "American Sonnets to My Father" in my second book of poems, *Word Wounds and Water Flowers*, written the year he died, 1981, honors his struggle to be an American and tells of how I've attempted to fulfill his desire to be a published author. I managed to win a scholarship to the Millay Colony for the Arts the year he died. While there, walking alone in the woods, grieving his loss—he forever so dear to me—I wrote:

> **American Sonnets for My Father**
> **—for Donato Gioseffi 1906–1981**
> **written in Edna St. Vincent Millay's studio**
>   **at Steepletop, NY**
> You died in spring, father, and now the autumn dies.
> Bright with ripe youth, dulled by time,
> plums of feeling leaked red juices—from your eyes,

pools of blood hemorrhaged in your quivering mind.
At forty, I climb Point Pinnacle, today,
thinking of you gone forever from me.
In this russet November woods of Millay,
I wear your old hat, Dear Italian patriarch, to see
if I can think you out of your American grave
to sing your unwritten song with me.
Your poetry, love's value, I carry with your spirit.
take off your old black hat and sniff at it
to smell the still living vapor of your sweat.

You worked too hard, an oldest child of too many,
a lame thin boy in ragged knickers, you limped
all through the 1920s up city steps, door to door
with your loads of night and daily newspapers, each worth
a cheap labored penny of your family's keep.
You wore your heart and soles sore. At forty,
not climbing autumn hills like me, you lay with lung disease
strapped down with pain and morphine, hearing your breath
rattle in your throat like keys at the gates of hell.
Your body was always a fiend perplexing your masculine
 will.
You filled me with pride and immigrant tenacity. Slave
to filial duty, weaver of all our dreams, you couldn't be free
to sing. So be it. You are done, unfulfilled by song except
 in me.
If your dreams are mine, live again, breathe in me and be.

You never understood America's scheme.
Your wounded dream, father,
will never heal in me, your spirit mourns forever
from my breath, aches with childhood memory,
sighs for my own mortality in you,
which I, at last accept
more completely than ever when we

> laughed together and seemed we'd go on forever—
> even though we always knew
> you would die much sooner than I
> who am your spirit come from you.
> Remember, "a father lost, lost his!" you told us,
> preparing us with Shakespearean quotation
> and operatic feeling for your inevitable death.
>
> Good night, go gently, tired immigrant father
> full of pride and propriety. We, your
> three daughters, all grew
> to be healthier, stronger, more American than you.
> Sensitive father, I offer you this toast,
> no empty boast, "I've never known a man braver!"
> The wound that will not heal in me
> is the ache of dead beauty.
> Once full of history, philosophy, poetry,
> physics, astronomy, your bright, high flying psyche
> is now dispersed, set free from your tormented body,
> but the theme you offered, often forlorn,
> sheer luminescent soul, glistened with enough light
> to carry us all full grown.

Yet, my immigrant father, with all his passions and despite his sensitivity, had told me it was a useless endeavor for a female "meant for cooking and bearing children" to go to college. When I dared to defy him by going to college, I commuted only a few miles from home to a state institution in Montclair, New Jersey. It was the men of my generation who left the home to achieve as professionals, not the women.

The message I heard from him—that a daughter was less than a son—drove me into a kind of feminist rebellion and made women's themes important in my early work, particularly my first book, a novel called *The Great American Belly*, which was a comic feminist satire published in 1977. It dealt with an Italian American heroine named Dorissa Femfunelli, who traveled the country performing a feminist ritual dance celebrating childbirth and women's nurturing ways. Dorissa—a Goddess-worshipping eco-feminist—rebelled against patriarchal religions and her Italian father. At the same time, she was always anxiously seeking his approval.

An early poem, "Birth Dance, Belly Dancer," celebrated womanly powers and the ability to bring new life into the world. It portrays an ancient folk ritual performed by women as a birth dance in imitation of birth contractions. Its performance was a primitive Lamaze type of exercise to prepare women for natural childbirth—the quintessential feminine dance of life and birth—counterpart to the male war dance or dance of the hunt. It became a café spectacle when put on display at The World's Fair at the turn of the century, but had been a folk art ritual of the Middle East and the vineyards of Italy and Greece. The poem was used at the end of my novel to show the triumph of the birth-dancing heroine, Dorissa Femfunelli. I began to travel the country performing the poem as part of a multimedia dance piece.

Birth Dance/Belly Dancer
An Etruscan priestess
through whom the earth speaks,
enters veiled; a mystery moves toward the altar.
Unknown features, shadow of death, of brows,
of eyes, mouth, lips, teeth of the night,
jaw thrust forward like a pelvis,
navel hidden, mysterious circuit,
electrical wire of the first cries
thrust from the womb.
Silk veils hover over her,
turn with a whirling gestures
—the moon glows in her belly.
Her navel winks in an amorous quiver.
Amazing belly that stretches large enough
to let a life grow. She glides, dips, shimmies,
thrusts one hip, then another.
The music breaks. Pain fills the drum. She

falls to her knees, doubles over, leans back on her heels
as her stomach flutters, rolls with contractions, upward,
downward. She raises her pelvis, arching, widening.
Arms rise like serpents from a flesh basket,
beat, caress, nip, shimmer the air with rhythmic
pulse. At last the bloody mystery emerges,
inch by inch the head presses through the lost hymen.
Her pain works into a smile.
as the decked and bejeweled mother
pushes out her ecstasy.
Formless fluid shot into her,
molded, fired in the secret oven,
emerges, a child crying: it lives!
Its voice rings in her finger cymbals.

She rests her body, slowly rises from the earth.
Her breasts fill with milk. She shakes them:
these are food; I am life; I give food!

Woman, whose nerve-filled clitoris
makes her shiver, ecstatic mother, dance with a fury
around your circle of women.
Spin out the time locked in your own womb,
bloom from your uterus, Lady of the Garden.
The moon pulls you, crashes waves on the shore.
Undulate the branches of your arms in the wind,
Goddess of Trees, of all living things.
Your flesh is not defiled by
men who can't contain your mystic
energy of woman. Belly
that invites life to sleep in you,
breasts of mortal ambrosia,
Amazon groin that lit the hearth,
altar, oven, womb, bread, table, Earth
Mother, pagan witch of magic birth,

> from whom all suck leaves that flow
> through the body's blood,
> cave of your sex, our home,
> moon of earth, Great Mother!

Early on in the 1970s, I created an experimental poetry piece, with visuals titled "Care of the Body," which won me a grant from The New York State Council for the Arts. I used the grant to create the first "Brooklyn Bridge Poetry Walk," a multimedia street theater piece with David Amram, famed jazz flutist, as Pied Piper, and poets reading poems about the bridge. We walked over "The Eighth Wonder of the World," Hart Crane's "harp and altar of the fury fused," reading Lorca, Mayakovsky, Walt Whitman, and others through megaphones. We carried hand-painted placards I'd adorned with poets' names. Seeing mine as the only Italian name on the list of grantees for the State Council for the Arts had given me license and ambition to forge on in *that* mode or form. It was a great impetus to my sticking with writing as a career.

I'd based "The Brooklyn Bridge Poetry Walk," a street-theater piece, on an Italian Renaissance custom expounded by Florentine historians. The people of Florence, for example, are known to have paraded Michelangelo's statue of David through their streets to celebrate its creation. Also, Italian street fairs were an experience of my youth, when huge sculptures were carried through ghetto thoroughfares to celebrate saints' days with festivals. Such influences explain why much of my early work was performance poetry for theater and street theater.

I had chosen to acquire my higher degree in world drama, not poetry—probably because of my father's and grandmother's histrionic way of performing stories. I had wanted to be an actress and had acted early on with Helen Hayes and Ann Revere in Brechtian and classical dramas. In my thirties, I made a slow segue from poetic drama and theatrical performance to poetry for the page.

"The Birth Dance of Earth: A Celebration of Women and the Earth" was a choreo-poem with music and dance for theater presentation. I performed it on campuses and in theaters around the country, traveling from Miami to Milwaukee, San Francisco to Buffalo, culminating in a performance at The Brooklyn Museum where the leading feminist artists of the day had a show of their works. If my father had taught me that women were meant only for bearing children, I devised a liberating way of celebrating the fact and making it a feminist ritual. The poem was published by MS. in a centerfold spread titled "The New Dance of Liberation." My earliest publications in the first issues of MS. were what encouraged me to persist in these womanly themes to the present day as The Feminist Press prepares to reissue my international anthology of women's writings, *Women on War: Voices for Survival in the Nuclear Age*. The poem "Birth Dance, Belly Dancer," quoted earlier and written during the 1970s at the height of the feminist movement, became an important part of that theatrical performance "The Birth Dance of Earth," wherein I danced, with other women joining in at the finale, joyously celebrating birth-giving and nurturing abilities—as counterpart to the dance of war. Those were the early days of Soho and performance poetry in which I'd become deeply involved. Antiwar themes came to permeate my writing.

My work was no doubt influenced by the growing eco-feminist movement, as well as by Italian street theater and tarantella festivals during that decade. I fondly quoted Emma Goldman's declaration, "If I can't dance, I won't join your revolution," and I greatly admired Isadora Duncan's rebelliousness. I began to read such feminist sociopolitical critiques as those written by Goldman, and toured many campuses throughout the country with performance poems, which included music and dance.

Although my feminist writing takes delight in all aspects of women's lives, the women in my family—my grandmother, mother, and aunts—seemed to be bound to the home, the kitchen, and the sewing machine and did not seem to find much joy in being women. In my view at that time, they were repressed. Their limitations inspired me to write about women's lives and their need for liberation from the patriarchal culture in which I was raised, where only men's opinions mattered and were spoken publicly.

From 1968 through 1972, off-Broadway theaters produced my poetic monologue, "The Sea Hag in the Cave of Sleep," which tells of the sexual and mothering adventures of three women of different ages. I think my "sea hags," characters inspired by James Joyce, represented my Italian aunts and grandmother telling the stories of their struggle as women in a male-dominated world. They tell of how Pandora and Eve are blamed for all the troubles in men's lives, although all the while macho ways are causing destructive conflicts, famines, and other brutalities that follow war. The poem ends with the lines: "I come out of my own legs into this world," which is meant as an affirmation of women's self-actualization. Woman is born of woman, and that's a different phenomenon than being man born of woman. It was a tribute to Grandma Lucia.

Based on my father's Neopolitan mother, Lucia, I wrote a poem that seemed to embody all that was self-sacrificing and limiting for women in a patriarchal culture and performed it at Casa Italiana, Columbia, in 1978 at the dawning of the current Italian American renaissance in literature. To give an historical perspective, some years earlier, Richard Gambino of Queens College had joined with Dr. Ernesto Falbo in editing *Italian Americana* at the State University of New York, Buffalo. When I'd performed my work at SUNY Buffalo in 1976, Dr. Falbo was in the audience and spoke to me afterward, which inspired my writing of the following poem, originally titled "Bi-centennial Anti-poem for Italian American Women, in 1976:"

> **For Grandma *Lucia La Rosa*, "Light the Rose"**
> *You're one of only two or three Italian-American women poets in this country. You're a pioneer. There are fewer of you known than Black or Puerto Rican women poets.*
> Pr. Ernesto Falbo, SUNY Buffalo, N.Y. 1976.

On the crowded subway,
riding to the prison to teach
Black and Puerto Rican inmates how to write,
I think of the fable of the shoemaker
who struggles to make shoes for the oppressed
while his own go barefoot over the stones.

I remember Grandma Lucia, her olive face
wrinkled with resignation,

content just to survive
after giving birth to twenty children,
without orgasmic pleasures or anesthesia.
Grandpa Galileo, immigrant adventurer,
who brought his family
steerage passage to the New World;
his shoemaker shop where he labored
over American factory goods
that made his artisan's craft a useless
anachronism; his Code of Honor
which forced him to starve
accepting not a cent of welfare
from anyone but his sons;
his ironic "Code of Honor"
which condoned jealous rages of wife-beating;
Aunt Elisabetta, Aunt Maria Domenica, Aunt Raffaella,
Aunt Elena, grown women huddled like girls
in their bedroom in Newark, talking in whispers,
not daring to smoke their American cigarettes
in front of Pa;
the backyard shrine of the virgin,
somber blue-robed woman,
devoid of sexual passions,
to whom Aunt Elisabetta prayed
daily before dying in childbirth,
trying to have *"a son"*
against doctor's orders, though
she had five healthy daughters already;
Dr. Giuseppe Ferrara, purple heart veteran
of World War II, told he couldn't have a residency
in a big New York hospital because of his Italian
name; the Mafia jokes, the epithets:
"Wop, guinea, dago, grease-ball."
And the stories told by Papa
of Dante, Galileo, Leonardo, Fermi, Caruso
which stung me with pride for Italian *men*;

how I was discouraged from school,
told a woman meant for cooking and bearing
doesn't need education.

I remember Grandma
got out of bed
in the middle of the night
to fetch her *husband* a glass of water
the day she died,
her body wearied
from giving and giving and giving
food and birth.

Some of my feminist writings were experimental performance pieces like "The Birth Dance of Earth." I also wrote a playlet titled "Daffodil Dollars." Again, the theme was women's empowerment. I was a part of the early experimental poetry scene in New York's Soho—creating happenings, or multimedia poetry events involving performance, music, and dance. All of this bravado for performance, I believe, came directly from my father Donato's operatic way of storytelling.

Though I devoured Nancy Drew mysteries in grammar school like any other American girl, in my teens I discovered Edna St. Vincent Millay. The drama of her life, the fact that she won a scholarship to Vassar for a poem she wrote and her subsequent rise from poverty into the light of poetry, impressed me. It was a dramatic story like the ones my father told of his struggle to become educated and respectable from humble beginnings. Millay was a woman and a feminist, and to see that a woman could work hard to become a writer—from humble beginnings—and be respected for her work really influenced me. She was such a great beacon to me, both her life and her craft with language. I was pleased to find how Millay had marched for Sacco and Vanzetti. Her poem "Justice Denied in Massachusetts," is a tribute to the Italian immigrant struggle in America. Her example as a liberated woman and her involvement with social justice inspired me greatly.

My father didn't teach us Italian, not for lack of pride in it, but perhaps because he'd experienced so much prejudice for being an Italian immigrant. It's a little-remembered fact that there were concentration camps for Italian immigrants in the United States during World War II, similar to those in which Japanese immigrants were unjustly incarcerated. I remember a poster I saw in my ghetto neighborhood as a child living in the Ironbound section of Newark, New Jersey. I wrote this poem as a result. It explains why I, born during World War II, am not fluent in Italian.

> **"Don't Speak the Language of the Enemy!"**
> reads the poster at the end of a gray alleyway of childhood
> where the raggedy guineas of Newark
> whisper quietly in their dialects on concrete steps
> far from blue skies, olive groves or hyacinths.
> Bent in a shadow toward the last
> shafts of sunlight above tenement roofs,
> Grandpa Galileo sadly sips homemade wine
> hums moaning with his broken mandolin.
> Children play hide-and-seek
> in dusty evening streets as red sauce simmers,
> proverbially, hour after hour, on coal stoves,
> garlic, oil, crushed tomatoes blended
> with precious pinches of salt and *basilico*—
> a pot that must last a week of suppers.
> The fathers' hands are ugly with blackened finger nails,
> worn rough with iron wrought, bricks laid, ditches dug,
>   glass etched.
> Wilted women in black cotton dresses wait in quickening
>   dark,
> calling their listless children to scrubbed linoleum kitchens.
> In cold water flats with tin tables, stale bread is ladled
>   with sauce,
> then baked to revive edibility. Clothes soak in kitchen
>   laundry-tubs,
> washboards afloat. Strains of opera caught in static
> are interrupted by war bulletins.

> The poster pasted on the fence at the end of the block
> streaked with setting sun and rain reads:
> "Don't speak the language of the enemy!"
> But, the raggedy guineas can speak no other,
> and so they murmur in their rooms in the secret dark
>   frightened
> of the government camps where people like them
> have been imprisoned in the New World.
> They teach English to their children by daylight,
> whispering of Mussolini's stupidity—
> stifling the mother tongue, wounding the father's pride,
> telling each other, "We are Americans. God bless America!"

Grandpa Galileo Gioseffi was also a great influence on my life and writing. From him I learned to question and rebel. Galileo was an iconoclast who loathed the church's hypocrisy, and his rebellious attitude rubbed off on my father, and then onto me. No doubt the prejudice he suffered inspired me to join the Civil Rights Movement in 1961, at which time my writing turned to journalism for a spell. I became a television journalist in Selma, Alabama, on WSLA-TV during the days of the freedom riders and lunch counter sit-in protests. Because television programming was not integrated in Alabama in those days, I was beaten and sexually abused by the Ku Klux Klan for making an announcement on an all Black gospel show. There were burning crosses and broken watermelons on the lawn of the television station the next morning. It took me many years to write about that as I wanted to spare my father the truth. He never knew what happened to me, and I was ashamed of it, too. I was more than fifty years old when I finally published "The Bleeding Mimosa," a story about my rape and abuse at the hands of the Ku Klux Klan. Luciana Polney, a younger Italian woman writer, adapted it to the stage at the Duplex Theatre in Sheridan Square in New York in 1994. It was a liberating experience for me to view it acted out by others. I felt healed as I watched it played out to a survivalist's conclusion, as I saw the scenes between the immigrant father and the American daughter—that conflict: to be a good daughter and at the same time the struggle to overcome prejudice toward liberation.

Now, as I've reached the age of sixty and look back over my career as a writer, I can see clearly that my Italian father's passionate nature, his frustrated desire to be a respected writer in America, the prejudice he suffered, the reading he taught me to love, the education in literary art and science that he worked hard to acquire were a large influence on my tenacious desire to forge my way into the mainstream of American letters. On the other hand, my Grandmother Lucia's subjugation to my grandfather's will; my coming from an immigrant family that rebelled against the church's ways, but in some measure upheld its patriarchal values; my own rebellion against Old World ways and my search for truth and anarchistic liberation from the past; my desire to keep my father's surname and strive for acceptance as a woman, a daughter who could not be a son, but who wanted to make a loving father proud—*all* of these factors had a profound influence on my drive to become the first educated woman of my family and strive for an accomplished voice imbued with feminist themes in American literature.

My immigrant Italian forebears have made me who I am for worse or for better, and I can never deny that rich heritage of passionate emotions—the suffering and joy that art portrays—which I learned early on from my Old World Italian father. Despite my feminism, I have to say that my Italian patriarchal father's love of literature—his tenacity to fulfill the American Dream—was my greatest inspiration to being a writer. Sandra Mortola Gilbert, Diane di Prima, Josephine Gattuso Hendin—we feminists of that era of the 1970s—have, I hope, offered some impetus to the women who began to publish later. The following poem says it all for me. It was written when I finally made the pilgrimage back to my father's village of origin, Orta Nova, near the Gargano—the spur of the boot—not far from Bari. I went there in 1986, five years after his death.

> ***Orta Nova, Provincia de Puglia***
> "Land of bright sun and colors,"
> you're called in *Italia*.
> Near Bari and Brindisi where the ferry
> for centuries has traveled the *Adriatico*,
> to and from Greece.
> Orta Nova, city of my dead father's birth.

How strange to view you, *piccolo villaggio*,
with ladybugs, my talisman, landed on my shirt.

They show me your birth
certificate—"Donato Gioseffi, born 1905,"
scrawled in ink, on browning paper.
When I tell them I'm an author, first of my American family
to return to my father's home, I'm suddenly "royalty!"
They close the *Municipio* to take me in their best town car
to an archeological dig near the edge of the city.
There, the Kingdom of Herdonia, unearthed with its brick
   road
leading to Rome, as all roads did and still do,
back to antiquity's glory! Ladybugs rest on me at the dig
of stone sculptures the Belgian professor shows me. I buy
   his book,
"The Kingdom of Herdonia: Older Than Thebes."

Ah, *padre mio*, the taunts you took as a thin,
diminutive, "guinea" who spoke no English
in his fifth-grade class
from brash Americans of an infant country!
You never returned to your ancient land where now the
   natives,
simpatici pisani, wine and dine me in their best
ristorante. I insist on paying the bill. They give me jars
of *funghi* and *pimento* preserved in olive oil—their prize
produce to take back home with me. They nod knowingly,
when in talking of you, I must leave the table to weep—
alone in the restroom, looking into the mirror
at the eyes you gave me, the hands so like yours
that turn the brass faucet
and splash cold water over my face.
For an instant, in this foreign place, I have met you again,
Father, and have understood better, your labors,

your struggle, your pride, your humility,
the peasantry from which you came to cross the wide
sea, to make me a poet of New York City.
Which is truly my home?
This *piccolo villaggio* near Bari, with its old university,
the province where Saint Nicholas's Turkish bones are
   buried,
in hammered-gold and enameled reliquary,
the province of limestone caves full of paintings older than
   those of Lescaux,
this white town of the Gargano, unspoiled by *turisti*, this
   land of color
sunlight and beauty. This home where you would have
   been happier
and better understood than in torturous Newark tenements
   of your youth.
This land of sunlight, blue sky, pink and white flowers,
   white stucco houses,
and poverty, *mezzogiorno*, this warmth you left to make me
a poet from New York City, indifferent place,
mixed of every race, so that I am more cosmopolitan
than these, your villagers, or you
could ever dream of being. This paradoxical journey
back to a lost generation
gone forever paving the way
into a New World from the Old.

Works Cited

Gioseffi, Daniela. *The Great American Belly*. New York: Doubleday, 1978; Dell Books, 1979; London: New English Library, 1979.

Gioseffi, Daniela. "Birth Dance, Belly Dancer: The New Dance of Liberation." In *Eggs in the Lake*. Rochester, New York: Boa Editions, Ltd., 1979. Previously published in Ms. *Magazine* 6:1 (1978): pp.68–67.

Gioseffi, Daniela. *Women on War: An International Reader*. 2nd ed. New York: The Feminist Press City University of New York, 2003.

Gioseffi, Daniela. "For Grandma Lucia La Rosa." In *Word Wounds and Water Flowers*. West Lafayette, Indiana: VIA Folios/Bordighera Press, 1995. Also published as "Bicentenial Anti-Poem for Italian American Women." Previously published in *Newsletter of Casa Italiana*, Fall-Winter (New York: Columbia University, 1976) and *Eggs in the Lake* (Rochester, New York: Boa Editions, Ltd., 1979)

Gioseffi, Daniela. "Don't Speak the Language of the Enemy." Previously published in *VIA: Voices in Italian Americana* 13:1 (Fall-Winter 2002) and *Symbiosis: Poems* (New York: Rattapallax Press, 2002).

Gioseffi, Daniela. "Orta Nova, Provencia de Puglia" In *Going On: Poems*. West Lafayette, Indiana: VIA Folios/Bordighera Press, 2000.

Josephine Gattuso Hendin

A Usable Past*

Writing to the Hybrid Future

I began to write *The Right Thing to Do* in the aftermath of my father's death. I wrote in a white heat, in an almost obsessive need to relieve the turmoil in my heart caused by all that I had never said to him. I had left home to make my own way through college and graduate school, and spent my professional life teaching and writing about American literature, infatuated with the American past and the unruly, transgressive brilliance of contemporary writing. Although my parents and I had grown close again, much had been left unsaid to them, or even to myself, about the turbulent past that remained between us. I had written about Italian American subjects, but I had regarded my own experience as an encrypted language, suitable for my own private thoughts, but never for public speech. I wrote about American literature and culture for *The New York Times Book Review*, *Harper's Magazine*, *The New Republic*, and popular and academic journals, but I had kept the code of *omertà*, never writing about the practices and ways of the world in which I had grown up.

---

*Used with permission of Josephine Gattuso Hendin, New York University.

Many Italian American women scholars have experienced a gap between their professional and personal identities. Linda Hutcheon coined the word *cryptoethnics* to describe herself and other English scholars who, by custom or choice, had used married names that masked an Italian American heritage and defined their public identity. Becoming a novelist meant more for me than shifting forms from criticism to fiction. It involved an awakening of the voices, ethos, and emotions of my childhood that had formed me. It involved a fuller realization that, much as I carried around more than one way of expressing myself, I carried around more than one culture. Any shift in the way one looks at the world and experience can be looked upon as a cultural shift that requires forms of self-examination that critical work does not.

Willa Cather once remarked that the most influential experiences of a writer's life occur before the age of eight. She was certainly right about that. Identity as a writer is invariably bound up with that formative identity. Writing for me has always been a way of wrestling precise meaning from the jumble of emotions and experiences life so often is. However, I had never written to put my own emotions in order or to sort through why I was so driven to resist them or the Italian American world that had shaped me. Although I set out to write a novel about a young woman's coming of age in turbulent times, and encountering obstacles and attitudes that affect virtually all women, I found that the experience of writing meant confronting my own relation to a past I loved but had not been able to probe. It meant sorting out my own ancestry and the love and anger it had often inspired. It meant thinking through what being an Italian American meant to me, and how its power had developed and changed for me over time.

Narrative is language's bottom line—the placing of what matters into a meaningful order. It was fortunate that my novel was first published in 1988, and reprinted in 1999, a time that coincided with a renaissance in Italian American studies and the emergence of a larger group of critics, novelists, and poets who were redefining what it meant to be an Italian American woman writer. In retrospect, I believe that exploration of Italian American heritage and my personal narrative have intertwined.

Writing *The Right Thing to Do* focused a bittersweet cultural heritage of feeling torn apart—drawn to the unruly larger world, but also pulled by claims of loyalty and love to a family both secure and suffocating, loving yet destructive of larger hopes. To want to escape into American uprootedness and possibility or embrace what I already knew, to want the unknown or crave the comfort of the familiar, is to feel every cut of ambivalence, that double-edged sword goading painful choices. Although my novel is fiction, not autobiographical and not literally true, it is true to the mores, attitudes, humor, and difficulty of the world I knew.

My fictional Italian American father, Nino, suspects that his daughter, Gina, is up to no good with a handsome young man with a blond beard. He is determined to save her from ruin and hedonistic times and end the affair; Gina is determined to continue it. What ensues is a struggle between them in which the conflict of generations and the war between the sexes converge. A Sicilian father's protective love is hard hit in the post pill paradise, but what is at stake is not any abstract double standard but the lived engagement of father and daughter in each other. Uncovering the energies of their struggle and their similarities meant recognizing the mingled difficulty, power, and value of their connection in a larger culture in which the upheavals of the 1960s and 1970s had left the power of authority and family connections foundering in a culture of experimentation.

The poet Marianne Moore described the family tree as a kind of "living genealogy which is in its branching, unified and vivid." (Dearborn 160). The effort of assimilated women writers to grapple with issues of inheritance and identity inevitably brings ancestry into a collision with newness, and memory into an encounter with disruptive social forces and the historical moment. These all erupt in the conflict of generations that had most often been seen as a male phenomenon. When Marcus Lee Hansen, describing a renewal of desire for once-rejected ethnic traits, remarked in what was to become a classic formulation—"what the son forgets the grandson wishes to remember"—it probably did not occur to him that he had forgotten about daughters and granddaughters. His succinct phrase implied those universal conflicts between fathers and sons that were being newly seasoned in what was then imagined as the melting pot of American life. From that cauldron, third-generation sons could presumably emerge so purged of immigrant insecurities that they could reclaim that distinctive heritage their fathers had hoped to abandon or at least conceal in order to succeed.

There was reason to consider men the front line in the battle between Italian and American mores. It was once primarily men who went out of the home to workplaces where they felt the direct blows of the American world. Pietro di Donato described the result as crucifixion in *Christ in Concrete*. Mario Puzo depicted it as driving the father insane in *The Fortunate Pilgrim*. In his warm memoir, *Mount Allegro*, Jerre Mangione celebrated his father's stoic endurance while lamenting his narrowness and fatalism, but also conveyed his certainty that he himself would construct a broader, more promising life. For women writers, the path was complicated by the very idealization by successful male writers of forms of female power that were restricted to the home and its preservation.

Women were, and still are, largely expected to be peacemakers who made homes a haven from harshness and provided traditional stability and love amid the claims and challenges of the competitive larger culture. Given the odds against them, women faced a daunting task requiring intelligence, energy, and compassion. For many male writers, that sainted mother who offers unconditional love, who can always be relied on for strength of character and support, and who fully understands them, represents a lost, idealized world. Women writers have been no less grateful to such mothers, but they have taken a more complex and even ambivalent look, mindful and even hopeful that they would never follow in their path.

It is safe to say that the lives of immigrant Italian women were as much affected by America as those of men. Yet the transformation in expectations that women experienced was far more radical and their journey toward affirming their heritage was far more complex than has generally been acknowledged. In the encounter with America, the prized qualities of *serietà* that encompassed women's shrewd understanding of their situation, ability to manage inventively within it, and the necessity for both hard work and competence readily expanded into a desire for self-realization and self-expression that often was accompanied by frustration, depression and despair. Carla Cappetti sensitively quoted the relevant issues that had been explored by urban sociologist William Isaac Thomas in his study of delinquent Polish immigrant girls:

> the modern revolt and unrest are due to the contrast between the paucity of fulfillment of the wishes of the individual and the fullness, or apparent fullness, of life around him. All age levels have been affected by the feeling that much, too much, is being missed in life. This unrest is felt most by those who have heretofore been most excluded from general participation in life—*the mature woman and the young girl* (82).

Scholars of literary ethnicity and even specialists in the role of gender were, until recently, not engaged in identifying what is distinctive about the female journey. Irving Howe, in his pointedly titled study, *World of our Fathers*, attributed this absence to the fact that differences in the assimilation of women were submerged in Jewish immigrant life because both American and Jewish tradition saw marriage as the female goal. He cites the examples of Mary Antin and Anzia Yezierska, two Jewish immigrant writers who wrote of their longing for change but who had to contend with the expectation that the lives of women would remain homebound or that their labor in any workplace would be ideally followed by tradition-bound marriages and motherhood. Wherever women were, they would meet the same expectations and feel the claims of caring for children, working, doing laundry, cleaning, cooking—all those family responsibilities that filled the time between sunrise and sunset.

Advocacy of universal processes of acculturation first brought the subject of gender and ethnicity into the mainstream of scholarly consideration. *Pocahontas's Daughters*, published in 1986 by Mary Dearborn, is a seminal work on women and ethnicity. Dearborn claims Pocahontas as the true godmother of all ethnic women. Pocahontas is legendary for her role as savior of Captain John Smith—she protected him from the warriors sent to kill him by her father, Powhatan, Chief of the Confederacy of Algonquin tribes in what is now the state of Virginia. By wrapping her arms around Smith's head to prevent the warriors from beating him to death, she saved his life. She eventually left her tribe for the English, and, by marrying the English settler John Rolfe, joined the new culture. To assimilate, Dearborn's ethnic woman must follow a comparable path by rejecting her own family to embrace the Founding Fathers and figuratively adopt George Washington as her new father. To do so is, presumably, to enter the mainstream through substituting America's patriarchy for one's own. To contest the dominance of men by assertions of different female strengths or claims of matriarchal forms of power would, Dearborn believed, only "continue the long and sorry tradition of exoticizing and excluding . . . Pocahontas." (193).

The growth of interest in gender and ethnicity over the past twenty years has enabled deeper and more expansive explorations of the acculturation of women in scholarship and fiction. Italian American women novelists and scholars of literary ethnicity are exploring the variety and power of women's roles and have brought an awareness of findings in gender studies and ethnic studies over the last decade to bear on the issue of what constitutes the "living genealogy" of women's ancestry encoded in fiction. Mary Jo Bona's groundbreaking study, *Claiming a Tradition: Italian American Women Novelists*, provided the first book-length critical analysis of the subject and highlighted how varying configurations of family life, represented in fiction ranging from the immigrant memoir to current novels and stories, provided a baseline against which changes in the role of women could be measured. Exploring the problem of defining the ethnic identity of Italian American women and recognizing, as she said in her introduction to *The Voices We Carry*, that "immigrant fiction and autobiography were primarily written by Italian male immigrants," she situates her literary analyses in *Claiming a Tradition* in the context of intergenerational and marital relationships as they affect women, are changed by their perspective, and alter their view of the larger world. In doing so, she addresses some of the primary cultural codes operating in the Italian American family.

Bona notes that the code of silence (*omertà*) forbids revealing anything to strangers and applies with particular force to women, who are the guardians of family relationships (Claiming 14). Yet she challenges the fear embodied in the proverb: "To whom you tell a secret, you give your freedom," and finds that telling family secrets reflects, for women, "a profoundly courageous act of autonomy" (Claiming 14). Bona gives equal weight to the refusal of Italian American women writers either to abandon *Italianità* or to embrace it without revision. *Claiming a Tradition* provides an account of the ethnic novel through reevaluations of the roles of women in families. Analyzing a broad spectrum of Italian American women writers, it explores earlier works in which a woman's "pragmatism, shrewdness and assertiveness" are devoted to protecting her family, sometimes through defying the family patriarch, and current fiction, which underscores the tensions of a female individualism that make "going home . . . a radical act: an act of faith and defiance" (Claiming 32, 197). In effect, Bona's work establishes a lively and inventive intellectual tradition amongst Italian American women writers.

A striking recent addition to definitions of what it means to be an Italian American woman stresses the matriarchal sources of power. *Strategies of Empowerment in the Writing of Italian American Women*, by Mary Ann Vigilante Mannino, theorizes a unifying strategy that can reconcile cultural collisions between Italian and American practices by recognizing sources and symbols of female power that may transcend discord. In the process, Mannino discusses a variety of Italian American women writers and explores their relation to women writers from other ethnic groups. For example, Mannino presents one origin and resolution of cultural discord in the conflict with religious authority precipitated by Italian immigrants' encounters with an American church that was shaped by the Irish, who were antagonistic to their emotionalism. Southern Italian religion stressed the endless compassion of God, celebrated the saints in earthy festivals, and was often most passionate in its worship of the Blessed Virgin, the all-compassionate Mother of God, who may be the ultimate matriarchal force. Mannino notes:

> because the legacy of the southern Italian peasant is a value system that in many central issues is in marked opposition to the American culture that the children of these immigrants absorb in the public schools, in the church and in the movies, the daughters and granddaughters lack a certain clarity and decisiveness

about their choices. The post-modern age, in which most of these women write, is an era of flux and uncertainty as well. Italian/American women who write are uncertain of their identity in an age of uncertainty. They are women born into conflict searching for stasis. This is not to suggest that conflict is wrong and that stasis is good, but rather that conflict is disconcerting and uncomfortable and people try to remove themselves from it. People long for what they rightly or wrongly believe to be the blissful existence of stasis (41).

Mannino persuasively argues for the discovery of a redeeming stability through invoking powerful, secular female ancestors. She celebrates the potential influence of the peasant grandmother and analyzes the role of strong female ancestors in a variety of Italian American and other ethnic works. For example, Mannino explores how Helen Barolini's *Umbertina*, a novel of four generations, tells the tale of the strong and intelligent peasant, Umbertina, who comes to America, creates a successful business, nurtures her family, and provides a potential model for later generations.

Not everyone can find the path to the heritage of female power. Mannino incisively argues for the inspiration provided by Umbertina for those who can embrace the earthy and passionate Italian culture she represents. Mannino sees Umbertina's granddaughter, Marguerite, as doomed to insecurity and ambivalence because she was raised to shed her peasant heritage by upwardly mobile parents determined to make her, as Mannino says, an "American lady" (133). She represents

> the privileging of rationality over emotion, and the internalization by Italian/American women of the American sex-gender system which forces women to become cheerleaders for their husbands rather than having meaningful work of their own, and which scripts them as sexual objects rather than sexual subjects (133).

Marguerite is plagued by self-doubt and disappointment at the lack of physical passion in the literary, intellectual world of Rome into which she has married to escape her wealthy, American upbringing. In contrast, her own daughter, Tina, searches for a female tradition of empowerment in her peasant ancestry. Her quest is projected metaphorically as her journey to her great-grandmother Umbertina's birthplace in Calabria.

Exploring the harshly impoverished mountain village of her great-grandmother, Tina comes to understand the achievement represented by Umbertina's immigration, her emergence as the shrewd architect of her family's American success in the food business, and her ability to raise sons who could prevail in an American world. That empathic understanding of the magnitude of her great-grandmother's drive and intelligence constitutes a refutation of female self-doubt and subordination. Mannino explores a variety of texts in which the energy and acuity of a peasant grandmother can inspire female empowerment.

Intergenerational bonds highlight the extent to which Italian Americans are bearers of two cultures. The codes of silence (*omertà*) and of proper public presence or behavior (*bella figura*) that shaped the solidarity and practices of the traditional family are bound to be at odds with a thirst for self-expression and self-affirmation in the larger tell-all culture of today. For the Italian American woman writer, the clash between authority and freedom, silence and speech, loyalty to family and the craving for escape from its confines are all richly dramatic subjects that have cultural resonance. What are the effects of such conflicts on the meaning of memory or family history and the viability of tradition? The question with a thousand answers, addressed differently by Italian American women novelists and poets, turns on the usability of the past. Can the codes, sources of meaning, and expressive styles of the past, which are perfected within the coherent world of family, address the needs of current lives spent in an individualistic, competitive culture beyond the family?

As critics and novelists, Italian American writers have stressed the fluidity of the relationship between mainstream America and marginal ethnic groups. In his *Italian Signs, American Streets: The Evolution of Italian American Narrative*, Fred Gardaphé formulates a developmental view of that relationship and argues for the susceptibility to change and adaptability of traditional ethnic signs and codes as they affect and are affected by historical, social, and economic change. Anthony J. Tamburri, in *A Semiotic of Ethnicity: In (Re)cognition of the Italian/*

American Writer, formulates a vision of that fluidity based on transformations in ethnic consciousness developed over time by the interaction between ethnic groups, as well by their dynamic relation to mainstream America. Both formulations are based on presumptions of a reflexive relationship between margin and mainstream that have helped shape American cultural historiography. "Once I thought to write the history of American immigrants. Then I discovered that the immigrants were American history," wrote Oscar Handlin, in his influential study, *The Uprooted*, which announced the inseparability of immigrant and mainstream (3). This was true when Handlin wrote in 1951, but it is even more accurate today.

Current writers from different ethnic groups who stress a confident hybridity are heirs of the redefinitions at work in mainstream America, which have substituted a discourse of cultural pluralism or cultural mosaic for an earlier assimilationist rhetoric of homogenization in the melting pot. The willingness to do so has multiple causes, but among them is the loss of faith in and growing cynicism about disparities between our secular religion of civic virtue that gave a self-righteous energy to the will to erase ethnic differences and the actual conduct of those in power. The rise of the multicultural movement goes hand in hand with the decline since the 1960s of the dominant culture's unchallenged authority. Growing recognition of the power of difference as a renewable source of creative energy has proved a stimulus to ethnic studies and to Italian American scholarship (Hendin 142).

Women scholars and writers have found in the female experience of otherness a vantage point that permits them to question or even to revise and adapt traditional codes for lives in a multiethnic, cosmopolitan America. Italian American women novelists have fused personal and collective experience in sharply realized fiction that positions ethnic conflict against larger American social unrest. For me, the family as a primary social institution is not only the bulwark against the competitive strife of the larger culture, but also the crucible in which cultural changes are registered in intensely personal and dramatic form. The family is affected and even invaded by the lure of the world outside. Fictional families serve as a means of showing how the culture, operating through the family, achieves incremental changes. My focus as a novelist has been on the experience of that unrest within the family.

In this context, I believe I share with other Italian American writers two factors that help provide a distinctive creative heritage in depicting families. First, we have available a sharply codified set of rules—ideals of family loyalty, proper public behavior *(bella figura)*, matriarchal compassion and *serietà*, patriarchal authority, and silence and proper speech *(omertà)*. All of these clarify the nature and belief system of the family as a central unit and help define a coherent set of values to contest, defy, adopt, or compare with the larger culture. The second factor concerns a style of expression that seemed natural to me and that, I have noticed, has been widely used by other Italian American writers. This expressive style borrows from traditions of Italian folk storytelling. It emphasizes communicating through illustrative tales or anecdotes, dramatic dialogue, and clarity of meaning. It involves a rejection of abstraction. It uses stories and anecdotes characters tell each other within the frame of the novel to encode and dramatize a relational vision of identity that can register the stress exerted by larger cultural forces in personal relations. Even when issues of estrangement or escape are crucial signs of stress, a focus on relational identity lends dramatic intensity to visions of alienation.

The tendency to move away from abstraction and employ rich residues of folktale tradition can affect even experimental Italian writers who concretize estrangement or uprootedness as an experience. For example, Italo Calvino's postmodern fictions draw on his command of folktales and blend the ordinary, the absurd, and even the miraculous in compressed formulations. Calvino's experimentalism perfected the meaningful anecdote as a postmodern parable. In "The Man Who Shouted Teresa," one of the stories collected in *Numbers in the Dark*, a man in the street enlists a crowd to help him shout "Teresa" louder and louder. Not attached to anyone he knows or hopes to find, the name and the calling of a female name selected at random cast a kind of magic spell against isolation. It is a means of finding support, of affirming solidarity with strangers in a crowd that lasts no longer than the effort of shouting a woman's name together. Connectedness is balanced with loneliness in Calvino's representation of the strangeness of a man shouting a name in an effort to bury his solitude in a chorale.

In Italian American writing, connection and separation are polar opposites that are invariably placed into sharp and surprising relation to each other. I believe a struggle between these opposites shapes the struggle for individuation or identity for many Italian American women writers. In such fiction, the crowd that counts is often not one of strangers but the family itself. The struggle to individuate by redefining connection and the question of female identity are central issues that are affected by storytelling traditions. These traditions can be applied to the new purpose of establishing the nature of connection as the context for any form of separation. Women are traditionally keepers of family solidarity and stories which, like folktales, often instruct the listener in tales of harmony and conflict.

The voice of the family is female. Rooted in interviews and research with Italian American and other ethnic groups, Elizabeth Stone believes family stories shape us. She writes:

> Family stories—telling them and listening to them—belong more to the women's sphere. When I interviewed married couples, it was not unusual for the woman to know more of her husband's family stories than he did, usually because she'd heard them through her mother-in-law. In this way, despite the convention of patrilineality, the family is essentially a female institution: the lore of family and family culture itself—stories, rituals, traditions, icons, sayings—are preserved and promulgated primarily by women (19).

Contemporary writing by Italian American women writers often casts the family saga into a demonstration of crises of ambivalence over the nature and intensity of family connections. Ambivalence as a thematic device structures narratives through division or opposition, pitting family identification against feelings of alienation. The play of connectedness and separation from family is shaped by the fact that even separation narratives—whether of diaspora from Italy or of widening gaps between parents and children or lovers—are told in female voices that stress connectedness as much as individuation and make ambivalence a central element. That ambivalence takes many forms and can focus on conflicts between expression and self-expression.

Crises of language can be used to express crises of the ambivalent self. Italian American writers can call into question a bifurcation of communicative power forged by attitudes toward the use of Italian or English. For example, Carole Maso's *Ghost Dance* deals in part with a family in which a successful Italian American stockbroker father has buried his ancestry, his family stories, and his tongue. His own father refused to speak or acknowledge the Italian language at home. His wife, a German Armenian, is a successful poet in English. For their daughter, Italian defines a world of silence and suppression; English is the vehicle for expression and self-assertion in an open, vocal world. The attitude toward the language of ancestry and the retention of Italian traits is quickly gendered—Italian is seen in terms of a patriarchal code of silence, but English is emancipatory as the language of expression of a non-Italian mother. Attitudes toward speech blend with attitudes toward the father and emerge in a critique of the code of *omertà*. In an interview about *Ghost Dance*, Maso remarked: "The way to resist [silence], to speak against silence is very much what [the] book is about. To live next to silence but to speak" (Bona 177). Maso's command of the craft of writing permits her to layer cultural memory and language—English and Italian provide the voices of expressive feeling and secrecy and self-containment. The title *Ghost Dance* expresses, among other things, the reawakening of ghosts, of long-suppressed tales and memories that might be revived through the lyrical voice of fiction, the voice of the daughter as writer. This is the legacy the daughter adopts along with a determination to develop new ways of communicating the hidden past.

Italian American writing often grounded crises of behavior in economic exploitation by mainstream America. Recent writing by assimilated Italian American women in more prosperous times focuses on the impact of horrifying American experience in sexual humiliations. The very content of those humiliations calls into question gender roles, and the value of silence and even family solidarity. Sometimes these are expressed in an identification with the oppression of the family as a whole and the determination to identify with that humiliation and to retaliate for it. The magnitude of the ensuing violence and violations of propriety, or *bella figura,* can be suggested by a tendency on the part of the author to mask extreme critiques of Italian American themes of family solidarity in a different ethnicity.

In Carole Maso's darkly brilliant, beautifully written novel, *Defiance,* a dysfunctional and impoverished family of Irish Americans in Boston cannot protect their son from being raped by a priest or help their promising and intelligent daughter withstand her brother's tormented needs. The son seeks out his own death in the Vietnam conflict. The daughter identifies with her abused brother, who "marries" her when she is eight years old and joins him in hatred of all those who seem to have escaped the poverty, rage, and humiliation both have known. Maso's use of Irish ethnicity masks a core Italian American theme of family identification and loyalty, but recasts it as a crisis of being that equates the family bond with experiences of sexual exploitation, violence, and death. In this crisis of being, loyalty to a brother extracts a price in lives.

Maso's fictional sister, Bernadette, is driven by a will to retaliate with violence against all of those she sees as holding untroubled power. Although she becomes a Harvard physics professor and is, in a sense, an American success, she refuses to abandon the emotions that bind her to her past or to separate from her brother's victimization. She uses her position to retaliate by becoming an oppressor. She sexually humiliates, degrades, and eventually murders two rich and talented students she sees as emissaries from an untroubled world of WASP privilege. She hopes for a reunion with her brother through her own death. Here gender stereotypes of *bella figura* are outraged by Bernadette's predatory sexual violation and murder of men. The theme of family loyalty is grimly satirized by a union that is possible only through death. This family cannot survive together; it can only embody a negative solidarity in a harsh critique of the price of loyalty.

The critique of family codes is often bound up for Italian American women writers with a critique of patriarchy. The experience of authority and the iron law of family codes can precipitate a desire for strong, revolutionary speech that attacks male power and freedom from pregnancy and child care, and uses the family constellation subversively. The most powerful woman poet among the Beats, Diane di Prima invoked abortion as a form of harsh, retaliatory violence against the failed father. In di Prima's "Brass Furnace Going Out: Song after an Abortion," the poem's persona speaks to her fetus:

> I want you in a bottle to send to your father
> with a long bitter note. I want him to know
> I'll not forgive you, or him for not being born
> for drying up, quitting
> at the first harsh treatment
> as if the whole thing were a rent party
> & somebody stepped on your feet.

The "father" is to be rebuked by the dead fetus that serves as the proof of his failure. The transgressive power of "Brass Furnace" derives in part from di Prima's ability to invest rage at the feckless lover, and even the fetus, with moral intensity. Its impact derives precisely from the clarity of codes of speech and behavior it violates and from its inversion, rather than abandonment, of moral ferocity. The speaker is the voice of righteous female aggression. Nowhere in this poem of matriarchal, female violence is there the cool indifference or meaninglessness that characterizes the treatment of failed love in much contemporary art.

Both Maso's *Defiance* and di Prima's "Brass Furnace" use extreme acts to underscore agonies of a cultural heritage in which separation and connection are life or death issues. These works represent transgressive extremes that highlight the dramatic form in which the encounter with male power, family responsibility, and clear cultural codes provide a framework that permits Italian American women writers to explore or exploit the situation of women in a larger American world.

A central concern of my own writing is the nature of a woman's identity conceived of in the dramatic forms Italian American culture enables. However, I subject female identity to the pressure exerted by the mainstream on gender roles and male authority. I see narrative as a means of reconciling extremes of separation and connection, individuation from the family and identification with it, patriarchy and matriarchy.

These concerns correlate with the revision of gender roles at work in the larger culture and disclose the relationship between the family and turbulent times. I use the pattern of forms and themes of my writing as pathways to representing a quest for that attrition of differences that can lead to moral poise.

The Right Thing to Do expresses in its title the abiding moral obsessions of Italian American life. However, it also implies a question contemporary writers face: What is the right thing to do in our world of indeterminate, relativistic choices, changing gender roles, and skepticism toward all authority? Gina's coming of age and challenging of her father, Nino, are meant to situate the encounter with the patriarchy in contemporary, close, personal terms. Nino, in pursuit to retrieve his daughter from what he sees as the worst mistake a young woman can make, finds himself examining his past, as well as her feared future. Each is ambivalent about the other's choices. They are locked in an intense interaction between the poles of family obligation and a thirst for complete autonomy.

In the relation between father and daughter, the conflicts of sex and intergenerational strife intertwine in ways ranging from the humorous to the painful. For the father, conflict with his daughter forces him to confront and identify what his expectations of women have been in the past. His life as a man in which he has claimed all the benefits of the double standard may well be in conflict with his feelings as a father. Nino wants greater freedom, opportunity, and success for his daughter than he himself has tolerated from women in his own life. The most enlightened Sicilian father may well find his heart flooded with an atavistic protectiveness that originates in love and in his need to define his daughter's path to fulfillment in a life he sees as safe for her. His daughter, on the other hand, experiences that concern as suffocation. What is at stake for him is her soul, her allegiance to those values that place him at the head of the family as arbiter of what is best. He has fought against all odds to earn and keep this role. To reject those values is, he believes, to reject him.

Gina is in a terrible bind. She knows he cares for her and wishes only to protect her. He is willing to make her miserable for the sake of what he believes is right. If she obeys him, she loses her individuality, her lover, her newfound freedom, and a gateway to the larger world. *The*

Right Thing to Do calls into question the nature of parental authority and filial responsibility; it turns on the issues of sexual identity, both in the daughter's coming of age and in the father's recognition of the sexual attitudes evident in his own past as a man and in her future as a woman. Nino's authority is fueled by his greater knowledge of the world, his genuine concern for her, and it is tinged by his bitter awareness that all his values are under siege in what he perceives as an amoral culture. In making a claim for independence from him, Gina finds she has gone to war.

Ambivalent bonds tightening and intensifying the struggle between father and daughter are a structuring device for me. They shape the form of the novel in the placement of sequences told from his perspective and hers, and in the interpolation within the novel of family stories based on traditional folk forms and told by different characters. Ambivalence also structures Gina's responses to the sophisticated, cosmopolitan life of her lover and his family, which is presented in parallel sequences. Such tales and episodes are used to thicken the double edge of meaning and emotion that every encounter between father and daughter, and Gina and her lover, displays. In contrast to the representation of strife between fathers and sons, who are typically locked in an isolating struggle, Gina, like other fictional Italian American women, finds in her mother only a partial ally.

The quarrel among women of different generations is often diminished by a shared impatience with restricted lives and male authority. If sons are protected from knowing their mother's impatience with the double standard, daughters are amply informed of it as essential protection against making the same mistakes. Shrewd about what she has missed out on, Gina's mother is nevertheless able to find strong meaning in her life and unable to provide a clear, alternative model. A wealth of possible errors is illustrated by the family stories she tells. There are cautionary tales of hopes dashed by early marriages to those wrong men who are not serious, who gamble or drink or lapse into solitude behind the sports news. Rarely if ever rising to an indictment of marriage itself, such stories are not restricted to warnings.

Some tales are about surprisingly strong and unconventional women. Gina's mother tells her a story about a woman whose unsparing and unsentimental realism about her faithless husband enables her to appeal to and make a mutually beneficial arrangement with a woman he has gotten with child. Such stories, which seem to promote not only independence but a cool rationalism in dealing with emotionally charged issues, are meant to instruct. Through them, Gina is encouraged to win the war against masculine authority lost by her mother. Yet none of the stories her mother tells deals with a viable future beyond marriage and family. There are no women, no mentors, no role models in Gina's family who know how to translate those strengths into a road map through the competitive complexity of the life she is moving toward. Gina must put together her father's ability to manage in the world outside and her mother's emotional wisdom. She is on her own.

The lessons Gina takes from her mother's stories are not always the ones her mother intended her to learn. Ironically, Gina comes to value the cool rationalism, self-discipline, self-control under pressure, and discretion that her mother saw as aspects of matriarchal *serietà*, but that she has learned from her father and is translating into an individualistic sense of how to deal with the obstacles in the world outside. Another meaning of the title, *The Right Thing to Do*, bears on such questions of strategies: what actions will *implement* sensations of freedom and autonomy and use traditional codes to approach a driven, competitive world of unruly appetites?

Gina's struggle with her father is a chess game in which Nino realizes, as he deals with her moves and countermoves, that she has learned all her best tactics from him and can use them against him. In short, she has adapted character traits that check him at his own game and deprive him of female vulnerabilities to exploit. In a series of conversations, chase scenes, and confrontations, the two engage in strategic maneuvers: when he retreats, she strikes. When he pursues and advances, she disappears. He never backs down. However, he comes to understand that she will not either.

What redeems their struggle from occasional brutalities on both sides is the fact that each retains a stake in the other. The need to do the right thing surmounts the need to score points. For her, that may involve compassion for him; for him, it may involve accepting her separateness. At the climax of their relationship, he tells her a story he claims is drawn from the deep well of his Sicilian childhood. His tale orchestrates multiple views of the fate of a father and daughter of his invention; its open questions are his ironic gift to her. *The Right Thing to Do* goes further though. It suggests that the borders of the domains of the patriarch and matriarch, family and world, have grown porous and that survival in current times depends on the appropriation of the assets of both by a younger generation.

Narrative is, for me, an ordering of *experience* as well as language. It enables me to choose a pattern and meaning that dispel confusion. Writing that draws on ethnic experience and gender is, I think, the intimate voice of the hybrid American world in which immigration and history are inseparable, inclusiveness is an increasing necessity, and so many of us are shaped by more than one culture. As children of a large and older migration, Italian American writers today are in a good position to explore and disclose the impact of cultural change and to address what hybrid lives mean to personal as well as public life in a cosmopolitan world.

Writing *The Right Thing to Do* was an adventure in discovery and self-discovery for me. Through writing it, I found out what I know about identity and its relation to culture. When so many women readers who were not Italian Americans told me that Nino was exactly like their fathers, I came to understand something more—that the experience I described was somehow specific in its Italian American expression but wider and perhaps even universal in its meaning and its hopes.

Storytelling, for me, means continuing the dramatic forms of Italian narrative traditions and Italian American culture. I prize their stress on the intense immediacy, moral force, and feel of life that—even in its fantastic, miraculous aspects—is always lived face to face. I hope my storytelling extends those traditions into the maelstrom and excitement of American reality. Balancing an Italian American heritage with the claims of an unruly contemporary world, those traditional codes, styles, and expressive forms will be revised and repositioned. I believe they will always be bright beacons for any journey down new and different paths.

Works Cited

Barolini, Helen. *Umbertina*. New York: The Feminist Press, 1999.
Bona, Mary Jo. *Claiming a Tradition: Italian American Women Writers*. Ad Feminam Series, edited by Sandra M. Gilbert. Bloomington: Southern Illinois University Press, 1999.
———.*The Voices We Carry: Recent Italian/American Women's Fiction*. Montreal: Guernica Press, 1994.
Cappetti, Carla. "Deviant Girls and Dissatisfied Women: A Sociologist's Tale." In *Writing Chicago: Modernism, Ethnography, and the Novel*. New York: Columbia University Press, 1993, 73–108.
Dearborn, Mary V. *Pocahontas's Daughters: Gender and Ethnicity in American Culture*. New York: Oxford University Press, 1986.
di Prima, Diane. "Brass Furnace Going Out: Song after an Abortion." In *Selected Poems 1956–1976*. Plainfield: North Atlantic, 1977.
Gardaphé, Fred L. *Italian Signs, American Streets: The Evolution of Italian American Narrative*. New Americanist Series, edited by Donald Pease. Durham, North Carolina: Duke University Press, 1996.
Handlin, Oscar. *The Uprooted: The Epic Story of the Great Migrations That Made the American People*. Boston: Little Brown, 1952, 3.
Hansen, Marcus Lee. Lecture to the Augustana Historical Society 1938, "The Problem of the Third Generation Immigrant." Reprinted as "The Third Generation in America." *Commentary* 14 (November 1952), 492–500.
Hendin, Josephine Gattuso. "The New World of Italian American Studies." *American Literary History* 13.1 (Spring, 2001), 142–157.
———.*The Right Thing to Do*. New York: The Feminist Press, City University of New York, 1999.
Hutcheon, Linda. "Cryptoethnicity." In *Beyond the Godfather: Italian American Writers on the Real Italian American Experience*, edited by A. Kenneth Ciongoli and Jay Parini. Fairfield, Connecticut: University Press of New England, 1998, 247–257.
Mannino, Mary Ann Vigilante. *Strategies of Empowerment in the Writing of Italian/American Women*. New York: Peter Lang, 2000.
Maso, Carole. *Ghost Dance*. Hopewell, New Jersey: Ecco, 1980.
———. *Defiance*. New York: 1998. Plume. 1999.
Stone, Elizabeth. *Black Sheep and Kissing Cousins: How Our Family Stories Shape Us*. New York: Penguin, 1988.
Tamburri, Anthony Julian. *A Semiotic of Ethnicity: In (Re)cognition of the Italian/American Writer*. SUNY Series in Italian/American Studies, edited by Fred Gardaphé. New York: SUNY Press, 1998.

Carole Maso

Notes of a Lyric Artist Working in Prose*

A *Lifelong Conversation with Myself Entered Midway*

An EROTIC song cycle.
 AVA could not have been written as it was, I am quite sure, if I had not been next to the water day after day. Incorporating the waves.
 Making love those afternoons at dusk, just as the shapes were taken back. Afterwards darkness. Provincetown in winter.
 The design of stars then in the sky. I followed their dreamy instructions. Composed in clusters. Wrote constellations of associations.
 Loving the world, and needing it, as I did. Wanting to transmute it into shapes Begging it to—
 "Stay a little."
 Virginia Woolf: "The idea has come to me that what I want to do now is to saturate every atom. I mean to eliminate all waste, deadness, superfluity: to give the moment whole; whatever it includes. . . . It must include nonsense; fact; sordidity; but made transparent."

---

*From *Break Every Rule* by Carole Maso. Copyright © 2000 by Carole Maso. Reprinted by permission of Counterpoint Press, a member of Perseus Books, L.L.C.

The desire of the novel to be a poem. The desire of the girl to be a horse. The desire of the poem to be an essay. The essay's desire, its reach towards fiction. And the obvious erotics of this.

Virginia Woolf knew the illusion of fiction is gradual even if moments are heart-stopping, breathtaking. There is a pattern, which is only revealed as patterns are, through elongation and perspective, the ability to see a whole, a necklace of luminous moments strung together. How to continue the progression, the desire to go beyond the intensity of the moment or of moments. Like sex, one has to figure out how to go on after the intensity of the moment-how in effect to compose a life afterwards, how to conjure back a world worth living in, a world which might recall, embrace the momentary, glowing, obliterating, archetypal. One longs for everything. For the past one never experienced, for the future one will never know-except through the imaginative act. One longs to be everything. To have everything.

A certain spaciousness. There would be time and room for it all.

The creation of an original space. The desire for an original space in which to work.

Passion of the mind. Persistent desire for form to meld with idea and emotion in organic ways.

Restlessness of the form. *Every rose pulses.**

Gertrude Stein: "It can easily be remembered that a novel is everything."

Accuse me again, if you like, of over-reaching.

The novel's capacity for failure. Its promiscuity, its verve. Always trying to attain the unattainable. Container of the uncontainable. Weird, gorgeous vessel. Voluptuous vessel.

Room for the random, the senseless, the heartbreaking to be played out. A form both compressed, distilled, and expansive enough to accommodate the most difficult and the most subtle states of being.

Musings, ideas, dreams, segues, shifts in key, athletic feats of imagination, leaps and swirls. Or small, nearly imperceptible progresses. The unarticulated arc of our lives.

---

*All italicized material is from a Carol Maso novel or from a work-in-progress.

Many fiction writers do not, I believe, acknowledge reality's remoteness, its mysteriousness. Its inaccessibility to us and-to our modes of expression, though the novel is one of the very few good places for this sort of exploration.

Together, many novelists, now commodity makers, have agreed on a recognizable reality, which they are all too happy to impart as if it were true. Filled with hackneyed ways of perceiving, clichéd, old sensibilities, they and the publishing houses create traditions which have gradually been locked into place. They take for granted: the line, the paragraph, the chapter, the story, the storyteller, character.

I love most what the novel might be, and not what it all too often is.

Reach.

The novel as a kind of eternity. A kind of infinity. Inevitable progressions of beauty—with room and time enough for it all.

Not to worry.

Lyrical novels imply a formal design—an aesthetic patterning in order to achieve the desired intensity.

A personal sensibility projected through the minds and actions of others so that both the lyric and the narrative might be achieved. The lyric self coupled with the novelist's "omniscient" visions.

My relationship to poetry was always one of reverence: How could I ever approach such beauty, such perfection? An unhealthy relationship, finally. With fiction I feel far less reverent. What has been done? Maybe not that much.

The novel might be musically or visually conceived—pictorial relationships, symphonic turns rendered in prose.

The novel's design, for me, being an abstract relationship between parts.

Recognition of the patterns, the relationships, so they might be destroyed if necessary or deviated from or tampered with.

The ability to manipulate shapes and space. Writing AVA I felt at times more like a choreographer working with language in physical space. Language, of course, being gesture and also occupying space. Creating relations which exist in their integrity for one fleeting moment and then are gone, remaining in the trace of memory. Shapes that then regather and re-form, making for their instant, new relations, new longings, new recollections, inspired by those fleeting states of being.

Complexities.

How to prolong the lyric moment?

Andrey Tarkovsky: "Writing which links images through the linear, rigidly logical development of plot . . . usually involves arbitrarily forcing them into sequence in obedience with some abstract notion of order. And even when this is not so, even when plot is governed by characters, one finds that the links which hold it together rest on a facile interpretation of life's complexities."

Room as well for the random, the accidental, and the associations and shapes that arise from allowing accidents to happen.

It's not easy to keep this thing from that. At other times I feel most like a composer. More than anything else I aspire to the state of music. It's not desirable or possible to keep things separate. Many things arise:

The child draws the luminous letter A.

As a girl my favorite novel was *Wuthering Heights*. But I could not find a book anywhere else remotely like it. It created a hunger.

And my father playing his trumpet. Lying in the dark listening to that aching music. And how it seemed to approximate all we could not say.

Always I have loved poetry most, but at the same time felt the need for a larger canvas: a series of panels, a series of screens.

My form is always an odd amalgam—taken from painting, sculpture, theory, film, music, poetry, dance, mathematics—even fiction sometimes.

Reread: Goethe's *Werther*, Hölderlin's *Hyperion*, Gide's *Le Voyage d'Urien*, Barnes's *Nightwood*, Melville's *Moby Dick*.

To sit next to the great mysteries, or to lie in the dark next to them and find shapes, ephemeral and changing as they may be, for this. All this:

A beautiful passing landscape.

Our uncertainties, hopes, fears, longings, disappointments, our forgetfulness. Our relationship to language.

Huddled around the fire of the alphabet.

A free and large enough notion of story so that it does not coerce. All too often novels are narratives of coercion because they are too narrowly conceived.

A novel presumes a story and a storyteller. But who is the self who is telling? And what is the story? And where have we gotten our small definitions of story? And why?

And what if the story is:

The way you sound in letters, or on the beach, or at the moment of desire.

Three P.M. when the shadows cross the border.

The way you looked that night on your knees.

The way the swing swung.

And if not the real story, then what the story was for me.

The pull and drag of the tide.

Gertrude Stein: "I have destroyed sentences and rhythms and literary overtones and all the rest of that nonsense, to get to the very core of this problem of communication of intuition. If the communication is perfect the words have life, and that is all there is to good writing, putting down on the paper words which dance and weep and make love and fight and kiss and perform miracles."

To use all and everything that is available to us through observation, memory, fantasy, desire, imagination—so as to get up close next to one's vision.

Miracles might occur.

Jean-Luc Godard: "Cinema is not a series of abstract ideas but rather the phrasing of moments."

New definitions of story and character may be required. To. imagine story as a blooming flower or a series of blossomings. To change the narrative drive, to better mimic one's own realities, drives. So that narrative might be many things. *One hundred love letters, written by hand.*

Understand and accept the limitations and contours of the traditional narrative. In *The American Woman in the Chinese Hat*, my third novel (published fourth), there is an end to narrative as I once understood it. Without going there first, I do not believe I could have gotten to AVA—which is something quite else.

And characters may be perceived as a light or a force or a pressure, or as an aspect of possibility.

In the negotiations between poetry and prose one might like something neater. Let's put our mind to it:

To each—both lyrical fiction and poetry, a certain irresistible music. An Orphic voice speaking. A childish belief in the whole.

Is the sustaining of the lyric voice (certainly a kind of stamina) dependent on an insistent and pervasive sexuality? One feels an intimate link between the two.

The desire for—

Miracles.

Miracles. Helen reading my father the recipe for ravioli dough. He remembers his family drying pasta on all the beds in the Brooklyn house of his childhood. "Dig a well. Then put in eggs:" And I type it directly into the text of AVA, which I am working on in the next room. A place for the random, the accidental, the overheard, the incidental. *Precious, disappearing things.*

"Stay a little."

I love you.

An expansive narrative. Bela Tarr's *Sátántangó*—a terrifying film, filled with exhilarating narrative choices.

In my new work I want music, meditation, narrative, philosophy, more—and all at once.

I give myself room. The drama of the creative imagination being my one true subject. A continuous exploration made concrete, somewhat palpable, through fiction.

My aim in *The American Woman in the Chinese Hat* was to dramatize the breakdown of language, and with that carrying off of language, a belief system, a world. Much of the book's dram is linguistic. The novel, being a spacious form, allowed me to establish the rules of language within a temporal framework and then, once established and understood, I could subvert them. This is one of the things novels do well. The world falls apart as you read. One hopes, by the end that the impact of the fractures are not only understood, but felt. Because having been engaged, involved in the fluency of images, when they begin to dissolve, one feels dissolved as well. Only shards remain, disrupted syntax, words detached from their meanings. A bleak code calling up the lost, the fluent, the integrated world, once whole: Language enacts the speed and degree and manner of breakdown. We are forced to witness an entire history: a world is born, evolves, warps and finally breaks. Breakdown is dramatized, imaginative and linguistic ways of escape are cut off.

She hears a high sound. Like mermaids or birds. She's watching her hat. Strange angel. Butterfly.

To lose fluency. To become speechless.

The choice of lyrical techniques must augment and enhance the narrative decisions. Only then will the result be radiant, authentic, inevitable, grave.

Tarkovsky: "I think in fact that unless there is an organic link between the subjective impressions of the author and his objective representation of reality, he will not achieve even superficial credibility, let alone authenticity and inner truth."

Much of my work is propelled by, the desire to be reunited with lost, unremembered aspects of self and world.

Who were we, and why did we live?

Aspects of self, aspects of personality, temperament, take an outward shape and then are animated. Often, my obsessions, fears, hopes, all that matters most, grow heads, arms, legs and then move, interact with one another, in the form of characters.

Character, rather than well-rounded carriers of story, might work more like images do.

She waves. Wavers. In the agony of the afternoon. In a red dress. The American Woman in the Chinese Hat. She's not American at all. She is German maybe, or Suedoise. And she has no hat.

Poetry and prose. How to reconcile poetic forms with the narrative requirements of an extended prose work? Because finally, yes, it is the novel I have to work in.

A new energy is needed to sustain a contemporary lyric fiction. The energy of writing into one's desires, passion. The energy derived from many things might sustain such a voice. The energy from writing outside of fashion, against the fictive fashion, even. Easy to be a renegade in such an inauspicious fiction milieu. Use it to your advantage.

How to prolong the lyric moment?

What might the phrasing of moments look like in prose?

Rent Godard's *Pierrot le Fou.*

The novelist's lyric "I" engaged, as the epic poet is, in the world. A singer singing *in relation* to others. This perhaps defines the difference of the enterprise between lyric novelist and lyric poet. The novel as huge, shifting, unstable, unmanageable canvas. Smudged with lipstick, fingerprints, crumpled, tear-stained, many-paged.

The novel as a geometry of desire.

A high sound like burning . . . Stranger. Light. The sound of water over stones. She waves. Each word in its watery globe. Pulses. Once, twice, goodbye. Love. Forever. A woman. Floating like a heart. And roses.

How to prolong the lyric moment?

In *The American Woman with the Chinese Hat,* the reiteration and, gradual mutation of images mirror the disintegrating psyche of a narrator in the process of mental breakdown. The novel makes this acting out possible.

In a lyric novel, objects often are emanations of the unconscious.

I love winter most because it's the most recognizable outward correlation I know of my interior life. There is recognition. *Snowfalls like music.*

What is narrative? Narrative might be:

I wrote you one hundred love letters. One thousand love letters, written by hand. This is probably the last love letter I will ever write. One thousand love letters—you probably never got them all.

Prose, it seems to me, has the great ability to *dramatize* states of mind, as well as incorporating other kinds of "action" and development.

In *AVA* though there are elements of story everywhere, I am still reluctant and unprepared to say what the story is.

A polyphony. A bouquet of voices.

The storyteller as chameleon. Fluid, mutable.

The novel is all potential. All what might be. All what might have been. A record of all we cannot remember, all we've lost—never to be retrieved.

Despite my efforts, it resists me, eludes me. Perhaps it might be possible to write a perfect poem, but I do not believe it is possible, or even desirable, to write the perfect novel. That is what I love most about the form.

It is as rebellious, as unruly as I am.

There is another kind of novel other than the novel of adventure, the novel of manners, the psychological, the realist novel. It is strange, exotic, hybrid—and it is beautiful.

Lyrical fiction introduces the conventions of poetry (image, metaphor) into a genre dependent on causation and time. Characters, scenes, plots are turned into patterns, designs of imagery. Life and manners are sensually apprehended and then turned into design.

Lyrical novels are concerned with aesthetic relations—space, temporal and shape relations, tone and tempo. They are sensitive to tensions and pulls, resistances—gatherings and release.

An imaginative act, a design in which life is simultaneously brought up close and also viewed from afar at a more detached distance.

As in my *The American Woman in The Chinese Hat*, where figs, roses, butterfly, angel, fire, floating, stranger, red achieve a measure of impersonality, universality, love, dread. Inner emotion transforms the outer world into a fever dream, a hallucination where images from the exterior world are thrust into strange, glowing relief and reflect both a verisimilitude, a portrait of the outer world, as we can know it, and a private, interior, symbolic reality.

This sort of work requires a strange combination of both utter control and complete recklessness.

A leaping and staying in one place at the same time. Paradoxically what is closest and most personal is also turned into the universal, outside and removed from the self. Abstract and concrete at the same time.

Characters, too, weave patterns. Voices overlap as do motifs, echoing one another, reiterating, enlarging. Many techniques are employed: call and response, rubato, counterpoint, and these strategies heighten and formalize the ordinary narrative ploys.

The Waves by Woolf to my mind being the precursor to my *AVA*. Symbolic qualities are felt, perceived through voice and rhythm. Whole worlds are conjured in scraps of dialogue, a turn of the head, a pause, a deletion, a last extravagance. One feels, if I've been at all successful, their colors, tones, pressures, their human presences.

There is compression in lyric fiction, yes, but also expansion. Elongation. The longing for clearings. An opening up of perceptions, possibilities, every time the writer or the reader sits down. And duration, and the obvious erotics of this.

How to reconcile succession of time and sequence, of cause and effect, with the instantaneous moments of the lyric?

Tarkovsky: "All must come from inner necessity, from an organic process. Any artificial move is easily detected:"

Reread Poe, Novalis.

Is the loss of self in lyrical fiction like the loss of self in poetry?

One thing is evident: the conventional psychological novel with its phony or simplistic truisms and its grasping at straws doesn't approximate experience sufficiently.

Portraits of the mind and the moves the mind makes.

And if not the real story, then—

A girl in a striped bathing suit sits at the water's edge. She digs deeply in the sand and from the vast beach makes shapes: an arch, a pyramid, two towers.

And if not the real story, then what the story was for me.

A feminine shape—after all this time.

Virginia Woolf in "Modern Fiction"(1919) criticizes Joyce's *Ulysses* for not ever going beyond the self. And this is always my problem, too, with Joyce, and why for me he fails finally to be a great novelist.

Not to own or colonize or dominate.

The known world dissolves into feelings and groups of feelings, into music, which then might escape the dilemma, the trap of the personal.

Perversely, I find Joyce too confining.

To sing in prose, to somehow get the urgency of bone and blood and hair, entire histories, into prose.

Prose which remains lyrical in intention eschews consecutive action for other kinds of narratives. The narratives are not merely associative either; it's rather more mysterious and elusive.

The identification of self and world transmuted into shapes.

Virginia Woolf's "Mr. Bennett and Mrs. Brown."

In Woolf I think more than any other writer the conventions of the novel blend most perfectly with poetic technique.

The narrative beliefs that animated and propelled with such authority writers like Jane Austen no longer hold. Writers are forced into a reexamination of what are useable forms, if they are serious writers. What forms might be opened up by our particular predicament. This is a poetic as well as a fictive concern.

Woolf writes in "How it Strikes a Contemporary" that twentieth-century writers "cannot make a world, cannot generalize. They cannot tell stories because they do not believe that stories are true."

As we try to make meaning—
The shattered glass might mend.
—where maybe there is none.

Woolf implies that the writer may have to write notebooks rather than masterpieces. Notes instead of coherent, authoritarian, beginning-middle-and-end, thesis-and-conclusion pieces.

Virginia Woolf from *The Writer's Diary:* "The idea has come to me that what I want now to do is to saturate every atom. I mean to eliminate all waste, deadness, superfluity: to give the moment whole; whatever it includes. Say that the moment is a combination of thought, sensation, the voice of the sea . . . It must include nonsense; fact; sordidity; but made transparent."

The problem of course is that a sequence of illuminations is simply not enough.

A kind of liberation, a freedom, occurs by assuming the concentrating and illumination, the saturation of the moment as in poetry; and the prolonged temporal ability to stay where one's vision is and watch it evolve, change, double back on itself, augment, amplify, come to uneasy terms, resolutions-of a sort, as extended prose is capable of doing.

A poetic unity. An ecstatic, even mystical, integrity.

What is perhaps most astounding is the typical novelist's almost total disregard for language, as if it were only some bothersome means to an end. Some way of imparting information. And most prose called "poetic" is turgid, purplish, overwrought, self-conscious.

An intimate knowledge of the workings of language is as essential for prose writers as it is for poets. No matter what sort of fiction one writes.

The external world, facts, history, politics, manners, and the natural world shall be embraced. Also dreams, loves, fears—all aspects of the interior life.

Symphonic forms. Fugue forms. The improvisations of jazz. Montage. Jump cuts. Slow dissolves. Cubism, Cortázar, abstraction, the troubadours, the left-handed child. Love songs.

Woolf in *The Common Reader:* Forget that "appalling narrative business of the realist: getting from lunch to dinner."

Jane Austen ended forever a certain tradition. Reread Austen, Balzac, and all those you made facile enemies of back when you were struggling for a vision, for a voice. She had taken a certain kind of novel to its limits. I needed, I suppose, as a result to demonize her. Had no room for her.

We have witnessed the demise of the belief system that made Jane Austen's confidence and coherence possible.

In Chicago, I step into a small foyer before entering the magnificent lobby. It has been designed this way so we might feel and experience the space, the grandeur. The architect understood this. The novelist could well benefit from becoming an architect in prose.

The question persists: can poetic insight ever truly be reconciled with the novel's form? On the side of narrative—a plot of motives, time, and causality. Poetry—image and pattern.

The attempt in *AVA is* that narrative motifs might produce a design of images. To interweave motifs through the text by use of recurrences, repetitions, etc., which often act contrapuntally and trigger through theme, rhythm, and other mysterious methods associations in the reader as well as the writer. Often it is the act itself, the association-making process rather than the subject, that is recognizable.

My favorite literature, that which really lives for me, is always an experience in itself: a drama of language and shape and rhythms, and not just the record of an experience.

That language is feeling. That syntax is feeling. One should feel in one's whole being the necessity and inevitability of tense, point of view, tempo, voice, etc. That where the paragraph breaks is not taken for granted. That the notion of chapter is not taken for granted.

And that the formal patterns not constrict. Ephemeral, imperfect, stories without their old authority. "Notebooks" maybe "rather than masterpieces:"

Somewhere around seventh grade it seemed everyone was killing themselves or being killed. I was often afraid. Jimi Hendrix. Janis Joplin. RFK. Martin Luther King. The desire of the girl to be a horse. To run away or save. Save anyone. Just once.

The brother draws the letter K. The mother guides his hand. Says: *try.* Says: *you can.*

To use scenes, to ask scenes to function as image. I think unconsciously this was what I was trying in my first novel, *Ghost Dance. So* that scene by scene it makes the kinds of leaps that poetry makes line by line.

How to get character to function as image without contrivance. Time as character.

To witness the unfolding of the imagination across time and space. Like the sun rising on the bay. Provincetown in winter.

As we walk through plane after symbolic plane. In *The American Woman in the Chinese Hat* the fountain, the roses, the figs, the light, the forever.

In *The American Woman in the Chinese Hat* to find the formal arrangement of words in that limited and constantly diminishing set of possibilities that might save both protagonist and author. The struggle enacted on a formal plane.

Each word a fig.

After all the betrayals.

To orchestrate color in *The American Woman in the Chinese Hat*: pink and sea-green drinks, yellow drinks, a poet in a white dress, a young

Arlesian in a bright blue robe, like hope—and then to systematically drain the world of every color—except red.

Vin rosé, Cotes du Rhône—so many roses, and a red dress.

A red-drenched ending.

To take one to the point of no return—and then somehow, I don't know how, to return.

Fidelity to one's perceptions. Trust. *We look out the window at the red sign that says PSYCHIC.*

One of the direct challenges of poetry is to make language work again. Something fiction, although it is made of language, tends to relegate almost always to the basement. To be responsive and responsible to thought, to emotion, to the body, in language.

Poetry to my mind rejects habitual thinking far more readily than fiction. There seems less reverence for the accepted, the tired, the cherished gestures and forms. Fiction, too often, has substituted plot for structure. Fiction writers must be structuralists in order to realize the potential of the novel or the story, but for the most part they are not.

Only now and then, I realize, do I get anywhere close to a real insight, anywhere near. As usual, I grope in the dark. Aim at the thing.

The ultimate trust. To let go in the dark.

Not to fear being ludicrous. Not to fear failing magnificently. Like the films of Kieslowski, for example. Walk the fine line between being simply preposterous and utterly convincing.

Not to protect oneself. Expose your heart. Your circular, flawed, contradictory thought process, your hopes, ambitions, vulnerabilities.

To write risking ridicule. To risk being ridiculous, inappropriate, over the top. *Defiance* will be such a project.

Fiction might allow miracles to arise in the luxury of its space and time. It has the capacity to dramatize interior states. To dramatize longing, to dramatize distance.

As a girl when she was sad she would turn herself into a horse. Her left-handed brother. He's very sick.

I don't remember the knife from before, the American woman says near the end to the young Arlesian—*or your blood red robe.*

Every rose pulses.

In a novel far away longings can be quite literally far. The text can mirror, approximate, distance. The text can incorporate longing through its formal structures. It can make tentative approaches or bold, operatic gestures. It can enact reunion. It can double back on itself, revise itself, simulate larger postponements, resignations: Incorporate giddiness, dizziness, lust, love even. All this is possible in the novel's structure.

Music often performs similar feats. But the novel is different in that it conveys literal meanings simultaneous to the meaning it conveys through form and through the color and timbre and rhythms of language.

Miracles might arise.

The permission to make peace, forgive, admit when you've been wrung. The permission to be afraid.

My friend who makes glass books, far away, calls to say—

I look out at my spring garden. Hear the pulsing rose of her heart. One might stop time for awhile . . .

But a series of radiant tableaux are not enough.

A healing, a suturing, a reconciliation . . . everything having been broken, or taken away.

The dream all along: to be free.

There will be room and time for everything. This will include missteps, mistakes, speaking out of turn. Amendments, erasures, illusions. The creation of a kind of original space will mean:

Everything I ever wanted was there. Everything I ever feared or desired. Yes, time and place enough for everything. I've come closest to this, thus far, in *AVA*.

A place where there would be time and opportunity enough to turn old hierarchies on their heads. A place to re-imagine epiphany.

And if not the real story, then what the story was for me.

Mallarmé's "Le Nenuphar Blanc." Each image devolving until all that is left is the pure, white strangeness of the water lily.

I don't remember the knife from before, or your blood red robe.

She remembers the little emperor and how his hands turned the water red. Rose trout. She slept with a girl with crimson hair once. Objects are emanations of the subconscious. As in poetry there is a juxtaposition of themes and motifs. A manipulation of sound. Sound as desire.

Ava Klein in my *AVA* on the last day of her life with her one last late hope: Chinese herbs. World traveler, she had wanted to see China. This longing called up as she swallows one tablet after the next. She may have had lovers there, friends: Shi Sun, Steve Ning, Victor Chang. A line of beautiful boys—which recalls her friend Aldo, an opera singer, dead of AIDS, and his beautiful boys. Chinese tablets, China, Chinese boys, a poem: (She was a lover of literature, a professor of literature and desire.) Healing herbs, the healing lines of a poem by an ancient and forgotten poet. The one thousand Chinese murdered in a square. The desire to heal them. And all those who have been murdered. Her family in Treblinka, the whole universe, the breaking heart of the world. "The desire to speak in a language that heals as much as it separates," as Hélène Cixous says. And maybe this after all is narrative.

And if not the real story—

The ability to embrace oppositional stances at the same time. Contradictory impulses, ideas, motions. To assimilate as part of the form, incongruity, ambivalence.

To make a place for ambivalence or uncertainty to be *experienced* and not just referred or alluded to seems one of the most interesting challenges of the novel. The tentative, the unresolved, the incomplete might be enacted. Played out in the theater of one's imagination.

The potential for celebration. Exuberance. Virtuosity. Joy.

What did you think was beautiful there?

The intricate pattern on the scarf on the head of a Yugoslavian woman is beautiful, and the way you tried to hide your disappointment at not winning the prize so as not to spoil the evening Is beautiful. And the small bird as it arrives elegantly on the plate. And how surely if I have loved anyone it is you. And how you understood in the end why we could not make it work, despite love—despite everything we had going.

I have come to celebrate. I have come to praise.

The American Woman in the Chinese Hat for me is a novel of black celebration, a riot of language and exhaustion and despair. *AVA* on the other hand is a novel of bright celebration, of coming together, of all possibilities, of joy, jouissance.

Ecstatic dancing to klezmer and nonsense texts.

As lyric as *The American Woman in the Chinese Hat* is, as patterned, as dependent on image and design, the book would not work in a shorter or more truncated form. It could not work even as a long poem. A novel of loss, told simultaneously with hothouse vibrancy and an odd, detached, cool ferocity, it could not have approximated loss without first suggesting and then suggesting again and again through the fictive conventions of narrative, what exactly was at stake.

We were working on an erotic song cycle. It was called: *Everything I Owned*. Everything I loved or wanted or feared was here.

To be fierce, strict, smart, like Woolf. Woolf thought Meredith created figures of large, universal, elemental structure, but that these characters lacked concreteness and depth. They were too general to be collective. The qualities of both poetry and prose simultaneously must be achieved by the lyric novelist. The poet novelist must also measure up as a novelist; yes, how silly, of course. Few are up to this. And yet it is crucial, of great importance.

Stein: "Who can think about a novel. I can.

Themes in *The American Woman in the Chinese Hat* are reiterated, expanded, echoed as part of the plan, and in this way very dependent on song: "Row, row, row your boat . . . life is but a dream." It is not a casual reference, as nothing in this kind of work can be casual—but rather speaks again and again to what is happening in the narrator's psyche. The transformation of Catherine's psychic world is constantly mirrored in the outside world. Each word is a boat, a small saving thing in this increasingly dark, blood-drenched dream. Sea.

Language engenders language. Language itself presents unexpected and often extraordinary solutions. It leads you to the what next? To the how and why. To the *what if,* and *if only.*

Think about Camus, Malraux, Sarraute, Robbe-Grillet.

Throughout, images such as boats, dream, figs, swans, roses, horses; gloating; angel, butterfly endlessly repeat themselves in varying configurations as the imagination gropes and tries to make sense of chaotic experience. As the imagination tries to save, the outward world distorts to speak of the interior world. The internal world informs the external one. A hallucination. A fever dream. The way often of prose poems, I think.

Reread Baudelaire's prose poems.

There's a kind of glittering out there—a dark aching, a longing that can only be adequately, felt through form. In *The American Woman in the Chinese Hat* for instance, tentative gestures give way over time to inevitability. The move towards a radiant place, a place of rigorous disintegration, a place the architecture of the novel allows and makes possible.

And all day pretty girls dip their arms like swans into the fountain . . .
The dark swan of her desire floating out into the pool . . .
At the cemetery flowers float in their watery globes . . .
You said: swans. He can't help but see swans now at the fountain . . .

The search still remains, after all this time, (the search that was *The Art Lover's* search, 1985–1989) in finding a language in which to speak and the forms that might approximate.

All this:

Forever. For the languages of star and ash and music and numbers. The search for the blue flower of poetry or a red dress.

As we mimic the heartbeat in our upright walk, home.

Someone puts on Madame Butterfly in the square and they cry.

Woolf: "Stand at the window and let your rhythmical sense open and shut, boldly and freely until one thing melts into another, until the taxis are dancing with the daffodils, until a whole has been made from all the separate fragments."

How to get it even a little right:

My mother whispering in the next room during the years of my childhood. She's worried about my brother again. He's got a hole in his heart. He's very sick. And on the television now Bosnia. And floating in that room *won't die*. How do winds, the first crocuses (I'll bring them to my teacher), the passage of stars, of time—that's Orion's belt; what Mrs. Smith is calling out across the yard (sounds like bar talk) and birdsong. The body next to mine in bed, warmth and then warmth gone away. Where? To work?, To the store? What year is: it? Mrs. Smith said, *it's Bartok*. I hear the music now she's playing for me and her daughter Alison. The cuckoos when I finally got to France sounded just like that clock. For a moment it is the room of my child-

Notes of a Lyric Artist Working in Prose 233

hood, three girls in the same bedroom, the cuckoo clock. Another baby, maybe on the way. *No!* I say emphatically and then traffic—the apartment in New York. On the television, the weatherman. The girl picks up the magic book and reads it at night by flashlight. That's me; of course.

The illusion of including, of having it all. So many desires. A mélange of influences, techniques, pressures.

As a child my favorite book was the poetic, mystical *Wuthering Heights*. A somber, lonely, ecstatic meditation. So much solitude in the midst of everything. Three girls in the bedroom. Many children. So much going on. Why was I always so lonely? And still am. In the midst of much joy, such estrangement. How to get some of that down right.

As I take what I perceive, what I see out there, and abstract it, returning with a coherence, a solace of form, a shape.

The challenge: To turn the world, and the workings of the world, into song.

I love the things that continue. That never end. I love the long haul. Is this the novelist's disposition? The forever.

The ancient consoling tradition. The impulse to sing. The impulse to tell a story, to want to know insatiably, at times, what happens next.

That said, I must admit that conventional storytelling byres me silly. The analytic bits, the dreary descriptive impulse, the cause and effect linearity, the manufactured social circumstances.

To create whole worlds through implication, suggestion, in a few bold strokes. Not to tyrannize with narrative. Allow a place for the reader to live, to dream.

All of sex called up in an apartment vestibule. All reckless, incandescent desire. As in illuminated manuscripts, an emblematic approach to narrative.

Careful of the intercom.

Now in America they call this coffee, but I remember coffee. Let the reader linger there. Go where she will.

The novel is something, even when stopped, which is continuous.

I wanted to be obliterated by light, stunned, dazzled, stopped, and also to never die. To go on.

Each word a boat.

I wanted in my books prayers, bells, arabesques, dervishes, a doomed blood, a remote chorus, the static of cats, the way you looked that night, turning away—modulations to other keys. I wanted it all: the moment and the elongation of the moment, and then another moment, and the cumulative pleasures of an intensifying, building content. I was greedy. I believed it might all be possible.

Not to forget the lost songs of the troubadours and the unfixed relationship between words and music. A way in prose perhaps of speaking to some of my extraordinary solitude?

To fail. To Miss the mark. To not even come close.

In the midst of ecstatic possibility, sometimes, even then, no way out.

No longer the hunger for figs. The hunger for an arrangement of anything.

Shattering of glass.

Rilke's *Malte Laurids Brigge* is like my *American Woman* in that both, as lyric novels, move image by image toward intensity. Images follow a progress through interplays and modulation until they reach a level of nearly unbearable intensity. Action is a concern, but a secondary one.

The beauty and terror of silence intrigues me. Poetry reveres silence. Fiction too often tries to fill it up. And sound, voluptuous, reinsisting itself against that backdrop of silence, takes on a different quality.

As we form our first words after making love.

Not to take anything for granted.

But digression seems more built into the potential of the novel. Is true digression more possible in fiction, in that one may completely forget one strand of reality, having replaced it by an equally compelling and lengthy one, which might wipe out for awhile, obliterate what has preceded it? And then to be returned to the first world again, bewildered.

And so we get to the notion of home. The move towards home and the longing called home and all that memory, imagination, desire, belief, doubt can conjure as we circle and circle on this extraordinary journey. The novel filled with acting out, rehearsals, meditations, games from childhood, melancholy rainy afternoons or bright sunlight where you bounced a little ball and picked up glittering stars called jacks in one hand.

Where you bounced a large ball, "A," and you went through the precious alphabet. A my name is Alice. And yes,

It is true my name is Carole Alice.

Perfect the action in your mind that will keep the hula hoop up, or the brother safe, or the dress red.

Allow, because you must allow, the broken glass to speak.

And sometimes when she wasn't sad, but was furious and wanted to get away from all the brothers and sisters, she'd turn herself into a horse.

Time passes: It's shocking. You change shape. Your parents age and eventually die. You remember your mother in a bathing suit, beautiful on a dock at a lake. And when you put on your bathing suit now, she is exactly back at age thirty-five, in you.

Time passes. I digress.

A progress. A child is born. Grows. Learns to write. One day has children. Those children too sing the old songs, teach beloved things to the next children. A progress of numbers. They grow old.

My father playing his trumpet in the moody half-light.

I got to dance in a circle. I got to kiss you on the cheek.

The left-handed boy lived.

I wanted—

The pleasure of accumulated meanings, of accretion, which is the narrative act. A fragile constellation, through time and space, of relationship. An architecture of stars, of—

The joy has been in watching you grow. The joy has been in loving you.

I talk to a faraway friend and ask what will happen next. How did she find out? Who will leave whom? Where did the other woman go? And what about the child? She's not sure. My dear friend, a glass artist, tells me she is making glass books. Will there be further fractures?

One makes shapes.

K.

I wrote you one thousand love letters. You probably never got them all.

I imagine the progress of the glass books as she speaks.

The fragility of her voice trembling over the thin wires.

The relatives place the white ravioli on the beds to dry. I open my mouth to receive the host. Where have you gone?

And when she was joyful as well—she remembers now—ecstatic, she would turn herself into a horse. So that the horse took on many meanings.

The desire of the girl to be a horse. The novel to be a poem. The desire to change shapes again and again.

Is the lyric Orphic voice reliant for its energy and power on an insistent and intense sexuality?

Careful of the intercom.

As I write these notes to myself, I traverse the country "promoting," as they say, my *American Woman in the Chinese Hat*. Right now I am flying from Los Angeles to New York. We're going *fast*, at some 33,000 feet. The nose of the plane is already dipped in night. At the tail, where I sit, last day. This tells me something important, but I don't know what yet, about novel writing. There's movement and stasis. The sun setting at my side.

I'm reading a magazine with Nirvana's Kurt Cobain on the cover in between jotting these things in my notebook. I'm flooded with memories, associations, the history of a lifetime, my lifetime—and these things make Kurt Cobain's suicide even more painful today. Without my points of reference this pain could not exist in this way. The novel can create these responses, these states by the gradual, leisurely building up of moments though space And time. The novel possesses the sound, the structure, the spaciousness, the heart to get some of it down. Let's hope.

Jenny Holzer: "In a dream you saw a way to survive and you were full of joy."

Row your boat, row your small boat.

And, only a little after this it will be Kristen Pfaff, the bass guitarist from the band Hole—good-bye.

My dear glass friend has had a second breast removed now. Now what? Emotion as narrative: sadness, ferocity, fear, can give integrity, as we through fiction rehearse, pray, conjure, bring the night closer and also, simultaneously, dispel it. A beautiful, passing landscape.

Tarkovsky: "The allotted function of art is not, as is often assumed, to put across ideas, to propagate thoughts, to serve as example. The aim of art is to prepare a person for death, to plough and harrow his soul, rendering it capable of turning to good."

How to incorporate the joys and pleasures, tenderness, delicacies, the generosities and seductions of the novel and its narrative capacities with the extraordinary, awesome capabilities of poetry? There's the challenge. Who is up to it? I wonder:

A girl in a striped bathing suit sits at the water's edge. She digs deeply in the sand and from the vast beach makes shapes: an arch, a pyramid, two towers. Not child, but not yet adult, she is at that tender age of becoming.

The glass might mend itself.

A small voice rises in me. I *am*, it says.

And then the plane is enveloped in darkness.

For Cynthia
April–December 1994

Mary Jo Bona

"But Is It Great?"*

The Question of the Canon for Italian American Women Writers

> ... [T]he revision of the literary canon has ... been necessary because in the 1920s processes were set in motion that virtually eliminated black, white female, and all working-class writers from the canon.... The literary canon is, in short, a means by which culture validates social power.
> —Paul Lauter, *Canons and Contexts*

> For when the record is not recognized, it is in effect denied. This was the case for Italian American women writers.... Yes, the Italian American woman writer exists, and her experience is registered in an honorable literary record.
> —Helen Barolini, *Chiaroscuro: Essays of Identity*

DEFINING THE CANON AND THE CREATION OF ITALIAN AMERICAN LITERATURE

Classroom anecdotes often illustrate how easily persuaded students are by the status quo. Students traditionally are not encouraged to question the reasoning behind a professor's literary choices. In general American literature classes and special topic courses, such as a class on Italian American literature, students are used to completing the reading assignments

---

*Used with permission of Mary Jo Bona, SUNY at Stony Brook.

with little discussion about the aesthetic virtues of a work. As a case in point, during a discussion of the 1896 American novel *The Country of the Pointed Firs* by Sarah Orne Jewett, I required English majors at my former university provide the class with their judgment of Jewett's work. When the class initially fell silent, I wondered if the modernist structure of Jewett's novel unmoored the students, throwing them into confusion about how to read itself. Once their tongues loosened, however, several students spoke of the novel in convincing ways. They spoke of Jewett's devotion to storytelling: transmitting stories orally from one generation to the next, they saw, helped unite the author's fictionalized community and made living in a post-Civil War environment emotionally viable. They recognized how incorporating the Western tradition of the quest allowed Jewett to revise this narrative to explore the needs of a female community largely bereft of men, and how the quest for Jewett's community of women in Maine is just as much about adventure as it is about coming home.[1] A couple of the usually spirited students, however, remained unusually silent.

In an effort to engage them, I wrote on the board a value judgment made by Willa Cather, who was mentored by Jewett. Cather placed Jewett's *The Country of the Pointed Firs* alongside Hawthorne's *The Scarlet Letter* and Twain's *The Adventures of Huckleberry Finn*—in effect granting Jewett's lesser-known novel equal status with established American texts. Hawthorne and Twain already were deemed foremost literary talents during their lives; students in high school and college had been exposed to their most famous works for well over a half century. However,

---

[1] See Sandra A. Zagarell's essay "Narrative of Community: The Identification of a Genre" for an analysis of works of nineteenth-century literature, including Jewett's *The Country of the Pointed Firs*, that take as their primary subject the life of the community and portray a communitarian aesthetic that "deliberately refuses linearity in order to achieve an inclusive circularity" (pp. 521–22). Several twentieth-century novels by Italian American writers, including Mari Tomasi's *Like Lesser Gods* and Pietro di Donato's *Christ in Concrete*, also portray the ordinary processes of the community constructed around "continuous small-scale negotiations and daily procedures through which communities sustain themselves" (p. 503).

Cather's gesture of canonization on behalf of Sarah Orne Jewett was an effort to grant an American *woman's* work permanent recognition, akin to Hawthorne's and Twain's work achieved decades earlier:

> I can think of no others that confront time and change so serenely, . . . I like to think with what pleasure, with what a sense of rich discovery, the young student of American literature in far distant years to come will take up this book and say, "A masterpiece!" (as quoted in Pryse, p. v).

Nodding their heads in agreement, many of my students found the comparison between Jewett and her male compatriots apt. They also recognized their own participation in rendering a judgment of Jewett's work. However, when I asked one of the silent students to contribute her thoughts on the merit of Jewett's novel, she answered that she did not think *The Country of the Pointed Firs* should be judged alongside a novel like *The Scarlet Letter*, which she considered truly great. I asked her to explain what it was about Hawthorne's work that gave it such literary merit. She replied that she had not read *The Scarlet Letter*—yet—but she already knew that it was great. Clearly, certain American works, Hawthorne's among them, have become, as Lillian Robinson explains, "institutionalized as canonical literature," and therefore putatively immune from further assessment (p. 118).

Such a classroom anecdote is not meant to deride a young student; rather, it reveals an omission that is regularly evident within syllabi and general curricula. Before a semester begins, professors already have made decisions about the content of students' reading based on the two closely intertwined phenomena of text availability and judgments about worth. In my effort to introduce students to lesser-known literary texts, I explain that people create canons and that they have not descended, as the stone tablets did for Moses, directly from God. I further elaborate by saying that professors (along with reviewers, editors, critics, and publishers) decide what is worthy, publishable, and therefore available to students in the classroom.

Wendell Harris explains that citing a Biblical parallel in discussions of literary canons is inappropriate despite the word's core meaning of "rule" or "measure,"

> and by extrapolation, "correct" or "authoritative," . . . the process of biblical canonizing was toward closure, whereas literary canons have always implicitly allowed for at least the possibility of adding new or revalued works. (pp. 110, 111)

Feminist literary criticism has been in the vanguard of countering the dominant canon not only by offering an alternative list of writers, a "female counter-canon," but also by "radically redefining literary quality itself" (Robinson, pp. 122, 124). Given the vituperative responses in the 1980s and early 1990s to the dismantling of the traditionally male-dominated literary canon, it is not surprising to hear Lauter and others call the question of the canon a "cultural battle" (p. ix).[2]

Lauter's description of the canon is instrumental in understanding the difficulty in achieving recognition for both male and female Italian-American writers: "By 'canon' I mean the set of literary works, the grouping of significant philosophical, political, and religious texts, the particular accounts of history generally accorded cultural weight within a society. How one defines a cultural canon obviously shapes collegiate curricula and research priorities, but it also helps determine precisely whose experiences and ideas become central to academic study" (p. ix). Without publishers and reviewers to make writers visible, without critics to assess the value of specific books, without professors in classrooms

---

[2] I am thinking of two 1987 works that became best-sellers and advocated a return to conservative educational values and a narrow understanding of the literary canon. They are Allan Bloom's *The Closing of the American Mind* and E. D. Hirsch's *Cultural Literacy*. For a spirited and well-reasoned response to such views, see Gerald Graff's *Beyond the Culture Wars: How Teaching the Conflicts Can Revitalize American Education*. For an analysis of the cultural locus of Italian America and its relation to a corpus of Italian-American literature, see Justin Vitiello's "Off the Boat and Up the Creek without a Paddle—or, Where Italian Americana Might Swim: Prolepsis of an Ethnopoetics."

teaching such works, and without marketing strategies to keep books in print, writers of significant strength find themselves locked outside the American literary canon.

Defining the canon of *American* literature helps illuminate the struggle of Italian-American women writers whose existence as an aesthetically resonant cultural group has only recently come to light. The American literary canon refers to "that set of authors and works generally included in basic American literature college courses and textbooks, and those ordinarily discussed in standard volumes of literary history, bibliography, or criticism" (Lauter, 1991). In his seminal article on canonicity (reprinted in *Canons and Contexts*)—"Race and Gender in the Shaping of the American Literary Canon: *A Case Study from the Twenties*"—Lauter offers a detailed analysis of the institutional, theoretical, and historiographic reasons for the exclusion of female, black, and all working-class writers from the canon. This description, of course, includes all Italian-American writers. Lauter, in *Canons and Contexts*, cites three important factors that account for the progressive elimination of such writers from the American literary canon:

> the professionalization of the teaching of literature, the development of an aesthetic theory that privileged certain texts, and the historiographic organization of the body of literature into conventional "periods" and "themes." (p. 27)

In 1919, Fred Lewis Pattee published his anthology, *Century Readings for a Course in American Literature*. In it, he included works by Harriet Beecher Stowe, Mary Wilkins Freeman, Sarah Orne Jewett, Helen Hunt Jackson, Rose Terry Cooke and more. Less than twenty years later, Howard Mumford Jones and Ernest E. Leisy published *Major American Writers*, which included no women at all. By 1948, when the National Council of Teachers of English (NCTE) reviewed American literature in the college curriculum, Lauter reported in *Canons and Contexts* that "only three women appeared in the ninety syllabi of survey courses studied" (pp. 25–26).

What happened? Many factors contributed to the exclusion of women and minorities from anthologies and syllabi, not the least of which was the way the teaching of literature was organized according to a historiographic model, which focused on periods and themes, such as world wars and male experiences abroad. What remains clear to Lauter and to me is a cold fact that constricted the canon until the inception of movements for social change in the 1960s and 1970s: "the arbiters of taste, scholars and critics alike were . . . drawn from a narrow stratum of American society" (p. 36). For sixty years, the dominant literati did not consider the literary works of women and other minority groups worthy of examination.

Professors and pedagogical agendas have changed in recent years. Thus, female, Black, and working-class writers increasingly appear in American literature anthologies and on syllabi. However, coming late to the conversation about canon formation, most Italian American writers have not yet achieved a cultural standing that exerts influence on American readers' choices. Nonetheless, I would not go so far as to suggest that Italian American writers would be permanently denied entrance to the hallowed halls of canonicity. To do so would be to overlook the malleable nature of canons themselves and the institutional context out of which they emerge. As John Guillory explains, an institutional context is "a setting in which it is possible to insure the *reproduction* of the work, its continual reintroduction to generations of readers" (p. 237). Certainly, such institutional viability is in its infancy within Italian American letters. In fact, we have increased the recognition and reproduction of works by Italian-American writers.[3] The view that Italian Americans are nonreaders harnessed by a heritage of *omertà* has diminished considerably in the past fifteen years. I do, how-

---

[3]Several publishing houses have been instrumental in increasing the recognition of Italian American women's writing. The Feminist Press has republished Tina De Rosa's *Paper Fish*, Helen Barolini's *Umbertina*, Dorothy Bryant's *Miss Giardino*, and Josephine Gattuso Hendin's *The Right Thing to Do*; Guernica Editions, Diana Cavallo's *A Bridge of Leaves*; Syracuse University Press, Helen Barolini's *The Dream Book*; and the University of Wisconsin Press, Marie Hall Ets's *Rosa: The Life of an Italian Immigrant*.

ever, concur with Dana Gioia, who reluctantly supports Gay Talese's statement that "there is no *widely recognized* body of work in American literature" that portrays Italian American immigration experiences (italics mine, p. 23).[4]

Recognizing that stereotypes about a culture are dismantled when "someone has first had the courage to enunciate [them] in all [their] unlovely specificity," Robert Viscusi moves beyond the predictable lament of Italian Americans who bemoan the preoccupation of editors and the general public with grotesque themes regarding Italian American behavior and values. Constructing an Italian American literary canon occurs, Viscusi affirms, when

> a people begins to possess its own charter myth—when a people begins, that is, to inquire into the sources of its own historical identity—then the books its writers produce have something to say to the general reader that it will be very much in the general reader's interest to follow and understand. (pp. 267, 272)

Inquiries into the historical life of Italian Americans have flowed not only from traditional academic disciplines such as anthropology, history, sociology, and English, but also from interdisciplinary fields such as Women's studies, American studies, and ethnic/cultural studies. Benefiting from a dual heritage, Italian Americans must explore the creative dimensions of their cultural hybridism, crossing borders "geo-intellectually" and defining the cultural specificity of Italian American identities (Tamburri, p. 129). Describing Robert Viscusi and Helen Barolini as the elder statespersons of an Italian American critical generation, Anthony Tamburri suggests that these two scholars have "paved the way for the rest of us to work in . . . with a . . . vast[er] critical arsenal"

---

[4]Talese's lead article in the book review of *The New York Times* is called "Where Are the Italian-American Novelists?" *Italian Americana* (a cultural and historical review journal) devoted two of its issues to a candid exchange on Talese's essay, including Dana Gioia's response, "Low Visibility: Thoughts on Italian American Writers" (pp. 7–12).

(125).⁵ As Justin Vitiello observes, "before Italian Americana can ever . . . stake a serious claim as an ethos contributing conspicuously to the development of American civilization . . . Italian Americans themselves need to figure out where they belong (or not) in relation to the United States mainstream" (23). Helen Barolini's groundbreaking 1985 publication of *The Dream Book* stakes a serious claim by opening up new vistas of literary writing, redressing long-neglected women writers of Italian American extraction. In doing so, Barolini began establishing the importance of these writers in the development of an Italian American literary canon.

BLAZING A TRAIL FOR ITALIAN-AMERICAN WOMEN WRITERS: BAROLINI'S MANIFESTO

Perhaps no other critic of Italian American women's culture has offered more insight into this ethnic group's literary cohesion than has Helen Barolini. According to Alice Walker's back-cover commendation, *The Dream Book* was a "heroic recovery and affirmation." Placing Italian American women writers on the map for the first time in American literary history, Barolini explodes the silence of these writers by exploring the historical and social underpinnings of Italian cultural life and the literary hegemonies and oversights of the American publishing world. Describing her anthology of fifty-six Italian American women writers as her "literary manifesto," Barolini intended to establish "once and for all, that we exist, we are writers, we are part of the national literature" (as quoted in Ahearn, p. 47). Establishing a list of writers, Barolini initiated the process of Italian American canonization.

---

⁵Without institutional support and a network of scholars in the field of Italian American studies, earlier critics of Italian America such as Giovanni Schiavo, Jerre Mangione, Olga Peragallo, Leonard Covello, Rose Basile Green, Rudolph Vecoli, and Betty Boyd Caroli nonetheless produced important work. For an appreciation of their contributions, including the formation of the American Italian Historical Association in 1966, see Frank Cavaioli's "The Rise of Italian American Studies and the American Italian Historical Association" (pp. 1–22).

A year after the appearance of *The Dream Book*, Barolini published an autobiographical essay called "Becoming a Literary Person Out of Context," explaining that her elusive identity as a writer was "completely out of context with my Italian American background": "An Italian American woman becomes a writer out of the void. She has to be self-birthed, without models, without inner validation" (p. 263). Similarly, when writing her first novel, *Umbertina* (1979), Barolini was moved by "the burden of history, the need to tell the story in order to understand myself" (as quoted in Ahearn, p. 47). Aware of the fact that Anglo-American literature dominated the literary landscape when she was growing up in the 1940s and 1950s and did not fully speak to her southern Italian background, Barolini took up the pen herself: "If books did not tell me who I was, I would write those that did" ("Becoming a Literary Person," p. 265).

For Barolini, becoming a literary person required that she simultaneously become a critic, a literary archaeologist digging up the voices of the past and the voices of those presently unheard. Since the emergence of her auspicious anthology, Barolini has managed to see each of her books back in print, including a 2000 reprint of *The Dream Book*. Her reintroduction to *The Dream Book* also appears in her revised book of essays, *Chiaroscuro*, which offers an update on the literary situation for Italian American women writers. Since the inception of *The Dream Book*, writers represented in it who once thought of themselves as unique, without literary models from their individual ethnic group, "became aware of each other, held joint readings, formed groups, began to appear in collections, were asked to talk at colleges and at women's history events" (*Chiaroscuro*, p. 172). This anthology triggered responses of deep emotion from the writers themselves, who had previously perceived, as Barolini did herself, that they were writing out of a void, without models and without inner validation.

In 1987, when actor and writer Emelise Aleandri staged "The Dream Book Revue" at the CUNY Graduate Center in New York, Italian American writers featured in *The Dream Book* "were visibly brought together for the first time as a collective presence and voice" (*Chiaroscuro*, p. 172). Italian American women finally became visible to each other.

Providing mentorship and continuity with each other, perhaps for the first time in their literary history, Italian American women writers were no longer without models from their ethnic background.

Barolini's update of *The Dream Book* also records the literary achievements of Italian American women writers throughout the decade of the 1990s. Although in 1985, Barolini was correct in lamenting the paucity of literary critics to probe the background of Italian American women and "unlock the reasons for silence" (*The Dream Book*, p. 32), her 1999 assessment of scholars in the field of Italian American studies is remarkably reticent and dated. In fact, Italian American critics have been at the forefront of the workaday tasks of making such books as Barolini's available in paperback and accessible to students and a general reading public. Most notable is Fred Gardaphé's landmark study, *Italian Signs, American Streets: The Evolution of Italian American Narrative*, for its application of Giambattista Vico's notion of *corso* and *recorso* to "illuminate the recent rise in power of minority American literature" (p. 13). According to Gardaphé, Italian American literature has been abandoned by its Italian and American cultures, and "relegated to the *vicoli*, or 'side streets' of literary discourse" (p. 8). Tracing the development of an "indigenous critical voice," Gardaphé deciphers the codes specific to Italian American culture, compiling an inventory of "Italian signs" from the early immigrant works to contemporary modernist writings (pp. 8, 11).

Using Vico's evolutionary paradigm of cultural history, Gardaphé applies this philosopher's ideas of a culture's three ages to a reading of the movement from an orally based Italian immigrant culture to an Italian American one based on literary tradition (p. 15). Utilizing a culture-specific approach to analyze the works of male and female writers, Gardaphé fulfills Barolini's requirements of the function of the critic: "the critic . . . takes the long view and decides what becomes part of the canon" (*Chiaroscuro*, p. 191). In an effort to design an approach to reading Italian American literature, Gardaphé also turned to the critical works on other minority literatures, most particularly those of Henry Louis Gates. Gates's following comment in "Criticism in the Jungle" provided Gardaphé with a strategic imperative—to provide readers with the long view:

> W. E. B. DuBois argued that evidence of critical activity is a sign of a tradition's sophistication, since criticism implies an awareness of the process of art itself and is a second-order reflection upon those primary texts that define a tradition and its canon.... All great writers demand great critics. (as quoted in *Italian Signs, American Streets*, p. 3).

Other scholars like Gardaphé recognize the necessity of establishing indigenous critical theories to analyze works that might present contrasting ideologies to those represented by the traditional literary canon. Barolini, Viscusi, Tamburri, and Gardaphé have been engaged in enlarging the discursive power of Italian Americans as a literary group.[6]

ITALIAN AMERICAN WOMEN'S WRITING: ROSA, AN UNCANONICAL CLASSIC

Recurring themes in Italian American women's literature transcend the topics of migration history, family culture, and gender identity, but those very topics help define Italian American literary traditions and efforts to authenticate them through reprints, classroom teaching, and scholarly essays. Like their male compatriots, Italian American women writers have been drawn to tell ancestral narratives of Italian family life in the homeland and the New World. A fidelity to the story of immigration and resettlement shapes the constructions of many narratives, from Rosa Cassettari's late nineteenth- and early twentieth-century experience in Italy and America in *Rosa: The Life of an Italian Immigrant*, to Renee Manfredi's late twentieth-century depiction of Pittsburgh's Little Italy in her first short story collection, *Where Loves Leaves Us*.

---

[6]Other critics include but are not limited to the following: William Boelhower, Theresa Carilli, Edvige Giunta, Josephine Gattuso Hendin, Blossom Kirschenbaum, Mary Ann Mannino, Mary Frances Pipino, Roseanne Quinn, John Paul Russo, and Justin Vitiello.

Keeping in mind Wendell Harris's assertion that literary canons always implicitly allow for the possibility of adding new or revalued works, the recent reprinting of *Rosa: The Life of an Italian Immigrant* might initiate an "ongoing critical colloquy" with other autobiographies (p. 111). Marie Hall Ets, who transcribed and edited the unlettered Rosa's story, and historian Rudolph Vecoli, who initially sponsored the book by writing the foreword to *Rosa*, knew a good story when they heard one. *Rosa: The Life of an Italian Immigrant*, is an as-told-to autobiography written down by Marie Hall Ets, a social worker at the Chicago Commons, a settlement house like its model, Hull House, that helped "Italian women in the assimilation process . . . [and] used education as a method of social reform" (Batinich, p. 165). Ets befriended Rosa in 1918 and transcribed her stories, many of which remain unpublished and stored at the Immigration History Research Center at The University of Minnesota.

As late as 1970, Vecoli bemoaned the fact that the historian who "aspires to write the history of this inarticulate or silent majority is hindered by the paucity of sources" (Foreword, p. vi). By 1979, however, he was able to note that research into ordinary lives was rectifying the situation. As Winifred Farrant Bevilacqua points out, oral histories were becoming central areas of immigration research:

> immigrant letters and diaries, organizational records, church archives, and other similar materials were becoming more readily accessible in the nation's libraries and research centers. . . . [S]cholars had started creating new documents by gathering oral reminiscences of members of ethnic communities. (p. 546)

Vecoli's initial sponsorship of this oral autobiography helped place an unschooled Italian immigrant woman at the center of the historical stage. Conferring upon *Rosa* literary as well as historical value, Vecoli enlarged the work's discursive power by suggesting that it bore more resemblance to fictional accounts of immigrant life than to immigrant autobiographies. By placing Rosa's story alongside Willa Cather's Antonia or Ole Rolvaag's Beret, Vecoli in effect offered a hermeneutical approach to a generically indeterminate work (Foreword, p. vi). As a "bicultural document," Rosa's story comes to readers "through the filter of an American recorder and editor," thus making this work generically complex (Gardaphé, p. 31).

Reprinted in 1999 in the Wisconsin Studies in Autobiography series, *Rosa* has achieved a life-support system that includes not only Vecoli's scholarly foreword, but also an introductory note by Helen Barolini, who earlier excerpted *Rosa* in *The Dream Book*. Apropos of such collaboration, Harris's description of "academic recirculation" as it relates to canon preservation reinforces the intersection between text availability and scholarly sponsorship: "what is easily available in print tends to be what is being taught and written about; what is written about tends to be what one is teaching or others are writing about" (p. 114). Not yet canonized, Rosa's nontraditional narrative of triumph—she never achieves upward social mobility and remains a cleaning woman all her life, but feels triumphant as an American—is a rare bicultural document bridging two centuries and two nations.

Told from the perspective of a working-class person, Rosa's story demonstrates how one woman overcomes the fears and superstitions of her peasant culture of Lombardy without jettisoning her lifelong commitment to the Madonna. A staple feature of Italian Catholicism, the cult of the Virgin is not only, as Marina Warner explains, "the refuge of a poverty-stricken peasantry" (p. xxii). On the contrary, Rosa's dependence on the Madonna as an intercessor helps sustain in several ways. Throughout her entire autobiography, Rosa relies on the Virgin Mary to support her emotionally, provide her with a strong sense of female identity, and give her courage during dire situations.

Rosa Cassettari's story charts her life from childhood in 1870s northern Italy to old age in Chicago, where she died in 1943. An expert teller of tales, Rosa learned the art of spinning in nineteenth-century Lombardy from the men in the stables, the central domicile of storytelling in communities with scarce resources. The warmest place of domesticity, the stable was also the area most accessible to family and people outside the household, and the place where most of the important community exchanges took place, including the telling of old stories. As folklorist Roger Abrahams explains, the stables were the places where "stories were spun and woven: the trope is not a conceit, for it is the traditional way in which storytelling is described in most of the world in which weaving is done" (p. xi).

That Rosa in childhood simultaneously became a skilled silk maker in the local mills and a storyteller should come as no surprise, for she was sent to work by her foster mother at the age of seven and used stories to entertain the girls in the factories. Rosa was abandoned at birth, withstood agonizingly long hours at the silk mills, and was kept ignorant and fearful by Italy's rigid economic and class system. In early adulthood, Rosa was forced by her foster mother to marry a much older man, whom she loathed. Despite the harrowing fact that Rosa only learned the connection between sexual activity and parturition when self-delivering her second child, she never lost hope in her future in America or her faith in the Madonna's worldly intercession on her behalf. As Gardaphé explains, Rosa's immigrant experience "strengthens her Italian-created religious convictions" (p. 35). However, Rosa ultimately maintains her individual sense of self through storytelling. Bevilacqua observes how Rosa refuses to retreat into "an attitude of victimization," adopting instead the major strategy of cultivating

> the art of telling stories, which earns her the attention of others, gives her an identity that is related to her community and expressive of her individuality, and is an outlet for the richness of her inner world, so in contrast to her external poverty. (pp. 548–49)

Despite her limiting circumstances in northern Italy and, later, in America (to which she immigrated in 1884), Rosa continued to assert herself through the art of storytelling, an activity nearly denied her by an abusive husband from whom she managed to escape by going to Chicago. Anyone who has read Rosa's story knows its breathtaking quality, which makes it comparable not only to other narratives of immigrant life (such as Mary Antin's *The Promised Land*), but also to the slave narrative in its emphasis on escape and transcendence. Having achieved canonical status in the past decade or so, Harriet Jacobs's *Incidents in the Life of a Slave Girl* (the quintessential female slave narrative) might be usefully taught alongside *Rosa: The Life of an Italian Immigrant*. For both women, the painful acquisition of a personal voice is related to the act of creating a public, historical self. Rosa learned to speak in her adopted tongue, which provided her the means to tell her stories to various audiences in Chicago. According to Marie Hall Ets, Rosa's storytelling was known throughout all the settlement houses in Chicago, as well as several women's clubs and universities ("Introduction," p. 5). Although Rosa remained unlettered in her native and adopted tongues, her verbal artistry stemmed from oral traditions, which she mastered as a child.

For both women, the decision to refer to themselves pseudonymously and the editorial supervision they received deeply influenced what they said and how they said it. Pervading both documents are silences, especially regarding matters of a sexual nature. Both prematurely sexualized, Jacobs and Cassettari are compelled to reexamine nineteenth-century sexual mores. Jacobs's status as a female slave denies her the capacity to fulfill the ideology of the cult of true womanhood.[7] The Italian cultural beliefs in *fare bella figura* (creating an image of tasteful style)[8] and *omertà* have particular resonance for Italian women. When these beliefs conflict with her unwavering faith, Rosa does not always maintain them. In fact, after she migrates to America, Rosa divorces her cruel husband, managing to win a sense of freedom from her Old World *destino*. Finally, both narratives are fundamentally about the quest to find a home, a safe place where Jacobs and Cassettari could be secure from the male prerogative of dominance, insult, and violence. Rescuing themselves from abominably treacherous living conditions, each woman manages to find reasonably safe living quarters.

Placing *Incidents* and *Rosa* side by side reveals important commonalities. In discussing curricular issues in the reconstruction of

---

[7]For an overview of the cardinal virtues comprising the cult of true womanhood for nineteenth-century American women, see Barbara Welter's *Dimity Convictions: The American Woman in the Nineteenth Century*, chapter two.

[8]See Gloria Nardini's *Che Bella Figura!* for an ethnographic analysis of the meanings and contexts of this cultural phenomenon.

American literature, Lauter examines the transformation in perception that occurs when a traditional category is shattered by adding different works: "familiar works change when we read them alongside others, less familiar, . . . that grew from the same historical soil" (p. 111). Although Jacobs and Cassettari may have come initially from different countries, their eventual escape to a free land and their nineteenth-century attitudes about faith, womanhood, and domesticity unite them vis-à-vis the literary study of American women searching for community.[9]

ITALIAN AMERICAN WOMEN'S WRITING: SOME THEMES, FORMS, AND INFLUENCES

Oral storytelling, autobiography, memoir, poetry, fiction, and creative nonfiction comprise the various genres to which Italian American women recently have gravitated to relate their ancestral narratives of Italian family life in America. Although a fidelity to the story of immigration and resettlement often shapes the construction of Italian American narratives, the familial experience simultaneously governs the movement of many of the stories. Moreover, many works are set in ethnic neighborhoods, which undergo gradual but inevitable dismantling due to changing demography and class mobility. This destruction of the Little Italies of the early twentieth century has produced elegiac narratives, perhaps the most poignant of which is Tina De Rosa's *Paper Fish*. De Rosa beautifully renders the wounds suffered by the West Side colony of Chicago's Italians, whose neighborhood was razed. Bearing witness to the dispersed Italian community of her childhood, De Rosa's epilogue functions as snapshots of people who are taking their leave: "The city said the Italian ghetto should go, and before the people could drop their forks next to their plates and say pardon me?, the streets were cleared" (p. 120). De Rosa's description supports Rudolph Vecoli's as-

---

[9]Rosa's narrative also might be usefully read alongside Gioia Timpanelli's *Sometimes the Soul* and Adria Bernardi's *In the Gathering Woods*. Each writer incorporates storytelling techniques in her narrative, resuming the traditional role of the *cantastorie*, a singer/teller of old tales.

sertion that the death of such a neighborhood marks "the end of the first chapter of the history of Italians in America" ("Are Italian Americans Just White Folks?" p. 4).

The Feminist Press's re-publication of De Rosa's novel serves as an important milestone in Italian American women's literature. The first in a series of Italian American women's narratives to be re-published by this press, *Paper Fish* is De Rosa's virtuoso performance as a modernist writer. Louise DeSalvo's front-cover commendation of De Rosa's novel is no exaggeration: "The best Italian-American novel by a woman of this century." Such high praise is indeed a gesture of canonization, paralleling Willa Cather's description of Sarah Orne Jewett's novel as a "masterpiece!" De Rosa's story of Little Italy in Chicago and her enormously evocative writing style distinguish her as an important voice of Italian America and a singularly compelling stylist.[10]

Other writers of Italian American background commemorate places long gone and, in doing so, recover and make historical an essential part of their ancestors' complicated development in the adopted land. In her novel *Like Lesser Gods*, Mari Tomasi's story of the quarrying industry in Barre, Vermont, richly details the lives and untimely deaths of northern Italian artisans in the first decades of the twentieth century. Dorothy Bryant's *Miss Giardino* portrays the effects of subsequent migrations after the transatlantic crossing when Italian male mine workers moved from the East to the West Coast and often suffered from debilitating illnesses. Josephine Gattuso Hendin's *The Right Thing to Do* explores the conflict between generations as the rebellious daughter strives to break away from her parents' ethnic neighborhood in Astoria, Queens. Rita Ciresi's collection of stories, *Sometimes I Dream in Italian*, traces the childhood and adulthood of two sisters who struggle to negotiate their ethnic and gender identities in an economically

---

[10]For close literary analyses of the aesthetic merits of De Rosa's virtuoso novel, see individual chapters of Gardaphé's *Italian Signs, American Streets* and Bona's *Claiming a Tradition*. Article-length analyses include Giunta's Afterword to *Paper Fish*, Bona's "Broken Images, Broken Lives: Carmolina's Journey in Tina De Rosa's *Paper Fish*" and DeSalvo's "*Paper Fish* by Tina De Rosa: An Appreciation."

depressed New Haven, Connecticut. Dissatisfied with their life choices in adulthood, these sisters long for a connection to their Italian background that has been lost in their parents' generation. Although the Italian American identities of Ciresi's characters are not as submerged as they are in Agnes Rossi's collection of stories, *The Quick*, Ciresi's stories, like Rossi's, examine with compassion the emotional costs of loving a harsh parent and losing the language of the ancestors.

Perhaps a principal feature of Italian American culture and of several of its literary texts is the appearance of sibling solidarity in the midst of family crisis. De Rosa's *Paper Fish*, Rossi's *The Quick*, Ciresi's *Sometimes I Dream in Italian*, Rachel Guido deVries's *Tender Warriors*, and Carole Maso's *Ghost Dance* are just a few of the narratives that incorporate siblings not only to reflect the duality of ethnic identity, but also to deflect some of the family's suffering. Although not overtly using Italian American characters, Mary (Bucci) Bush's collection of stories, *A Place of Light*, depicts the lives of rural working-class families in upstate New York. Siblings covertly inscribe their ethnicity through rituals of healing as Great Aunt Maria tries to heal the sick mother in "Cure" with a poultice and Josie in "Bread" uses a staple of Italian American culinary life—a fresh loaf of bakery bread—to give herself permission to heal from an operation *and* a difficult family.

Accompanying the narrative topics of immigration, geographical provenance, social class, and commemoration of the history and development of the Italian family in America, other features of *Italianità* give Italian American writing its distinct ethnic flavor. A few examples follow. An emphasis on the strength and inspiration of grandmothers and mothers, who are sometimes compared to the Madonna, the preeminent figure in Italian Catholicism, informs the narratives of several writers, including the traditionalist Mari Tomasi and the modernist Carole Maso. In *Like Lesser Gods* and *The Ghost Dance*, the mothers are associated with the Madonna: Maria Dalli of Tomasi's novel is compared by the town's maestro to Leonardo's *Madonna of the Rocks*; Christine Wing of Maso's novel is linked with flight and the Assumption, the Christian feast celebrating Mary's ascension to heaven.

Italian American women's writing also integrates spirituality and *festa* in which celebration of faith reveals the intense love Italians hold for the Virgin Mary and their favorite patron saints. Consider Susan Caperna Lloyd's spiritual memoir, *No Pictures in My Grave*, and Mary Caponegro's postmodern story "Materia Prima" in *The Star Café and Other Stories* for varying but nonetheless intensive renderings of Italian American spiritual beliefs. Closely related to *festa* is the respect and devotion to food and the pride taken in its preparation and in the garden, which, like the kitchen, is a sacramental place for Italian Americans. Sprinkled liberally throughout the writings of so many Italian American women, culinary references inform the narrative movements of such works as Helen Barolini's *Festa*, Lynn Vannucci's "An Accidental Murder," Louisa Ermelino's *The Black Madonna*, and the poetry of Maria Gillan, Sandra Gilbert, Rose Romano, and Maria Fama. Rose Romano unites the fundamental necessities of eating and composing a life for Italian American writers in her lines: "Everybody must know / that we eat. Until we have / a right to this place" (p. 26).[11]

Some Italian American women have chosen the topic of Italy itself and have traveled there in order to renew ancestral ties with relatives. In doing so, recent authors have reversed earlier portrayals of Italy by nineteenth-century American writers, who often depicted contemporary Italian culture as corrupt.[12] For Italian American writers who return to the homeland, Italy is not the malevolent force that strips Americans of their innocence; rather, writers such as Anna Monardo (*The Courtyard of Dreams*) and Anne Calcagno (*Pray for Yourself and Other Stories*), recognize the homeland as a source of nutrition, feeding them literally and imaginatively.

---

[11]The Feminist Press will publish an anthology of poetry and short works by Italian-American women writers called *The Milk of Almonds: Italian American Women Writers on Food and Culture*, edited by Louise DeSalvo and Edvige Giunta.

[12]In *American Novelists in Italy*, Nathalia Wright explains that nineteenth-century American writers such as Hawthorne and James often depicted contemporary Italian civilization as corrupt, but the Italian past as edenic. Several twentieth-century Italian American writers, on the contrary, often regard the Italy of their ancestors and of the present as a place of health. Illness and suffering are equated with America. See my *Claiming a Tradition*, especially chapter one.

The spirit of feminism and its placement of women at the center of the literary stage are reflected in all of the works discussed in this essay. Italian American writers also have inherited the aims of modernism by using unconventional modes of ordering their works and radically subverting their portrayals of character, replacing outward depiction of behavior with inward states of consciousness. Like many twentieth-century women writers, Italian American women unite the creative strategies of modernism with the political aims of feminism, recognizing a complex identity based on the intersecting topics of ethnicity, class, and sexuality. Diane di Prima's *Memoirs of a Beatnik* (1969) preceded second-wave feminism in her transgressive memoir about sexuality and the complication of female identity within a world devoted to male pleasure. Di Prima's depiction of lesbian sex appears quotidian when juxtaposed to the horrifying realization that Diane's female lover is trapped emotionally and sexually inside her home by a rapist father and brother, anticipating by nearly thirty years the novels of English writer Jeanette Winterson (especially *Art and Lies*).

Alongside their undertaking to create new artistic forms and styles, modernist writers also introduce silenced and often *verboten* subject matters. The sheer bluntness of Louise DeSalvo's memoir *Vertigo* (1996) makes it one of the first to reveal the unhappiness she felt inside the traditionally venerated Italian American home. Unwilling to tolerate a reality that would divorce her from the complexity of her life as a second-generation Italian American from a poor family, DeSalvo writes about the effects of suppressed rage, financial struggle, and family conflict. Breaking away from the familiar Italian American story of family continuity and cultural cohesion, DeSalvo pursues a deeper understanding of her mother's life of constant housework, thwarted literary aspirations, and fear of the outside world. The inspirational engagements in culinary traditions, spiritual celebrations, and extended family gatherings are markedly absent in *Vertigo*. For Italian Americans, a forbidden subject matter might well be the unfortunate fact that a mother cannot provide her family with delicious meals. Louise dutifully revises her memories of unappetizing meals by becoming the mother she did not have as a child. Happily, DeSalvo succeeds in rewriting her mother's life by becoming a writer *and* a good cook, two intimately related phenomena.

An important indicator of an ongoing tradition of Italian American women writers is literary influence. Since the publication of several anthologies of Italian American writing, reprints of novels, and recent publications by writers such as Carole Maso, Mary Caponegro, Beverly Donofrio, and Louisa Ermelino, writers have been actively engaged in reading one another's work. It is a testimonial to the emergence of a visible presence of Italian American women writers that makes the existence of influence so thrilling. For example, Mary Cappello's *Night Bloom* echoes the concerns of DeSalvo's *Vertigo*. In her emphasis on her mother's agoraphobia and her father's rage, Cappello, like DeSalvo before her, explodes the silences traditionally informing Italian American family life. DeSalvo's back-cover blurb of Cappello's debut memoir exclaims that she was "knocked out by [Cappello's] original voice." Similarly, Carole Maso's back-cover commendation of Cris Mazza's *Your Name Here: _____* describes the book as a "complicated, . . . unflinching portrait of violence" and Rita Ciresi's flap-cover blurb praises Louisa Ermelino's *The Black Madonna* as worthy as a *"festa."* Italian American women are reading and supporting their sisters, reinforcing their visible presence, and providing viable models for present and future writers.

* * *

When assembling her critical anthology of antebellum American women's writing, Judith Fetterley juxtaposed images of hunger and satiation to describe the process of introducing unknown women writers. In contrast to "their well-fed brothers," Fetterley writes, American women were "thin, starving, and on their own" (*Provisions*, p. 34). Pursuing with difficulty her anthology project, Fetterley first recognized that male American classics were

> surrounded by placentas . . . each firmly centered in a rich nutrient mass of critical books and articles, scholarly biographies, exhaustive bibliographies, special and regular MLA sessions,

hundreds of discussions in hundreds of classrooms, cheap and accessible paperback editions, richly elegant coffee-table editions, government-funded standard text editions. (p. 34)

Such evidence, Fetterley explains, testifies to the presumed worthiness of such texts to be fed. In stark contrast, women writers of the American literary tradition were like the fictional children of many nineteenth-century writers—motherless and starving. In an effort to "begin the task of feeding," Fetterley, like Barolini, began the arduous task of discovering, retrieving, and getting the literature of women back in print (p. 34).

In 1985, Barolini's *The Dream Book: An Anthology of Writings by Italian American Women* and Fetterley's *Provisions: A Reader from 19th-Century American Women* were published, each with impressive introductions. With almost no body of scholarly material in existence to aid either critic, each had no other choice but to blaze a trail individually. As Barolini says, "paths are made by walking. Books are made by questioning" (*The Dream Book*, p. ix). In 1985, Fetterley anthologized an excerpt from Harriet Jacobs's *Incidents in the Life of a Slave Girl* and the entire text of Rebecca Harding Davis's *Life in the Iron Mills*, which earlier benefited from publication by The Feminist Press and from Tillie Olsen's biographical introduction. Since then, both works have achieved canonical status; their representation in *The Norton Anthology of American Literature* epitomizes their revalued status. In contrast, Barolini in 1985 anthologized excerpts in *The Dream Book* from the works of such writers as Louise DeSalvo, Rosa Cassettari, Gioia Timpanelli, and Diana Cavallo, all of whose works are presently available or back in print, though none are represented in any major American anthology.[13]

---

[13]*The Norton Book of American Autobiography*, edited by Jay Parini, includes excerpts from Pascal D'Angelo's *Son of Italy*, Gay Talese's *Unto the Sons*, and Alane Salierno Mason's "Respect." For a more generous selection of Italian American women's memoirs, see *Beyond the Godfather: Italian American Writers on the Real Italian American Experience*, edited by A. Kenneth Ciongoli and Jay Parini.

Italian American literature does not yet have the placenta that can give it a rich nutrient mass of support. Nonetheless, this field of literary study does have its growing core of critics. With an increase in scholarly interest in Italian American women's writing, we are in the process of defining this body of literature, exploring its greatness and insuring the reproduction of this work. Like Willa Cather before us, we will be able to exclaim with complete clarity that a work like Tina De Rosa's *Paper Fish* or Diana Cavallo's *A Bridge of Leaves* is a "masterpiece!" and should be read by the young student of American literature.

Works Cited

Abrahams, Roger D. Foreword to *Italian Folktales in America: The Verbal Art of an Immigrant Woman*, edited by Elizabeth Mathias and Richard Raspa. Detroit, Michigan: Wayne State University Press, 1988, ix–xv.

Ahearn, Carol Bonomo. "Interview: Helen Barolini." *Fra Noi* (September 1986): 47.

Antin, Mary. *Promised Land*. New Jersey: Princeton University Press, 1969.

Barolini, Helen. "Becoming a Literary Person Out of Context." Massachusetts Review 27, no. 2 (1986): 262–74.

———. *Chiaroscuro: Essays of Identity*. revised edition. Madison: University of Wisconsin Press, 1999.

———, ed. *The Dream Book: An Anthology of Writings by Italian American Women*. 1985. Syracuse, New York: Syracuse University Press, 2000.

———. *Festa: Recipes and Recollections of Italian Holidays*. New York: Harcourt, 1988.

———. *Umbertina*. New York: Feminist Press, City University of New York, 1999.

Batinich, Mary Ellen Mancina. "The Interaction between Italian Immigrant Women and the Chicago Commons Settlement House, 1909–1944." In *The Italian Immigrant Woman in North America*, edited by Betty Boyd Caroli, Robert F. Harney, and Lydio F. Tomasi. Proceedings of the Tenth Annual Conference of the American Italian Historical Association. Toronto: Multicultural History Society, 1978, 154–167.

Bernardi, Adria. *In the Gathering Woods*. Pittsburgh, Pennsylvania: University of Pittsburgh Press, 2000.

Bevilacqua, Winifred Farrant. "Rosa: The Life of an Italian Immigrant—The Oral History Memoir of a Working-Class Woman." In *Italy and Italians in America. Rivista di studi anglo-americani* 3, nos. 4–5 (1984–85): 545–55.

Bloom, Allan. *The Closing of the American Mind: How Higher Education Has Failed Democracy and Impoverished the Souls of Today's Students*. New York: Simon and Schuster, 1987.

Bona, Mary Jo. "Broken Images, Broken Lives: Carmolina's Journey in Tina De Rosa's *Paper Fish*." *MELUS* 14, nos. 3–4 (1987): 87–106.

———. *Claiming a Tradition: Italian American Women Writers*. Carbondale: Southern Illinois University Press, 1999.

Bryant, Dorothy. *Miss Giardino*. New York: Feminist Press, City University of New York, 1997.

Bush, Mary. *A Place of Light*. New York: William Morrow, 1990.

Calcagno, Anne. *Pray for Yourself and Other Stories*. Evanston, Illinois: Northwestern University Press, 1993.

Caponegro, Mary. *The Star Café and Other Stories*. New York: Macmillan, 1990.

Cappello, Mary. *Night Bloom*. Boston, Massachusetts: Beacon Press, 1998.

Cavaioli, Frank. "The Rise of Italian American Studies and the American Italian Historical Association." *The Italian American Review* 5, no. 1 (1996): 1–22.

Cavallo, Diana. *A Bridge of Leaves*. 1961. Toronto: Guernica, 1997.

Ciongoli, A. Kenneth and Jay Parini, eds. *Beyond the Godfather: Italian American Writers on the Real Italian American Experience*. Fairfield, Connecticut: University Press of New England, 1997.

Ciresi, Rita. *Sometimes I Dream in Italian*. New York: Delacorte Press, 2000.

Davis, Rebecca Harding. *Life in the Iron Mills*. New York: The Feminist Press, City University of New York, 1972.

De Rosa, Tina. *Paper Fish*. New York: Feminist Press, City University of New York, 1996.

DeSalvo, Louise. *Vertigo: A Memoir*. New York: Dutton, 1996. *American Writers on Food and Culture*. New York: The Feminist Press, City University of New York, 2002.

DeSalvo, Louise and Edvige Giunta, eds. *The Milk of Almonds: Italian*

———. "*Paper Fish* by Tina De Rosa: An Appreciation." *Voices in Italian Americana* 7, no. 2 (1996): 249–255.

deVries, Rachel Guido. *Tender Warriors*. Ithaca, New York: Firebrand, 1986.

di Prima, Diane. *Memoirs of a Beatnik*. 1969. New York: Viking, 1998.

Ermelino, Louisa. *The Black Madonna*. New York: Simon & Schuster, 2001.

Ets, Marie Hall. *Rosa: The Life of an Italian Immigrant*. 1970. Madison: University of Wisconsin Press, 1999.

Fama, Maria. *Identification*. Philadelphia: Allora Press, 1996.

Fetterley, Judith, ed. *Provisions: A Reader from 19th-Century American Women*. Bloomington: Indiana University Press, 1985.

Gardaphé, Fred L. *Italian Signs, American Streets: The Evolution of Italian American Narrative*. Durham, North Carolina: Duke University Press, 1996.
Gilbert, Sandra M. *Blood Pressure*. New York: Norton, 1988.
Gillan, Maria. *Where I Come From: Selected and New Poems*. Toronto: Guernica, 1995.
Gioia, Dana. "Low Visibility: Thoughts on Italian American Writers." *Italian Americana* (Fall/Winter 1993): 7–12.
Giunta, Edvige. Afterword to "A Song from the Ghetto." In *Paper Fish* by Tina De Rosa. New York: Feminist Press, CUNY, 1996, 123–57.
Graff, Gerald. *Beyond the Culture Wars: How Teaching the Conflicts Can Revitalize American Education*. New York: Norton, 1992.
Guillory, John. "Canon." In *Critical Terms for Literary Study*, edited by Frank Lentricchia and Thomas McLaughlin. Chicago, Illinois: University of Chicago Press, 1990, 233–249.
Harris, Wendell V. "Canonicity." *PMLA* 106 (1991):110–121.
Hendin, Josephine Gattuso. *The Right Thing to Do*. 1988. New York: Feminist Press, 1999.
Hirsch, E. D. *Cultural Literacy: What Every American Needs to Know*. New York: Vintage Press, 1988.
Jacobs, Harriet A. *Incidents in the Life of a Slave Girl*, edited by Jean Fagan Yellin. Cambridge, Massachusetts: Harvard University Press, 1987.
Jewett, Sarah Orne. *The Country of the Pointed Firs and Other Stories*. New York: W.W. Norton and Company, 1981.
Lauter, Paul. *Canons and Contexts*. New York: Oxford University Press, 1991.
Lloyd, Susan Caperna. *No Pictures in My Grave: A Spiritual Journey in Sicily*. San Francisco, California: Mercury, 1992.
Manfredi, Renee. *Where Love Leaves Us*. Iowa City: University of Iowa Press, 1994.
Maso, Carole. *Ghost Dance*. Hopewell, New Jersey: Ecco, 1990.
Mazza, Cris. *Your Name Here: _____*. Minneapolis, Minnesota: Coffee House Press, 1995.
Monardo, Anna. *The Courtyard of Dreams*. New York: Doubleday, 1993.
Nardini, Gloria. *Che Bella Figura!: The Power of Performance in an Italian Ladies' Club*. New York: State University of New York Press, 1999.
Parini, Jay, ed. *The Norton Book of American Autobiography*. New York: W.W. Norton and Company, 1999.
Pryse, Marjorie. Introduction to *The Country of the Pointed Firs* by Sarah Orne Jewett. New York: Norton, 1981, v–xx.
Robinson, Lillian S. "Treason Our Text: Feminist Challenges to the Literary Canon." In *The New Feminist Criticism: Essays on Women, Literature, and Theory*, edited by Elaine Showalter. New York: Pantheon, 1985, 118–134.

Romano, Rose. *Vendetta*. San Francisco, California: Malafemmina Press, 1990.
Rossi, Agnes. *The Quick: A Novella and Stories*. New York: Norton, 1992.
Talese, Gay. "Where Are the Italian-American Novelists?" *New York Times Book Review*, 14 March 1993, 1+.
Tamburri, Anthony Julian. *A Semiotic of Ethnicity: In (Re) cognition of the Italian/American Writer*. Albany: State University of New York Press, 1998.
Timpanelli, Gioia. *Sometimes the Soul: Two Novellas of Sicily*. New York: Vintage, 1998.
Tomasi, Mari. *Like Lesser Gods*. Shelburne, Vermont: New England Press, 1988.
Vannucci, Lynn. "An Accidental Murder." In *The Voices We Carry: Recent Italian/American Women's Fiction*, edited by Mary Jo Bona. Montreal: Guernica, 1994, 371–76.
Vecoli, Rudolph J. "Are Italian Americans Just White Folks?" In *Italian and Italian/American Images in the Media*, edited by Mary Jo Bona and Anthony J. Tamburri. Proceedings of the 27th Annual Conference of the American Italian Historical Association. Staten Island, New York: American Italian Historical Association, 1996, 3–17. Reported in *Beyond the Godfather: Italian American Writers on the Real Italian American Experience*, edited by A. Kenneth Ciongoli and Jay Parini. Hanover, New Hampshire: University Press of New England, 1997, 311–322.
———. Foreword to *Rosa: The Life of an Italian Immigrant* by Marie Hall Ets. Madison: University of Wisconsin Press, 1999, v–xv.
Viscusi, Robert. "Where to Find Italian American Literature." *Italian Americana* 12, no. 2 (Summer 1994): 267–72.
Vitiello, Justin. "Off the Boat and Up the Creek without a Paddle—or, Where Italian Americana Might Swim: Prolepsis of an Ethnopoetics." *Beyond the Margin: Readings in Italian Americana*. Eds. Paolo Giordano and Anthony J. Tamburri. Madison: Fairleigh Dickinson UP, 1998. 23–45.
Warner, Marina. *Alone of All Her Sex: The Myth and Cult of the Virgin Mary*. New York: Vintage, 1976.
Welter, Barbara. *Dimity Convictions: The American Woman in the Nineteenth Century*. Athens: Ohio University Press, 1976.
Winterson, Jeanette. *Art and Lies*. New York: Vintage Press, 1994.
Wright, Nathalia. *American Novelists in Italy: The Discoverers Allston to James*. Philadelphia: University of Pennsylvania Press, 1965.
Zagarell, Sandra A. "Narrative of Community: The Identification of a Genre." *Signs* 13, no. 3 (1988): 498–527.

Fred Gardaphé

The Double Burden of Italian American Women Writers*

Scholar and poet Mary Jo Bona makes an observation in an important essay that brings awareness to a double burden carried by Italian American women writers:

> Italian American women writers have explored the vital connection between being a woman and being ethnic in a world (America) which traditionally has valued neither. ("Broken Images, Broken Lives," p. 91).

I suggest that because of this burden, many Italian American women writers have had to take on the dual role of creator and critic of Italian American literature. In the process, they have become strong leaders in the development and advocacy of Italian American literary culture, an accomplishment not formally recognized by historians and scholars of American literature. It is my contention that Italian American women writers, much more so than their male counterparts, have become the organic intellectuals of their ancestral culture.

---

*Used with permission of Fred Gardaphé, SUNY at Stony Brook.

In 1971, Michael Novak's *The Rise of the Unmeltable Ethnics* woke Americans up to the realities that "white" ethnicities were not lost in a fog of assimilation. Novak pointed to the ambivalent attitude of progressive intellectuals toward the early twentieth-century immigrant as one example of how the idea of a melting pot was, and would no doubt always remain, a myth. Their ambivalence, said Novak, resulted from their privileging of individual accomplishments over those of the family and community, something that many assimilated ethnics had to learn on the road to acceptance as mainstream academics.

For Italian Americans, the fifth-largest ethnic group in the United States, the years since the publication of Novak's book have been challenging in terms of developing leaders on all fronts, but especially in terms of developing intellectuals—those Novak describes as creators of, rather than distributors of, intellectual culture. The earliest Italian Americans who became intellectuals, more often than not, adopted a model in which alienation from one's birth community, and often one's birth class, was a requirement for acceptance into the club. Never stabilized by political lobbies, government grants, cultural foundations, or endowed university professorships, Italian American culture has only recently found its place in America's cultural and educational institutions. The Italian Americans who have found their way into those institutions have had to leave their ethnic identities at the door when they entered. This pattern applies to male and female intellectuals, but it is the women intellectuals who have challenged it more often than the men. This paper will present an overview of the dual role of creator and critic of Italian American literature that Italian American women writers have adopted in order to make their voices heard and their presence matter.

Italian/American women writers are struggling against the constraints placed on them from inside and outside their ethnic culture. Add to these cultural constraints the usual issues of negotiating one's place in the vast array of English and American literary history—the struggle to find a style, a voice, a publisher—and you begin to see why it is so difficult for Italian American women to become writers. Perhaps this is why so many Italian American women take on a dual burden in their work as writers. From Olga Peragallo's 1949 listing of Italian/American writers, to Rose Basile Green's 1974 encyclopedic study of the Italian American novel, to Helen Barolini's 1985 anthology of Italian/American writing, *The Dream Book*, Italian/American women have been nurturing the development of Italian/American literature as both its creators and organizers.

The first attempt at a systematic study of Italian/American literature was Rose Basile Green's 1962 dissertation at the University of Pennsylvania: *The Evolution of Italian-American Fiction as a Document of the Interaction of Two Cultures*. This primal text, published in 1974 as *The Italian American Novel: A Document of the Interaction of Two Cultures*, was the first major attempt to identify and critically examine the contribution that American writers of Italian descent have made to American culture. Green, also a poet, had to give up the time she could have given to her own poetry to capture the presence of Italian American literature. Green's hard work enabled the formation of new dimensions of critical examination of the Italian American contribution to American literature.

One of the critics who benefited from Green's pioneering work was Helen Barolini. Barolini, an essayist, novelist, and translator, knew the importance that creating and reading literature plays in self-development. "Literature," she says, "gives us ourselves." (Introduction, p. 51). Without experiencing models created by Italian American women, Barolini says, Italian American women cannot be expected to pursue literary careers. She believes that the Italian American women can contribute to a revitalization of American literature that might begin with writing about the self in journals, memoirs, and autobiographies. Achieving identity as an Italian/American woman, as Barolini explains, is difficult.

> ..., the displacement from one culture to another has represented a real crisis of identity for the Italian woman, and she has left a heritage of conflict to her children. They, unwilling to give themselves completely to the old ways she transmitted, end up, in their assimilationist hurry, with shame and ambivalence in their behavior and values. (Introduction, p. 13).

This shame and ambivalence often become the very building blocks of Italian American women's writing. As Barolini's own fiction demonstrates, writing for Italian American women became not only a means of discovering an American identity, but also a means of discovering and creating a human identity. It is this dual requirement that makes writing into extremely challenging work for Italian American women as they attempt to reconcile past and present, Old World and new. Barolini's search for self through her own writing, and the creation of her American identity through the creation of literature, once established, enabled her to go in search of her sister authors. The results of that search are found in *The Dream Book: An Anthology of Writings by Italian American Women*.

In the houses of Italian America were women writers, who, until Barolini gave them *The Dream Book*, often felt they wrote in a void, isolated from the Anglo-Saxon literary tradition and the incipient, male-dominated Italian American tradition. Barolini tells us that Italian immigrant families, in spite of embracing the freedoms America provided that Italy did not, kept up the traditional male/female double standard. Women were not expected to go on to college; when they did go, it was often with the parents' hopes that they would just find husbands. Faced with such restrictive barriers erected by family and tradition, the Italian American woman who would be a writer could only become one by directly challenging the forces that attempted to keep her tied down to traditional roles. Part of that challenge would require fighting the image that the larger society had created for her to emulate.

So Helen Barolini took it upon herself to recast the public image of the Italian American woman in her own likeness. In doing so, she proved not only that an Italian American woman could write, but also that any consideration of Italian American culture would be incomplete if the literary works produced by women were ignored. Thus, Barolini became an important model for women writers.

Shortly after the publication of *The Dream Book*, Rose Romano, a poet, editor, and freelance typesetter, undertook a pioneering literary project when she launched *la bella figura*, a literary journal devoted entirely to writing by Italian/American women. The first issue, entitled "*Omertà*," featured poetry, short fiction, and reviews from well-known and first-time-published writers. Maria Mazziotti Gillan and Rachel Guido deVries were two of the better-known writers featured in the debut issue.

Romano started the journal after literary magazines began publishing work in which she was using what she called "this ethnically unspecified presumed to be WASP persona" (Gardaphé, p. 194). When she started writing about being Italian American, all of a sudden nobody wanted to publish her work. This led her to start her own magazine. Thus, Romano joined Italian/American women such as Helen Barolini, who have taken the wheel when it comes to directing the promotional drive of Italian American writers. Romano's motivation comes from her feeling that Italian American women were not taken seriously. In an interview, she said, "We're not considered real; we're Europeans, and Europeans run the world; it seems that no matter where we go we get it for being something; you're never the right thing. Now it's like we're American enough that we can afford to be Italian. We're not foreigners anymore" (Gardaphé, p. 195). Through her own writing and the publications she created with her *Malafemmina Press*, Romano helped create a sense of a distinctive culture and a tradition of Italian American women writers that would serve as models in the future.

Intellectual and literary models are vitally important for Italian American writers, and something Louise DeSalvo longed for early in her life. As she tells in her recent memoir, "Though I had read scores of books, not one had been written by an Italian-American woman. I had no role model among the women of my background to urge me on. . . ." (*Vertigo*, p.9). For DeSalvo, and other Italian Americans born in the 1940s, a sense of Italian/American culture and identity would come from one's family and perhaps one's neighborhood, but certainly not from school. Without Italian/American models in educational institutions, those like DeSalvo who would choose to become teachers and writers would need to look elsewhere.

This need for artistic and intellectual predecessors is not peculiar to the Italian/American community. As Alice Walker said in "Saving the Life That Is Your Own":

> the absence of models, in literature as in life, . . . is an occupational hazard for the artist, simply because models in art, in behavior, in growth of spirit and intellect—even if rejected— enrich and enlarge one's view of existence (p. 4).

Toward the end of this essay, Walker writes: "It is, in the end, the saving of lives that we writers are about. Whether we are 'minority' writers or 'majority.' It is simply in our power to do this" (p.14).

This power, it seems, took a long time for Italian Americans to realize. But the impact of reading and writing on the development of Louise DeSalvo's intellect, no matter who the model was, was significant. "It is as simple as this," she writes. "Reading and writing about what I have read have saved my life" (p. 7). This power of the intellectual is too often taken for granted, and for Italian Americans, that power has too long been ignored. Although they may rise as teachers and managers of mainstream American culture, as many have done, Italian Americans have been conspicuous for their absence in the management of a culture consisting of their own ancestral histories and traditions. Conditioned by demands of objectivity in research and scholarship, Italian Americans have long avoided their own stories in developing their analyses and critiques of culture. However, this is changing.

The current trend in many fields of academic study—scholars incorporating the story of their lives into their life research—is something that was launched by the scores of feminist critics who found the personal in the political and had the strength of conviction not only to tell their stories, but to help others tell theirs, as well. At the 1995 annual convention of the Modern Language Association (MLA), one of the largest academic organizations in the United States, a forum on ethnicity was held. One of the presenters at that forum was Linda Hutcheon. In her talk entitled "Crypto-ethnicity," Hutcheon pointed out that a number of the leading scholars in American and English literary studies were women whose ethnicity was hidden during their rise in their academic careers. Hutcheon noted that Sandra M. Gilbert, then the president of the MLA; Marianna Torgovnick and Cathy N. Davidson, professors at Duke University; and herself, a leading scholar of postmodernism, all descended from Italian immigrant families—a fact that was hidden by their adoption of their husbands' surnames. Unfortunately, Hutcheon did not explore the impact this cryptoethnicity has had on the intellectuals she identified.

The question I raised in response to her presentation was this: What is the significance that lies in identifying one's ethnicity with one's intellectual work? When I posed this question to Hutcheon (who has since become president of the MLA), offering to give her space in the journal *Voices in Italian Americana* in our Fall 1996 issue, dedicated to Italian American women's writing, she hesitated and then excused herself, saying that it was not something she felt she could competently contribute to through her own research. Hutcheon subsequently republished that essay in a book entitled *Beyond the Godfather*, but her hesitation a few years earlier marks a reluctance all too common among mainstream academics.

Marianna De Marco Torgovnick, an established critic and scholar, has documented her story of assimilation in *Crossing Ocean Parkway: Readings by an Italian American Daughter*. She wrote:

> What I tell here is different from the story of arrival. It is the story of assimilation—one that Italian Americans of my generation are uniquely prepared to tell, and that females need to tell most of all. (p. x).

Although Torgovnick has acknowledged her ancestral culture in writing, she has only indirectly taken on the responsibility of contributing to the institutionalization of that culture.

Sandra Mortola Gilbert has a long history of acknowledging her Italian/American ethnicity more often in her poetry than through any critical consideration of Italian/American women writers. Her important contributions to American culture, often written in collaboration with Susan Gubar, include *The Madwoman in the Attic* and its three-volume sequel, *No Man's Land*. Most recently, Gilbert and Gubar have flexed their collective intellectual muscles through their satirical *Masterpiece Theatre: An Academic Melodrama*, which dramatizes the culture wars of the late 1980s and early 1990s. Through this publication, Gilbert and Gubar position themselves on the middle ground between the back-to-the-basics conservatives and what they call the "forward to instability" radicals. Although Gilbert and Gubar have become America's dynamic duo of feminist literary studies, and although they have both contributed significantly to a sense of community in women's studies, it is when Gilbert leaves the partnership to speak in her own individual voice that she identifies as an American writer of Italian descent. It is in this work, I will argue, that Gilbert presents the possibilities and the problems of becoming a model for the Italian/American intellectual.

In "*Piacere Conoscerla*: On Being an Italian American," published in *From the Margin*, Gilbert begins to articulate the dilemma of identifying with her Italian/American ancestry.

> [T]o be an Italian-American is to live in a world of perpetual mystery. Almost always to be wrong—and then, worse still to drown your troubles in American booze. *Omertà?* The silence? Not just overt (—the silence—about, as I will tell you, the life and lives of ancestors, but for some of us—second and third generation, whatever we are (and that's itself debatable)—a silence about our language, our food, ourselves. (p. 116)

This silence, I suggest, is broken in the underground of Gilbert's intellectual work, in her psychic "summer kitchen" where it can be argued that she goes to examine her past. In her essay, she tells of two kitchens, "a downstairs room, called 'the summer kitchen,' to which all of us descended when the heat rose in Brooklyn" (p.118). She later refers to this basement kitchen as "the Italian 'heart of darkness'" (p. 118). Mythically captured in the poem "The Summer Kitchen," this place is a "white, bare secret room" where women labored, turning the men's work into nourishment for all. This "summer kitchen," I would argue, is where Gilbert's major Italian/American signifying takes place and where Italian/American intellectuals must go to find what Gilbert offers to future generations of Italian American intellectuals. Gilbert, who has always signified her Italian ancestry in her poetry, excluded it from her criticism. However, her attention to her own ethnicity, through her poetry, perhaps prepared her to recognize the importance of the work of Mary Jo Bona and prompted her to consider publishing Bona's *Claiming a Tradition*, the first critical book about Italian American writers in her signature Ad Feminam series at Southern Illinois University Press. Perhaps this is a case in which the child is the mother to the woman. Well-researched and -written scholarship such as Bona's makes it possible for major writers of the mainstream to understand and connect to their Italian ethnic roots.

With *Claiming a Tradition: Italian American Women Writers*, Bona joins Olga Peragallo, Rose Basile Green, and Helen Barolini as one of the great advocates of Italian American literature. What separates Bona from the others is her command of cultural and literary theories that help place Italian American women's writing in the context of American history. Hers is a most important contribution to the field of American literature in general and women's studies and Italian/American culture in particular.

Claiming a Tradition is the first book-length study of Italian/American women writers, and Bona's clear writing and lucid arguments make it accessible to the casual reader, as well as the professional scholar. From the opening, a strong, authoritative, and confident voice guides the reader. A solid introduction places the literature in the context of American literary history and ethnic studies. Bona does an excellent job of setting up the background against which her readers are projected. She writes: "claiming a tradition for Italian American women writers is an act of assertion in the face of possible resistance." She then shows us the many sites, which generate that resistance in mainstream American culture and from within Italian American culture itself. Furthermore, a good summary of earlier critical work on the literature indicates that we are listening to someone who has done her homework.

The bulk of the study explores elements of *Italianità* that Bona finds inside each of the works she reads. These include the role of the mother, *l'ordine della famiglia*, *destino*, *la via vecchia*, *comparaggio*, and *omertà*. She structures her chapters by pairing texts that highlight concepts, such as: family in Mari Tomasi's *Like Lesser Gods* and Mario Benasutti's *No Steady Job for Pappa*; coming-of-age in *A Cup of the Sun* and Josephine Gattuso Hendin's *The Right Thing to Do*; personal identity in Diana Cavallo's *A Bridge of Leaves* and Dorothy Byrant's *Miss Giardino*; and recovering ancestry in Helen Barolini's *Umbertina* and Tina DeRosa's *Paper Fish*.

In many cases, the authors she covers have received little, if any, critical attention. We are witnessing an original contribution to the field of literary criticism and history that advances earlier thinking and scholarship. The study is well integrated; each chapter builds on the previous one the way a narrative might build a plot, except that her story is composed of critical arguments. Her organization helps us witness a tradition evolving.

Bona's keen sense of what has been missed by previous scholars stems from the thoroughness of her preparation, the precision of her execution, and her passion for the material. Based on her dissertation, *Claiming a Tradition* represents a mature rethinking and immense reworking of the ideas and the language that were ahead of their time even in the early stages of the development of her thesis. Bona has revised her earlier writing to reflect her continued passion for literary expression and her mastery of the field. Her methodology of pairing authors works well to bring out commonalities, as well as differences. This technique advances her argument that these women are, whether they know it or not, creating a real literary tradition. Beyond giving us insight into the past, this study serves the future development of Italian/American literature. Her final chapter, "Recent Developments in Italian American Women's Literary Traditions," is a survey of contemporary writers such as Rachel Guido deVries, Renee Manfredi, Agnes Rossi, and Carole Maso, and provides us with a good sense of what will be happening in the decades to come.

Bona, an accomplished and award-winning poet, has given up much of her career as a creative writer to criticizing and historicizing the writing of Italian American women. This is something that Edvige Giunta, editor of the Fall 1996 issue of *Voices in Italian Americana*, which was dedicated to Italian American women writers, pointed to in her Editorial Statement.

> For Italian/American women critics to write about Italian/American women writers does not mean merely to choose to write intellectual and literary history. Writing is often an act of defiance. Writing often means, directly or indirectly, daring to write of one's own life. It means asserting the right to break the silence imposed from the inside—the family and a culture which, in order to protect themselves, often choose to sacrifice their own—and from the outside—the American culture and media willing to accept and reproduce only stultifying images of Italian womanhood. It means shaping a place in-between, a "space/*spazio*" that cuts across the hyphen and whose elusive borders fluctuate between the real and the imaginary: a space which is being continuously re-invented by a community of writers, critics, and readers. (p. iii)

Bona's powerful study was published in Ad Feminam, a series edited by Sandra Gilbert. Although Gilbert may not have written critically yet about Italian American women writers, she became a powerful advocate of Italian American women's writing by publishing this fine study.

Other writers provide even more evidence of this dual responsibility taken on by Italian American women writers. Maria Gillan publishes writers and gets their books reviewed in *The Paterson Literary Review*; she also sponsors contests, organizes readings, and edits anthologies with major presses—all in addition to doing her own award-winning writing. Rita Ciresi takes time from her teaching and her award-winning fiction writing to comment regularly on writers in the journal *Italian Americana*. Mary Ann Mannino, in addition to publishing fiction and poetry, recently published her dissertation on women writers (Revisionary Identities, 2000), and Maria Famà has begun making Italian American women poets accessible to readers of Italian through her translations.

Now I don't want to give you the impression that this is something only the women of our community do. More so than the men though, it is the women who have a strong sense of community and of the need to support that community in any way possible. This was not the case, as Helen Barolini so strongly recounts in her essays, with Gay Talese, Mario Puzo, and Jerre Mangione.

Conditioned by demands of objectivity in research and scholarship, Italian Americans have long avoided their own stories in developing their analyses and critiques of culture. However, this is changing. Today, many American intellectuals of Italian descent are heeding Michael Novak's advice that "There is no other way but autobiography by which to cure oneself of too much objectivity." In the past few years, a number of major American critics of Italian descent such as Marianna De Marco Torgovnick, Louise DeSalvo, Sandra Gilbert, and Mary Cappello have departed from their professional intellectual pasts to publish autobiographical texts.

The development of this work of creating, cataloging, and criticizing Italian American literature is by nature a collective project that requires the interaction of all concerned so that Italian/American writers can achieve the cultural impact they so rightly deserve. The responsibility, then, of all intellectuals is to create knowledge that will not only nurture the next generation, but also enable intellectuals to connect to, and not shy away from, the communities that have created them. It is the Italian/American woman writer who has taken on this double burden and shown us best how to get this done.

Works Cited and Selected Bibliography

Barolini, Helen. "Becoming a Literary Person Out of Context." *The Massachusetts Review* 27.2 (1986): 262–74.

———. *Chiaroscuro*. Essays of Identity. Madison: University of Wisconsin Press, 1999.

———, editor. *The Dream Book: An Anthology of Writings by Italian-American Women*. New York: Schocken Books, 1985.

———. Introduction to *The Dream Book: An Anthology of Writings by Italian-American Women*, edited by Helen Barolini. New York: Schocken Books, 1985, 3–56.

———. Preface to *The Dream Book: An Anthology of Writings by Italian-American Women*, edited by Helen Barolini. New York: Schocken Books, 1985.
———. *Umbertina*. New York: Seaview, 1979.
Bona, Mary Jo. "Broken Images, Broken Lives: Carmolina's Journey in Tina De Rosa's *Paper Fish*." *MELUS* 14, nos. 3–4 (Fall–Winter 1987): 87–106.
———. *Claiming a Tradition: Italian American Women Writers*. Ad Feminam Series. Carbondale: Southern Illinois University Press, 1999.
DeSalvo, Louise. *Vertigo: A Memoir*. New York: Dutton, 1996.
Gardaphé, Fred. "Romano Cuts a *Bella Figura*." In *Dagoes Read*. Toronto: Guernica Editions, 1996, 194–196.
Gilbert, Sandra M. *Blood Pressure*. New York: W. W. Norton, 1998.
Gilbert, Sandra M. "Summer Kitchen." In *Blood Pressure*. New York: W. W. Norton & Company, 1988, 55–57.
Gilbert. *No-Man's Land*. New Haven, Connecticut: Yale University Press, 1991.
———. "*Piacere Conoscerla*: On Being an Italian-American." In *From the Margin: Writings in Italian Americana*, edited by Anthony J. Tamburri, et al. West Lafayette, Indiana: Purdue University Press, 1991, 116–20.
Gilbert, Sandra M., and Susan Gubar. *Masterpiece Theatre: An Academic Melodrama*. New Brunswick, New Jersey: Rutgers University Press, 1995.
Gilbert, Sandra M., and Susan Gubar. *The Madwoman in the Attic*. New Haven, Connecticut: Yale University Press, 2000.
Giunta, Edvige. Editorial Statement. In *Voices in Italian Americana* 7, no. 2 (Fall 1996): i–ix.
Green, Rose Basile. *The Italian-American Novel: A Document of the Interaction of Two Cultures*. Cranbury, New Jersey: Associated University Press, 1974.
Novak, Michael. *Unmeltable Ethnics: Politics and Culture in American Life*. 2d ed. New Brunswick, New Jersey: Transaction Publishers, 1996.
Romano, Rose, editor. *la bella figura: a choice*. San Francisco, California: Malafemmina Press, 1993.
Torgovnick, Marianna De Marco. *Crossing Ocean Parkway: Readings by an Italian American Daughter*. Chicago, Illinois: The University of Chicago Press, 1994.
Walker, Alice. "Saving the Life That is Your Own: The Importance of Models in the Artist's Life. In *In Search of Our Mother's Gardens*. San Diego, California: Harcourt, Brace, Jovanovich, 1983, 3–14.

Edvige Giunta

Speaking Through Silences*

Ethnicity in the Writings of Italian/American Women

> It's not easy being an angry poet when you come from a culture whose most profound statement of anger is silence.
> (Rose Romano, "Mutt Bitch")

> Remember me, Ladies, the silent one? I have found my voice and my rage will blow your house down.
> (Maria Mazziotti Gillan, "Public School No. 18, Paterson, New Jersey")

The force of acculturation in the United States pressures authors of ethnically and culturally marginalized groups to learn to speak the language of the dominant, Anglo-centric culture, to adhere to its aesthetics, even to mold their art within its parameters.[1] Being an immigrant means to be

---

*"Speaking Through Silences: Ethnicity in the Writing of Italian/American Women" was originally published in *Literature and Ethnic Discrimination*, edited by Michale J. Meyer (Amsterdam and Atlanta: Rodopi Press, 1997).
[1] In "I'm Here: An Asian American Woman's Response," Amy Ling questions of definitions of "fine literature" and argues for the need to study literature as "the written voice of a specific group of people at a specific time" (742).

an outcast in more ways than one: cut off from the culture of consent *and* from the culture of descent, which is reduced to a ghost culture in the new country, immigrants typically occupy a marginal position within the culture of origin prior to emigration.[2] To argue that emigration "forces a disintegration of self, culture, and society," and to posit an integration of such elements prior to emigration, though, would mean to ignore the factors that triggered departure from the country of origin (Ostendorf 577). In other words, the sense of loss and separation pre-exists emigration, and immigration, rather than healing the fracture between self and culture, re-enacts the drama of separation and marginalization.[3] Various forms of economic, social, and political subjection suffered in the country of origin constitute the baggage that immigrants carry with them to the new country, where the very conditions they escaped from are often replicated. The literature produced by immigrants and their children articulates the struggle to extricate oneself from the constraints of such conditions.

The self-silencing that acculturation entails resonates in language, cleansing it of ethnic ties. Lack of recognition generates a perception, both external and internal, of cultural invisibility.[4] Italian/American literature articulates the struggle of a culture caught between assimilation and exclusion.[5] As the poet Rose Romano argues, because Italian Americans can "hide" (*Wop* 35), by camouflaging—or even rejecting—their ethnic identity, they can assimilate into the mainstream, but at the cost of losing cultural identity and internalizing self-hatred. Ethnicity is characteristically expressed—and repressed—in traditional and culturally acceptable Italian/American narratives, as evidenced by the popularity of

---

[2]Sollors claims that the conflict between "descent" and "consent" "is at the root of the ambiguity surrounding the very terminology of American ethnic interaction" (5).
[3]"The difference is between a malintegration one has learned to cope with or whose hopelessness is fully understood and a more radical malintegration exacerbated by the greenhorn status" (Ostendorf 577).
[4]The same is also true, of course, for those who belong to groups that are marginalized because of their class or sexual orientation. In this essay I will focus specifically on ethnic discrimination.
[5]On the status of Italian Americans in American culture, see Tamburri and Bona eds., Tropea et al. eds.; and Gambino.

authors like Mario Puzo and Gay Talese and directors like Francis Ford Coppola and Martin Scorsese.[6] For Italian/American authors it is imperative to rethink the ways in which ethnicity can be represented in order to defy the stultified images of their ethnicity pervasive in mainstream American culture.[7] The literature of many Italian/American authors simultaneously verbalizes and silences ethnicity. This kind of writing, in which a thinly disguised accent reveals ethnic identity, dramatizes the cultural conflicts at the heart of the experience of hyphenation.[8]

The effort to articulate one's own ethnic voice and to construct narratives that claim a position of agency for members of immigrant communities is further complicated when an author also must transcend the cultural limitations linked to gender and sexual identities. She may translate her dual foreignness into a language that is acquiescent and rebellious at once.[9] Discussing Helen Barolini's autobiographical project, Fred L. Gardaphé argues that the autobiographies of Italian/American women are characterized by "an intense politicization of the self" (20) which, in Barolini's work, translates into a continuous effort to achieve both self-legitimation and the legitimation of an Italian/American female literary tradition.[10]

Indeed, many Italian/American women writers root their self-exploration in a relentless analysis of the place occupied by Italian/American ethnicity in American culture. In her essay "An Italian

---

[6]See Gardaphé, "What's Italian About Italian/American Literature."
[7]See Barolini's discussion of stereotypes of Italian/Americans in "Becoming a Literary Person Out of Context" (272).
[8]Anthony Tamburri has argued that the experience of hyphenation is literally reproduced in the signs used to refer to Americans of Italian descent. In *To Hyphenate or Not To Hyphenate*, he argues that the slash, unlike the hyphen, establishes an egalitarian and dialectical relationship between the terms Italian and American.
[9]On women and ethnicity, see Dearborn. On Italian/American women authors, see Barolini, "Introduction," *The Dream Book*, 3–56; Bona, Introduction, *The Voices We Carry*, 11–29; Gabaccia, Gardaphé, "Autobiography as Piecework"; and Giunta, "'A Song from the Ghetto'."
[10]On Barolini, see Gardaphé, "Autobiography as Piecework" and Giunta, "Blending Literary Discourses." See also Barolini's introduction to *The Dream Book* and her essay, "Becoming a Literary Person Out of Context."

American Woman Speaks Out" (1980), Tina De Rosa laments the isolation rooted in a deeply internalized perception of her culture of origin as an aberration from the standard of American middle-class life. Similarly, in her memoir, *Vertigo* (1996), Louise DeSalvo continues the exploration of Italian/American women's identity which she had begun in her novel *Casting Off* (1987), defying pious and stultifying images of Italian/American womanhood. In *Casting Off*, De Salvo had encoded Italian/American identity in the Irish surnames of her characters, thus articulating the silence enforced by a culture that does not allow for Italian/American characters who break away from the stereotypes inculcated by films such as *The Godfather* and *Moonstruck*.[11] In her poem "Public School No. 18, Paterson, New Jersey," Maria Mazziotti Gillan writes of the teachers who, "without words," tell the young speaker "to be ashamed" of being Italian and "to hate" herself (*Where I Come From* 12–13). She recalls the Psychology professor who had told her that she reminded "him of the Mafia leader/on the cover of *Time* magazine" (*Where I Come From* 13). The speaker of "Growing Up Italian" remembers: "In kindergarten, English words fell on me,/thick and sharp as hail. I grew silent,/the Italian word balanced on the edge/of my tongue and the English word, lost/during the first moment/of every question" (*Where I Come From* 54). Gillan thus interrogates American culture's tolerance for Italian Americans. However, like the speaker of "Public School No. 18, Paterson, New Jersey," Gillan and other Italian/American women writers have found the strength and the words to blow down the house of those who silenced them.

The work of Agnes Rossi, a writer of Italian *and* Irish ancestry, illustrates the kind of negotiations between cultural/ethnic identities undertaken by Italian/American women. Rossi's ambivalent treatment of her Italian background contrasts with a more direct and less complicated approach to her Irish ancestry in *Split Skirt* and, especially, in her unpublished novel, *Fancy*, set in Ireland and the United States. Rossi's narratives bear directly upon questions of ethnic (self-) representation

---

[11]On representations of Italian Americans in film see Giunta, "The Quest for True Love."

and identity politics, and capture notions of ethnic identity in postmodernity, in which ethnicity eschews static demarcations. Existing on the margins, postmodern ethnicity evokes the elusively defined borders of transnationality, migrancy, and homelessness.[12] Rossi's authorial development epitomizes the simultaneity of acceptance and denial of Italian ethnicity, suggesting an ongoing conflict that fuels her creative process. Her first book, *Athletes and Artists: Stories* (1987), silences the ethnic voice, while the protagonist of *The Quick* (1992) is identified through her name as an Italian American. The younger protagonist of Rossi's novel, *Split Skirt* (1994), is, like her author, of Italian and Irish descent, but the only explicit mention of her ethnicity "didn't survive the final edit."[13]

The disappearance of this reference evidences the suppression of the ethnic voice.[14] The editing process that unwittingly cancels traces of ethnicity functions as a form of self-censorship, one that is analogous to the hiding of the speaker of Gillan's "Public School No. 18, Paterson, New Jersey." "My face wants to hide," she confesses, juxtaposing her chattering voice at home, where her words are "smooth" in her "mouth," to her silence in school where she "grope[s] for the right English/words, fear[ing] the Italian word/will sprout from . . . [her] mouth like a rose" (*Where I Come From* 12).[15]

For contemporary writers such as Agnes Rossi, Rita Ciresi, and Cris Mazza, the Italian word often remains unspoken, or is erased. The characters in Ciresi's *Mother Rocket* represent a wide ethnic spectrum

---

[12]See Chambers and Bammer. As Micaela Di Leonardo points out, though "critics and advocates alike implicitly or explicitly assume that contemporary identity politics categories—gender, race or ethnicity, nationality, sexual orientation—are ur-identities, the most fundamental divisions in human experience, but depending on which era of American history we consider, we would want to later alter or expand this list" (109).
[13]Personal letter from Agnes Rossi, 5 January 1994. Early drafts of *Fancy* also contained Italian/American references.
[14]Rossi claims that the omission of the Italian/American reference had to do exclusively with the direction the narrative had taken. Telephone conversation, 28 February 1994.
[15]In her first book of poems, a chapbook entitled Taking Back My Name, Gillan turned self-silencing into the subject matter of her poetry.

because, as Joshua Fausty argues, the author "infuses her ambivalent sense of her own cultural identity into her characters, linking her quest for ethnic/authorial self-definition to their multicultural identities" (204). Mazza, whose experimental fiction escapes simple classification, creates a character, in *Your Name Here*, in search of her identity with no secure knowledge even of her name.[16] And the protagonist of Renèe Manfredi's novel *Running Away with Frannie*, when asked by his traveling companion, "Who are you again?", answers: "I'm not sure." For characters *and* their authors, living in a post-melting pot and post-white ethnic revival American culture, ethnic identity cannot be traded in for the promise of an American narrative of success; at the same time, the nostalgic evocation of the motherland no longer represents an option for third- or fourth-generation writers.[17]

Ethnic boundaries intersect in a postmodern world struggling to create viable methods for cultural identification and connection. Accordingly, Rossi's characters suffer from cultural displacement and psychological detachment, translated either into a third-person narrative, as in many of her stories—a seemingly uninvolved and isolated voice acting as a mere recorder of events—or into a detached first-person narrative such as that of Marie Russo, the protagonist of *The Quick*, whose last name strikingly resembles the author's. Marie's narrative articulates a disjunction between story and self which in turn mirrors a fracture between self and community. Rossi thus inscribes her own fractures in her characters' ambivalent choices and fragmented identities. As an Italian/American author, Rossi faces the difficulties of entering a literary market that, for the most part, perpetuates stereotypical and folkloric representations of her ethnicity.[18] Commenting on the lack of recognition

---

[16] See Pelton's review of *Your Name Here*. Examining issues of ethnic visibility and invisibility in Italian/American literature, Fred Gardaphé argues that writers such as Don De Lillo and critics such as Frank Lentricchia either suppress ethnic clues or portray their ethnicity obliquely through other ethnicities. See his article "(In)visibility."
[17] For a discussion of third-generation Italian/American writers, see Gardaphé, "A Third-Generation Renaissance."
[18] On the status of Italian/American literature see the introduction to *From the Margin*, eds. Tamburri, Giordano, and Gardaphé. See also Gardaphé, *Italian Signs, American Streets*.

for Italian/American authors, Gardaphé rightly calls Italian/American writers "cultural immigrants" on the "American literary scene" ("Third Generation," 72).[19]

As a woman author, Rossi must also confront a cultural background—Italian/American—historically hostile to female artistry and scarcely populated by feminine voices that might enable the emerging author to place herself confidently within a literary tradition.[20] As an Irish/Italian/American author writing two decades after the white ethnic revival, she negotiates between ethnic identities, crossing and blending cultural worlds that jar against each other, simultaneously attempting to establish the subject position from which she writes and to avoid the entrapment which speaking solely from that position would entail.[21]

Privileging memory, Rossi's novella *The Quick* strives to narrate an Italian/American story through a narrative in which, ironically, ethnicity goes unnamed. Scattered traces of ethnicity surface in the narrative to create the space in which this author inscribes her ethnic voice. This novella speaks with an accent, ever so slight, yet unquestionably present. The Italian/American background of the narrator, Marie Russo from Paterson, New Jersey, emerges obliquely, and neither the author nor the narrator give it much emphasis. Indeed Marie demonstrates very little awareness of her ethnic roots.[22]

---

[19]In his book *Italian Signs, American Streets*, reversing the association between Italian Americans and organized crime, Gardaphé argues for the need "to make sure that the cultural crimes of the past do not increase others' ignorance of Italian American culture" (4).

[20]On the development of a female Italian/American literary tradition, see the introduction to *The Dream Book*, ed. Helen Barolini. See also Barolini's "Becoming a Literary Person Out of Context," Bona's introduction to *The Voices We Carry*, Gardaphé's "Autobiography as Piecework," and Giunta, "'A Song from the Ghetto.'" See Caroli on the history of Italian women immigrants in North America.

[21]For a discussion of "positionality," see Brenkman 99–100.

[22]Rossi claims that she has developed a self-awareness of her ethnicity in the recent past ("On Being Italian American," unpublished notes, 2). Marie then actualizes the author's own relationship to her ethnic experience.

After a terrible fight with her father during which her mother's china shatters, however, Marie remembers that her mother's cabinet contained the "flowered vase" her "father's relatives sent from Italy." "Chris and I," she remarks, "never considered ourselves related to my parents' relatives, especially the ones we never saw, the ones who were just blue airmail letters that lay around the house for a while and then were gone" (85). The relatives are metonymically identified at first with the "vase," and then with the "blue airmail letters," that, like the character's ethnicity, have seemingly disappeared. Thus Marie internalizes the very invisibility of her ethnicity. Her inability to connect with her ethnicity may lie at the core of her psychological and cultural displacement.

In all her relationships, with the exception of her friendship with Phyllis, an older fellow worker, she experiences a discomfort that makes her acutely aware of the contrived quality of her cultural roles as daughter, sister, girlfriend, college graduate, teacher, wife, and mother. After accepting these roles, however, she eventually rejects them all. Moving into an empty and "shabby" apartment (57), she asserts her need for a blank space, devoid of cultural scripts, in which, abandoning herself to the seduction of emptiness, she can plunge into her past and begin to remember and tell. Marie Russo's storytelling, like Rossi's, acknowledges loss and despair with utter honesty, and claims the need for the storyteller to connect with the past, without being weighed down by it, in order to forge her voice.

Rossi confers a unique sense of unity on the complex narrative of her novella through the somewhat monotonous voice of its narrator, a seemingly detached commentator. The narrative opens in the present and then unfolds in a spiral of memories that the narrator weaves in and out of the present. Rossi's reliance on memory and storytelling connects *The Quick* to the traditions of the *bildungsroman, kunstlerroman* and memoir. But Rossi challenges the conventions of these genres by telling a story of failed development and failed artistic emergence, and by seemingly depriving her fictional memoir of direction and cohesion. Disrupting narrative continuity, the plot recapitulates Marie's life, a life punctuated by attempts at self-assertion as well as self-erasure: she remembers she could have "made a life" for herself, but she "didn't want to" (70). Ultimately, Marie's life story articulates a fracture between the narrator and her narrative: she disclaims any connection with her narrative subject, just as she disclaims her connection with her Italian relatives. By consolidating the intricate and seemingly disjointed narrative of *The Quick* around loss—loss of people, hopes, opportunities for self-realization—Rossi obliquely expresses her concern with the dying ethnicity of her characters. The vanishing of the ethnic identity is rendered through abrupt narrative shifts, textual fractures and narrative gaps as well as lack of narrative unity or final closure.

The link between Marie's ethnicity and her self-definition is expressed through her longing for a place that feels like "home," the very longing that leads her to go home after quitting her job: "I'd been away long enough to dream up a romantic notion of home as a safe place where I'd be able to get my bearings" (29). For Marie, the search for a "home" begins when, as a twelve year old, she glues a lock on the door of her room—but the glue gives out, "with no fight at all," when her father, completely unaware, pushes it open (63). His violence and ruthlessness haunt Marie's childhood and adolescence: "I knew then that my father would always crash through, without even meaning to, and, worse, without even knowing he'd crashed through" (64). This realization captures the sense of displacement and loss characterizing Marie's self-perception. The search for a home takes her to disparate places, such as Woolworth's, Phyllis' home, the burnt house of the Metuchens, the house where she lives during her marriage to Ralph, and finally the empty apartment where she begins to tell her story. The search articulates Marie's attempt to negotiate between self-definition and cultural definitions. Rejecting romanticized notions of home, Rossi chooses not to resolve Marie's conflicts and does not offer epiphanies that will transform her characters' lives.

Rossi's concern with social outcasts is not limited to *The Quick*. Marginal figures—truck drivers, waitresses, jobless men and women, ex-drug addicts, failed artists—populate *Athletes and Artists* and the stories in *The Quick*. These figures live on the borders, existing at such a distance from mainstream culture that often, its myths do not appeal to them. At the same time, they also appear to be cut off from the culture of descent. Marie's inability to mourn the loss of her ethnicity is bound up with the fact that she identifies it with the patriarchal ideology dominant in her parents' household. Marie's relentless remembering and her interpellation of her audience—"I want to tell you some of the things Phyllis told me that summer but I don't want to have to go on and one [sic] about what color blouse she was wearing when she said a particular thing" (58)—radically contrast her with her mother, who lives in silent expectation of her father's explosions.

In Josephine Gattuso Hendin's novel, *The Right Thing To Do*, the daughter realizes that she is "everything" to her father and that "he could only deal with losing her by controlling her life, so that whatever happened to her would show his mark" (32). It is this paternal mark that Marie tries to escape, often to no avail. The voicelessness and passivity of the maternal figure, however, pose a more pernicious threat to the daughter's self-definition than does the father's physical and psychological abuse.

Gianna Patriarca, an Italian/Canadian writer, powerfully depicts the heritage of maternal silence in poems such as "Italian Women," "My Birth," and "Daughter." The speakers of these poems must face the haunting image of women who "wrap their souls/around their children/ and serve their own hearts/in a meal they never/share" (9). Women writers of Italian ancestry have to fight both the culture that marginalizes their ethnicity and the ethnicity that silences their gender.

If Marie is, on the one hand, capable of rejecting the model of femininity offered by her mother, then, on the other hand, she lacks the tools to fashion a new role for herself. Marie's failed attempt to reconcile her desire for a "conventional life" with her wish to be "eccentric within that life" (69) parallels her inability to bridge the gap between two cultures, mainstream American culture and Italian/American culture. While the seductiveness of American mythology leads Marie to adopt it—she dreams of a "Cape Cod house" (70)—she is also capable of realizing that the "shabby" apartment she moves into after the divorce feels more "like home than the house with three bathrooms ever" did (57). On the other hand, her relationship to Italian ethnicity is confused, repressed both in Marie's life and in the text, emerging occasionally, but never enough to provide the opportunity for confrontation or resolution. In Rossi's novella, Italian/American ethnicity is represented as a ghost culture that the narrative vainly tries to evoke: it emerges infrequently, embodied in lost airmail letters or broken china.

Marie's account of her life as a series of scattered and seemingly disconnected episodes parallels her representation of her ethnicity as an accumulation of tokens. Italian art and religion are represented by a dwarfed "six-inch bust of Verdi," and a "plate" with the grotesque face of "the sixties pope," John XXIII, "the one with the little round head that looked like a newborn baby" (85). This satirically reductive image both reifies and infantilizes religion. Consequently, the objectification of Marie's cultural heritage is reflected in her detachment from her life, a life made up of broken pieces, like the shattered china in her mother's cabinet. "I never heard a louder noise inside" (82), Marie recalls: the failure to establish a clear referent for "inside" creates a syntactical ambiguity that collapses the "inside" of the house and the china cabinet and Marie's "inside." The china cabinet, with its old souvenirs and its rarely used dishes, functions as the repository of her ethnic past, inaccessible and now reduced to useless shards and splinters. The grotesque souvenirs, fragmented and commodified versions of Italian culture, parallel the phony cultural roles available to Marie. These codified cultural artifacts mirror the cultures that have produced them. While walking up and down the aisles of Woolworth's, where she spends "a good part" of her Saturday afternoons, "wandering amidst water pistols and perspiration shields and brands of cold cream nobody ever heard of" (53), Marie meets a friend who introduces her to Ralph, her future husband. As a synecdoche for a culturally impoverished society, the store that provides Marie with a husband represents the American alternative to the Italian souvenirs, capsules of a culture that neither Marie nor her parents ever experienced directly.

Marie "feels at home" at Woolworth's, a place where she can meditate (53). This grotesque image of meditation in Woolworth's is reminiscent of the "house with a supermarket-style door" (17) that Marie describes at the very opening of the novella as she begins reflecting on her past. Her cultural landscape is an assemblage of odds and ends from both Italian and American mythologies, all of which stifle her confused but emerging sense of selfhood. The narrative translates Marie's dissociation as detachment: only by identifying the sources of her dissociation can Marie experience her speech and her stories as her own. Molding her scattered memories of loneliness, loss, and death into a story becomes a self-created rite of passage for a woman who "felt like an impostor" (57) in the conventional life she had seemingly chosen for herself.

Helen Barolini writes that both of her parents,

> children of immigrants, passed on to their children conflicted feelings about their origins. In striving to get past the old generation they severed themselves too drastically from it; their lives became all in the foreground, without depth or ties to the past, all a surface of American success. ("Becoming a Literary Person" 263)

Marie's father's vaguely defined dreams of success, and his hope to attain vicariously, through his daughter, the education that would guarantee him access to mainstream society, are juxtaposed to Marie's rejection of success viewed as social recognition. Although Marie is not seduced by her father's dreams, she is unable to free herself from the cultural constraints linked primarily to her mother's passivity and to her father's expectations of success and dread of social failure. Moreover, she inherits from her parents a longing that can never be satisfied, a sense of cultural emptiness that can never be filled. By the end of the novella, Marie has not glued together the broken china, but she has at least started piecing together the fragments of her life. While her storytelling signals her emergence as a narrator, as a character she can not fashion her story or her part. As a first-person narrator, however, Marie becomes a producer of discourse—written discourse—and thus reverses her positions as a woman within Italian/American culture and as an Italian/American within American culture.[23] Rossi legitimizes

---

[23]"Perhaps the most revealing cultural difference between southern Italy and America, especially relating to literary representations of selfhood, is the Southern Italian's distrust of words itself [sic]. A firm belief in the value of deeds over words was held sacrosanct by the peasant stock in southern Italy.... the southern Italians' traditional distrust of words perpetuated a heritage of silence for both genders" (Bona 89).

Italian/American culture by creating it as a literary experience. Not only does her novella express a search for cultural legitimation, it also questions the forces that legitimize (or de-legitimize) cultural experiences.

In *The Quick* Rossi explored dialogic possibilities through Marie Russo's conversation with the reader. Rossi's implied audience in *The Quick*, however, differs greatly from the silent patriarchal "God" who motivates Celie's epistolary narrative in Alice Walker's *The Color Purple*. Marie wills into existence this elusive reader/listener, recognizing the necessity of an other who will listen. At the same time, the text of *The Quick* never produces a responsive voice such as Nettie's. Phyllis, the older woman with whom she establishes a relationship that defies the norms prescribed by Marie's social and cultural milieu, never plays a role as active as Phoeby's, Janie's friend and sympathetic audience in Zora Neale Hurston's *Their Eyes Were Watching God*. Walker's and Hurston's engagement in a literary exchange in which they act as each other's audience, but also as precursor/mother/sister/discoverer, translates into the epistolary relationship between Celie and Nettie, anticipated by the relationship between Janie and Phoeby. In contrast, the absence of a female interlocutor in *The Quick* reflects Rossi's lack of a literary community. If, as Barolini argues, Italian/American women authors "write out of the void" ("Becoming a Literary Person" 263), with no community to nurture their voices and no space to legitimize their stories, then Rossi's fiction articulates the search for a community of women to validate authorial speech.[24]

Such a search prompts the narrative structure of *Split Skirt*. In her first novel, *Split Skirt* (1994), Rossi draws upon and yet departs from the tradition of dialogic, communal ethnic narratives exemplified by such works as Alice Walker's *The Color Purple*, Cristina Garcia's *Dreaming in Cuban*, and Amy Tan *The Joy Luck Club* and *The Kitchen God's Wife*, in

---

[24]"That Italian American women have been underpublished is undeniable; just as exclusionary, however, is that the few who are published are not kept on record and made accessible, even bibliographically, in libraries and in study courses. Not only do Italian American women writing their own stories publish with great difficulty . . . but once in print, they must confront an established cadre of criticism that seems totally devoid of the kind of insight that could relate to their work" (Barolini, *The Dream Book* 44–45).

which the ethnicity of the author legitimizes the credibility of the narrative and establishes a relationship between character and author based on ethnic identity.[25] *Split Skirt* centers around the encounter between two married women, Rita and Mrs. Tyler, respectively of Italian/Irish and Irish descent. They meet in a place one might think unlikely to foster friendship, the Bergen County jail in New Jersey, in which they spend three days, Rita for drunk driving and possession of cocaine, and Mrs. Tyler for one of her escapades as a seemingly incurable kleptomaniac. While the narrative of *Split Skirt* overtly recognizes Mrs. Tyler's Irishness, it withholds Rita's Italian background. The names by which the characters refer to and address each other, Mrs. Tyler and Rita, act as age and class markers: Rita is a lower-middle-class, street-smart twenty-seven year old, while Mrs. Tyler is a sophisticated upper-middle-class woman in her fifties (though through her confessional narrative she retrieves her working-class origins).

Mrs. Tyler's ethnic self-revelation is instrumental in her self-presentation and in shaping Rita's perception of her. Mrs. Tyler generously informs Rita, and the reader, that she has no doubts about her origins—like her mother, she is Irish, a "Brennan" (157)—but Rita never mentions her own last name, thus preventing easy ethnic identification.[26] William Boelhower argues that "by discovering the self implicit in the surname, one produces an ethnic seeing and understands himself as a social, an ethnic, subject" (81). The issue of naming has been of particular relevance to many Italian/American women writers who, assuming their husbands' names, have surrendered the most immediate sign of ethnic identification.[27]

---

[25]For a discussion of identity politics and white ethnicity, see di Leonardo.
[26]Yet Mrs. Tyler herself questions her own identity as she slips "in" and "out" (98) of the clothes her mother in law purchases for her.
[27]Sandra Mortola Gilbert, Dorothy Calvetti Bryant, Marianna De Marco Torgovnick, and Linda Bortolotti Hutcheon are just a few Italian/American authors who relinquished their Italian names through marriage. Gilbert wrote to Barolini: "And my mother's name was Caruso, so I always feel oddly falsified with this Waspish-sounding name," which I adopted as a 20-year old bride who had never considered the implications of her actions!" (Barolini, *Dream Book* 22).

The absence of Rita's name, then, "produces" ethnic invisibility. Italian/American ethnicity surfaces, though, when Mrs. Tyler tells Rita about Judy Gennaro, her long-lost "best" friend, the only one she ever had (159). She quotes the reaction of her husband, John, after hearing screams coming from the Gennaros' house, where Judy is repeatedly the victim of her husband's violence: "goddamn Italians" (159). John's comment, which reproduces the common stereotype of Italian/American men as wife-beaters, represents the only direct reference to Italians in the book. When Judy first appears, Mrs. Tyler refers only obliquely to her background: she is "Mediterranean" (157). She never specifies her ethnicity. Moreover, John's remark does not elicit further elaboration on Mrs. Tyler's part or a response from Rita: Mrs. Tyler acts as if she is unaware of Rita's ethnic background, which is not surprising since Rita herself seems to have erased ethnic memory. Rossi inscribes her ethnic autobiographical narrative in a text which does not advertise itself as either a multicultural novel or an Italian/American novel. Nevertheless, it is noteworthy that in *Split Skirt* the two women who act as Mrs. Tyler's confidantes are Italian. These characters are the receptacle of their friends' secrets and their author's ethnic identity.

If Mrs. Tyler sees "secrecy" as the only means by which to maintain "her two separate realities" (122)—she sees herself as a "double agent" (120)—the narrative of *Split Skirt* self-consciously dramatizes Rossi's own "separate realities," her ethnic "split," by developing into a series of alternating sections in which the two characters take turns telling their stories, playing the parts of both author and audience. Destabilizing authorial power, the dual narrative of *Split Skirt* enables each character to recount her story as an autobiographical oral narrative, a genre characteristic of the early stages of ethnic literature, which typically present the speaker as an authorized witness.[28]

---

[28]Interestingly enough, the recent publication of ethnic memoirs by second- and third-generation Italian/American critics such as Frank Lentricchia, Louise DeSalvo and Marianna De Marco Torgovnick suggests that the cycle has come full circle, recreating the early literary forms of the immigrant experience.

In her study of ethnic writers, Bonnie TuSmith argues that the "specific motivation behind" the use of such strategies as vernacular speech patterns is the "artistic validation of one's ethnic culture and value system against a hegemonic European American standard in literature" (25).[29] Rossi's narrative, which emphasizes the oral aspect of storytelling, questions the "validation" of the ethnic experience by shifting the focus onto the individual and away from the group experience, and thus connects authenticity with self- instead of group-authorization. Throughout the novel, Rossi struggles to forge a viable relationship between self and other, rejecting notions of community based solely on loyalty to the ethnic group, and thus articulating her position as a writer who draws upon her ethnic experience by rewriting its narratives and rethinking ideas of authenticity and tradition.

While both Mrs. Tyler and Rita commit themselves to speaking the "truth" (23), to going back to origins, they soon realize that they are so enmeshed in roles and plots they did not fabricate for themselves that the "truths" they tell are always provisional and require scrutiny and questioning. Thus these narrators engage in a process of continuous re-authorization, which also includes re-evaluating their positions in old plots and even self-consciously questioning the plots they envision for themselves. What has distinguished Italian/American women writers

---

[29]TuSmith's common though somewhat facile distinction neglects to take into account ethnic intersections. Her juxtaposition of two large, broadly defined, groups, European/American and non-European/American, oversimplifies differences among various European/American groups and subgroups, such as the Northern Italians and Southern Italians. In addition, her juxtaposition ignores the way in which immigration policies have shaped the idea of "Americanness" developed by certain ethnic groups, including Italian Americans. To overlook the history of discrimination suffered by certain European American groups, especially Eastern and Southern European, would mean to ignore the history of citizenship in the U.S. In the early twentieth century "preparedness" experts argued that "military service was the only way to 'yank the hyphen out of the Italian Americans' and other 'imperfectly assimilated immigrants'" (Vaughan 450). "The history of citizenship," Brenkman argues, "is also the history of the denial of citizenship" (89). See Brenkman's critique of Sollors's classic distinction between descent and consent (98–99).

from their male counterparts has been a greater willingness to expose the evils of their culture, despite the ostracism that oftentimes follows from such a choice.[30]

Like other multicultural writers, Rossi rejects the notion of an exclusive narratorial power in favor of a decentered narrative that allows an egalitarian narratorial situation. In the last section of *Split Skirt*, Rossi resorts to a third-person narrative: acting as a removed camera-eye that privileges Rita's perspective, the narrative records the two protagonists' re-union outside the county jail. However, the seemingly omniscient narrative gaze does not come across as an all-powerful, all-controlling device, but as a shift towards yet another subject position, one in which the authorial voice brings together different perspectives.

In a multicultural society, John Brenkman argues, it is necessary that everyone become "fluent enough in *one another's* vocabularies and histories to share the forum of political deliberation on an equal footing," and that everyone engage "others' contingent vocabularies" (89) as well as one's own. *Split Skirt* illustrates such an engagement with "others' contingent vocabularies," through its inclusion of the voice of Luz, the Hispanic teenage prostitute who speaks in the first-person in the penultimate section. Luz's connection to Rita and her role as a "sister" (127), another sister, enables her to participate in the narrative space Rita and Mrs. Tyler have been forging together. Appropriately, Rossi dedicates the novel to her own "sisters." Typically, multivoiced narratives by "ethnic" authors create a space which, in privileging certain voices, also excludes non-members. *Split Skirt* departs from such exclusionary narratives. If Rossi employs the dialogue between her two characters as the means by which to establish a conversation between her own Irish and Italian ethnicities, the inclusion of Luz signals an effort to enlarge the ethnic space and to create a narrative that emphasizes not sameness and consensus, but difference and communication.

---

[30]Oral histories of immigrant families diverge along gender lines; women "more willingly discussed family problems than men, who more typically presented sanitized or romanticized memories" (Gabaccia 43).

Discussing what he calls a "third generation renaissance" of Italian/American writers, Gardaphé explains:

> When we examine later writers, those who are grandchildren of immigrants, we enter a period in which the immigrant past is recreated, not through self-reflection, but through a more distant historical perspective, a perspective gained by removal from the ethnic experience and resulting in the recreation of the immigrant experience in America through more distinctively fictional forms. ("Third Generation" 71)

Mrs. Tyler's recollection of her fear of being mistaken for an "immigrant" (49)—the only reference to the journey that brought her family to America—epitomizes in its uniqueness the status of ethnic memory for writers like Rossi. Her fiction represents an effort not so much to recover that memory, but to reinvent it. If the past, as Salman Rushdie writes, is "a country from which we have all emigrated . . . [and] its loss is part of our common humanity" (12), Rita, Mrs. Tyler, and Luz transcend the specificity of their experiences by sharing their memories and participating in each other's sense of loss and displacement.[31]

Yet clearly defined narrative boundaries prevent the other from being subsumed into the self. Rita and Mrs. Tyler cannot see Luz and Madeline, her cellmate. Separated by the walls of their cells, they can only hear each other's voices. Their words thus act both as self-centered monologue and self-less conversation, directed inward and outward, asserting both uniqueness—difference—and connection. Rossi's multi-voiced narrative maintains the specificity of Italian/American, Irish/American, and Latina experiences, but it also explores possibilities for a broader dialogue that recognizes the creative potential of intersections and opens the borders of the ethnic/authorial space.

---

[31]Gardaphé argues that when writers are free from "the chain of the immigrant's memory and reality, and have . . . to rely on imagination . . . their writing reaches into the more mythic quality of the Italian-American experience, thus creating literature that transcends a single ethnic experience" ("Third Generation" 83). Rossi's novel self-consciously transcends the "single ethnic experience" in more ways than one.

Demonstrating the specificity of the cultural displacement experienced by Italian/American women, Rossi compels the reader to define and question the kind of recognition sought by Italian Americans and members of other unrecognized or unlegitimated ethnicities. The inadequacy of prevailing stereotypical representations of Italian/American culture in the United States prompts authors like Rossi to narrate different and untold aspects of the ethnic experience—and Rossi is not alone. For example, in her poem "Ethnic Woman," Rose Romano proclaims: "My ethnicity isn't something I drag out/of a closet to celebrate quaint holidays/nobody heard of" (*Wop* 57), thus rejecting the label of "ethnic" that reduces cultural identity to a series of tokens, devoid of referential ties to the variety and richness of Italian/American social reality. In "Mutt Bitch," she claims: "If I have no culture/I can say nothing;/therefore, if I say nothing,/I have no culture" (*Vendetta* 37). Romano, like Rossi, rejects the notion of a quintessential Italian/American identity. These and other Italian/American women writers establish themselves as intellectual voices that move beyond nostalgic and blindly celebratory views of their ethnicity. In doing so, they demonstrate the power of literary texts to explore, interrogate, and offer forceful alternatives to current social and political realities. Their writings negotiate and trouble categories of the personal and the public, exposing how the lives and voices of individuals in the minority are products of dominant discourses of identity, even as they show how such people can become effective agents of resistance and change. These works challenge the mainstream imagination and its stereotyping; they present alternative visions of ethnicity that both include an awareness of the hostile powers working against its expression and dare to imagine a future—and to create a present—in which such forces would cease to have relevance.

Exposing the devastating effects of "good-natured bigotry," Romano claims that she could "write" her "life/story with different shapes in/various sizes in limitless patterns of/pasta laid out to dry on a thick, white/tablecloth," and she asks the implied audience/reader of "Ethnic Woman": "Must I teach you/to read?" The signs of Italian/American culture have become so stultified that for Romano it is imperative to reclaim those signs, and to re-inscribe new significance in them. Like Romano, in her work Agnes Rossi captures the problematic status of

Italian/American culture by simultaneously articulating and suppressing the signs of its presence, and similarly requires a reader willing to learn how to read the almost-silent signs, how to hear the voices that speak with an accent that wants to be heard.

Works Cited

Bammer, Angelika ed. *Displacements: Cultural Identities in Question*. Indianapolis: Indiana University Press, 1994.
Barolini, Helen. "Becoming a Literary Person Out of Context." *The Massachusetts Review* 27.2 (1986): 262–74.
—— ed. *The Dream Book: An Anthology of Writings by Italian American Women*. New York: Shocken, 1987.
Boelhower, William. *Through a Glass Darkly: Ethnic Semiosis in American Literature*. Oxford: Oxford University Press, 1987.
Bona, Mary Jo ed. *The Voices We Carry: Recent Italian/American Women's Fiction*. Montreal: Guernica, 1994.
—— and Anthony Julian Tamburri eds. *Through the Looking Glass: Italian & Italian/American Images in the Media*. Staten Island, NY: American Italian Historical Association, 1996.
Brenkman, John. "Multiculturalism and Criticism." *Inside and Out: The Places of Literary Criticism*. Eds. Susan Gubar and Jonathan Kamboltz. New York and London: Routledge, 1993. 87–101.
Caroli, Betty Boyd, Robert F. Harney, and Lydio F. Tomasi eds. *The Italian Immigrant Woman in North America*. Proceedings of the Tenth Annual Conference of the American Italian Historical Association, 1977. Toronto: The Multicultural History Society of Ontario, 1978.
Chambers, Iain. *Migrancy, Culture, Identity*. London: Routledge, 1994.
Ciresi, Rita. *Mother Rocket*. Stories. Athens: University of Georgia, 1994.
Dearborn, Mary V. *Pocahontas's Daughters: Gender and Ethnicity in American Culture*. New York: Oxford University Press, 1986.
De Rosa, Tina. "An Italian American Woman Speaks Out." *Attenzione* (May 1980): 38–39.
DeSalvo, Louise. *Casting Off*. Brighton, UK: Harvester, 1987.
——. *Vertigo*. New York: Dutton, 1996.
di Leonardo, Micaela. "White Ethnicities, Identity Politics, and Baby Bear's Chair." *Social Text* 41 (Winter 1994): 165–91.
Fausty, Joshua S. Review of Mother Rocket. *VIA: Voices in Italian Americana* 6.2 (Fall 1995): 204–207.

Gabaccia, Donna. "Women and Ethnicity: A Review Essay." *Italian Americana* 12.1 (Fall/Winter 1993): 38–61.
Gambino, Richard. *Blood of My Blood: The Dilemma of the Italian Americans.* Garden City, NY: Anchor/Doubleday, 1975.
Garcia, Cristina. *Dreaming in Cuban.* New York: Ballantine, 1992.
Gardaphé, Fred L. "Autobiography as Piecework: The Writings of Helen Barolini." *Italian Americans Celebrate Life, the Arts and Popular Culture: Selected Essay from the 22nd Annual Conference of the American Italian Historical Association.* Eds. Paola A. Sensi Isolani and Anthony Julian Tamburri. American Italian Historical Association, 1990.
———. "(In)visibility: Cultural Representation in the Criticism of Frank Lentricchia." *Differentia: Review of Italian Thought* 6–7 (Spring/Autumn 1994): 201–18
———. "Italian-American Fiction: A Third Generation Renaissance." *MELUS* 4.3–4 (Fall/Winter 1987): 69–85.
———. *Italian Signs, American Streets: The Evolution of Italian American Narrative.* Durham, NC: Duke University Press, 1996.
———. "What's Italian About Italian/American Literature." Paper presented at the Purdue University Conference on Romance Languages, Literatures and Film. Purdue University. West Lafayette, IN. October 13–15 1994.
Gattuso Hendin, Josephine. *The Right Thing to Do.* Boston: David R. Godine, 1988.
Gillan, Maria Mazziotti. *Taking Back My Name.* San Francisco: Malafemmina Press, 1991.
———. *Where I Come From: Selected and New Poems.* Montreal: Guernica, 1994.
Giunta, Edvige. "Blending 'Literary' Discourses: Helen Barolini's Italian/American Narratives." *Romance Languages Annual* 6 (1995):
———. "'A Song from the Ghetto.'" Afterword. Tina De Rosa. *Paper Fish.* 1980. New York: The Feminist Press, CUNY, 1996. 123–57.
———. "The Quest for True Love: Nancy Savoca's Domestic Film Comedy." MELUS. (Summer 1997): 75–89.
Hurston, Zora Neale. *Their Eyes Were Watching God.* 1937. Urbana: University of Illinois Press, 1978.
Lentricchia, Frank. *The Edge of Night.* New York: Random House, 1994.
Ling, Amy. "I'm Here: An Asian American Woman's Response." *Feminisms: An Anthology of Literary Theory and Criticism.* Eds. Robyn R. Warhol and Diane Price Herndl. New Brunswick, NJ: Rutgers University Press, 1991. 738–45.
Manfredi, Renèe. Excerpt from *Running Away with Frannie.* VIA: *Voices in Italian Americana.* Special Issue on Italian/American Women. 7.2 (Fall 1996).

Mangione, Jerre and Ben Morreale. *La Storia: Five Centuries of the Italian American Experience*. New York: Harper, 1992.
Mazza, Cris. *Your Name Here*.Minneapolis: Coffee House Press, 1995.
Ostendorf, Berndt. "Literary Acculturation: What Makes Ethnic Literature 'Ethnic'?" *Callaloo* 8.3 (Fall 1985): 577–86.
Patriarca, Gianna. *Italian Women and Other Tragedies*. Toronto: Guernica, 1994.
Pelton, Ted. *VIA: Voices in Italian Americana*. Special Issue on Italian/American Women. 7.2 (Fall 1996). 285–87.
Romano, Rose. *Vendetta*. San Francisco: Malafemmina Press, 1990.
———. *The Wop Factor*. San Francisco: Malafemmina Press, 1994.
Rossi, Agnes. *Athletes and Artists: Stories*. New York: Persea, 1987.
———. Fancy. Unpublished novel.
———. Letter to Edvige Giunta. 5 January 1994.
———. *The Quick: A Novella and Stories*. New York: Norton, 1992.
———. *Split Skirt*. New York: Random House, 1994.
———. "On Being an Italian American." Unpublished notes.
Rushdie, Salman. *Imaginary Homelands: Essays and Criticism 1981–1991*. New York: Penguin, 1992.
Sollors, Werner. *Beyond Ethnicity: Consent and Descent in American Culture*. New York: Oxford University Press, 1986.
Tamburri, Anthony Julian. *To Hyphenate or Not To Hyphenate. The Italian/American Writer: An "Other" American*. Montreal: Guernica, 1991.
———, Paolo Giordano and Fred L. Gardaphé, eds. *From the Margin: Writings in Italian Americana*. West Lafayette, IN: Purdue University Press, 1991. 357–73.
Tan, Amy. *The Joy Luck Club*. New York: Ballantine, 1989.
———. *The Kitchen God's Wife*. New York: Ballantine, 1991.
Torgovnick, Marianna De Marco. *Crossing Ocean Parkway: Readings by an Italian American Daughter*. Chicago: University of Chicago Press, 1994.
Tropea, Joseph et al. eds. *Support and Struggle: Italians and Italian Americans in a Comparative Perspective*. Staten Island, NY: The American Italian Historical Association, 1986.
Tusmith, Bonnie. *Community in Contemporary Ethnic American Literature*. Ann Arbor: University of Michigan Pres, 1994.
Vaughan, Leslie J. "Cosmopolitanism, Ethnicity and American Identity: Randolph Bourne's 'Trans-National America.'" *Journal of American Studies* 25 (1991): 443–59.
Walker, Alice. *The Color Purple*. New York: Harcourt Brace Jovanovich, 1982.

Mary Ann Mannino

Stains of an Immigrant Past*

Inherited Habits of Being

A current issue in Italian/American literary criticism is the discussion of literature written by Italian/Americans when there is no overt *Italianità*. By *Italianità*, I mean the presence, in the work of immigrants, of their language, their holiday celebrations, and the identifying customs they brought with them when they immigrated.

The mass immigration of Italian/Americans took place between 1880 and 1924, but a smaller number of Italians came to this country after World War II. As writers are further and further removed from the immediate experiences of immigration, either as immigrants themselves or as children or grandchildren of immigrants, their writing contains fewer and fewer of those obvious markers that would identify their ethnicity. What are we to say about this literature that is written by Italian/Americans but does not deal explicitly with an Italian/American subject matter? Is it ethnic writing?

Should we conclude that ethnic writing is short lived and will exist only as long as the writer has some memory of the migration experience?

---

*Used with permission of Mary Ann Mannino, Temple University.

This memory can be through personal contact with the immigrant generation or through contact with a parent who has had such a connection, or if the writer has researched the Italian/American immigrant experience, as a historical fiction writer would, to replicate the details of a culture that is no longer lived. Should literary critics interested in ethnic writing confine their study to literature with overt *Italianità* only?

Some people, Dana Gioia among them, feel that ethnic writing, in particular ethnic poetry, is only a transitional category and cannot exist past the second generation ("What Is Italian American Poetry?"). For Gioia, ethnic poetry implies a writer who was raised in an immigrant subculture and whose writing deals with ethnic subject matter.

Anthony Tamburri, by contrast, would broaden the category of ethnic literature by including within it writers who have deliberately chosen not to allow their cultural heritage to be overtly present in their work. Tamburri argues that one can speak of the Italian/American qualities of a Frank Capra film by reading the absence of *Italianità* "as an Italian/American sign in *potentia*" (p. 7). Tamburri suggests that as writers travel "from the margin to the mainstream," they do not abandon their cultural heritage, but they transcend a mere parochial allegiance to it (p. 7). In other words, the writers feel comfortable enough with the American half of their identity to place characters in a setting that is absent of *Italianità*.

Similarly, Edvige Giunta endows with ethnic meaning the absence of ethnicity in Agnes Rossi's *Split Skirt* and *The Quick* and in Nancy Savoca's direction of Bob Comfort's *Dogfight*. Giunta reads the loss and displacement that the characters experience in the narrative as representative of their loss of ethnicity and thus as an indication that these works have an Italian/American presence. Giunta argues that in Rossi's *The Quick*, "Marie's inability to connect with her [Italian/American] ethnicity lies at the core of her psychological and cultural displacement" (p. 166). Giunta further suggests that Agnes Rossi and Nancy Savoca "strive to narrate the Italian/American experience through a newly coined language in which ethnicity goes unnamed" (p. 165). Giunta speaks of the absence of obvious ethnic markers in their writing and the presence of a blending of different languages and cultural discourses as writing with "an accent." She argues that Savoca's direction of the film and Rossi's novella "speak with a foreign accent, ever so slight, yet unquestionably present"(p. 165).

I applaud Giunta's concept of an accent as the blending of two cultural discourses that identify the speaker/writer as a bicultural person and the work as Italian/American. Often, creative work by Italian/Americans without ethnic markers has an elusive quality that suggests an Italian/American experience "even if we can not readily define it" (Tamburri, p. 7). Of more interest to me, however, is Giunta's suggestion that a psychological dysfunction or ailment a character might be experiencing could somehow be read as a sign of ethnic writing.

Like Giunta and Tamburri, I believe that works of literature written by Italian/Americans can be considered ethnic writing whether or not there is overt *Italianità*. I would look to the motivation, internal conflict, displacement, psychic dysfunction, and choices made by the characters in fiction and the speakers in poetry to reveal a connection to an Italian value system and to the injury caused by immigration, which may, whether recognized or not, be buried in the psyche of the writer. Perhaps patterns of thought, which motivate characters in fictional pieces, could indicate a work's accent and signify Italian/American literature. The feelings of loss and displacement that Giunta reads in Rossi and Savoca's main characters are just the sign I'm talking about.

I looked at the works of four women whose writings are rich with *Italianità*—Maria Mazziotti Gillan, Rita Ciresi, Mary Cappello, and Maria Fama—for thought patterns within their characters that, if present in writings that did not contain *Italianità*, would still indicate a subtle Italian accent. I looked for features in the texts that reveal inner conflicts in the narrative characters and in the poetic speakers and that could in some way obliquely connect to an immigration experience.

I was able to find pieces by each of the writers that contained ancestral voices that affected the speakers in poems and the characters in fiction. In three instances, this ancestral voice was internal—fabricated or imagined by the character or speaker—not "real." In one, Mary Cappello's *Night Bloom*, the immigrant voice was represented by the journal of the immigrant himself but interpreted by his granddaughter, the writer.

The persistence of the voice of an immigrant ancestor who has a message informs Maria Mazziotti Gillan's poem "The Crow," Rita Ciresi's novel *Blue Italian*, Mary Cappello's memoir *Night Bloom*, and Maria Fama's poem "Tablecloth." In three pieces, the voice of the Italian ancestor is articulated directly. The immigrant voice in *Blue Italian* comes indirectly through the voice of Rosa Salvatore's mother, whose mother was an immigrant. I want to suggest that an interrogation of character motivation and action can provide a method of reading writers as Italian American even when ethnicity is not obvious.

In Ciresi's and Gillan's works, the immigrant voice is critical and judgmental, and it becomes for the speaker of Gillan's poem and the character, Rosa Salvatore, their superegos against which they struggle in order to succeed in America. Apropos of this dilemma, Freud tells us that "the tension between demands of conscience [the superego] and the actual performances of the ego is experienced as a sense of guilt" (Freud, *The Ego and the Id*, p. 33). I would like to look at the way guilt operates in these works.

For Freud, the superego is the heir of the Oedipus complex. It is constituted through the internalization of parental prohibitions and demands. Freud conceives of it as a part of the mind that has become separated from the ego and that seems to dominate it. He says that within the superego, we have "the representative of our relation to our parents. When we were little children we knew these higher natures, we admired them and feared them; and later we took them into ourselves" (Freud, *The Ego and the Id*, p. 32). When Freud further suggests that the role of the father is carried on by teachers and others in authority, "their injunctions and prohibitions remain powerful in the [superego] and continue in the form of conscience, to exercise the moral censorship," he allows for others besides the father to affect the superego (Freud, *The Ego and the Id*, p. 33). In *Civilization and Its Discontents*, he argues that in many adults "the place of the father or the two parents is taken by the larger community" (p. 85). The writers I will discuss confirm that for Italian Americans, the collective ancestral voice becomes a powerful internalized censor of everyday actions. I want to suggest that this voice, whose message has been influenced by the immigration experience, can be found in the superego of characters or speakers in works where there is no indication of Italian American writing except the writer's ethnicity expressed via Giunta's idea of a slight accent.

If we recognize the power of the superego in the development of a person, and if we then see the way the immigrant voice continues to remain in the Italian/American psyche in the form of a conscience, or when the Italian/American struggles against that voice as a generator of guilt, we can see that the beliefs and values of the immigrants persist in the writing of Italian Americans well after the third or fourth generation as a mind-set or way of viewing the world. Thus, overt *Italianità* is not required to signify its presence. The writer will either depict characters that follow or argue against the ancestral values not necessarily represented as ethnic voices.

One way to read Italian/American writers' works is to look within the characters for an immigrant conscience that causes conflict and often guilt.

Maria Gillan's poem "The Crow" begins:

> The voices of the old ones follow us,
> warnings in whispers,
> fear fed to us in bottles
> along with our milk.
>
> The first time alone,
> we stand, terrified
> and perfectly still,
> in the kitchen
> waiting for them to come home.
> (p. 9)

The speaker of the poem describes a childhood that is imbued with fear that comes not from society or the world outside, but from her family, parents, and grandparents. In describing it as being "fed to us in our bottles," the speaker insists that the fear is absorbed into her own body.

I would like to suggest that the fear about which Gillan speaks is a direct result of the original immigrant's trauma of diaspora and partial assimilation. The violent shock of migration permanently ruptures a way of life and rips away the immigrant's language, leaving him or her with losses that can never be recovered and with a permanent placement in an alien environment where everyday activities are reminders of his or her outsider status. According to Freud, a psychic trauma such as this causes the individual to develop defense mechanisms. As a defense mechanism to prevent further loss, the immigrant develops a deep-seated fear and mistrust of the environment that is communicated to his or her children.

Does this fear disappear when the immigrant dies? I think not. The fear is transmitted from parent to child long after the reason for the original fear has ceased to exist. Freud suggests that the defense process is more or less integrated into the ego and that it often takes on a compulsive aspect and works in an unconscious way. Thus, he implies that a person could experience a vague sense of terror that has no specific object or could displace his or her fear onto other objects and become phobic. In turn, the phobia censors action and prevents people from acting in their own best interest. On the other hand, if they act in spite of the internalized prohibition, they experience anxiety and guilt.

In the second stanza of "The Crow," the effects of the ancestral warnings leave the speaker terrified and paralyzed when she is alone because she has internalized them. She anticipates the criticism or punishment she might receive if she moves in any way against family taboos; therefore, she does not move at all. Freud suggests that it is a fear "of a loss of love" and "of punishment" that causes a person to adopt another's judgments (Freud, *Civilization and Its Discontents*, p. 85).

Part 2 of Gillan's poem describes a situation the speaker faces as an adult. She is at a poetry reading and is awed by the success of the person who reads before her. What is significant is that although the first reader is highly accomplished and respected within mainstream American culture, the poem's speaker recognizes the first speaker's concealed Italian/American heritage and her fear and lack of self-confidence, which mirror the speaker's own:

> When I meet you, your face
> is the glass in which I am reflected.
> In your voice, I hear a shaking so deep
> I expect you to fly apart.
> Though our names, changed by marriage,
> are anonymous, the immigrant faces
> line up in our heads. We count them,
> compulsively, as if they were beads.
> (p. 9)

Both women, successful or less so, hear the same crippling message, which the speaker connects to immigrant voices:

> In our ear,
> a voice,
> connected to us like a cord,
> whispers
> you aren't really very much
> you guinea, you wop,
> so we struggle
> to blot out the sound of the crow
> who sits on our shoulder and laughs
> blot out the voice
> that belittles all we do,
> and drives us to be best.
> 'My daughter,
> she's ugly, but smart.'
> (pp. 9–10)

The speaker of this poem is presented with a dilemma. She wishes to go beyond the limits that immigrant fear of loss has drawn around her. Her ego has allowed her to write poetry about her life and family and read it before an audience, but her superego represented by a voice "connected to us like a cord" disrupts the pleasure she should have in her success and instead belittles her. The speaker feels an unconscious guilt for her transgression. By writing and reading her poetry, she is ignoring the voices that would limit her, but she is still afraid that their predictions of dire but amorphous consequences will come true because she has gone in a direction unknown and inaccessible to her ancestors. The poem's final stanza delineates fully the psychological dilemma for this Italian American speaker:

> You know,
> I know,
> we know,
> who always has to be best?
> We are driven women,
> and we'll never escape
> the voices we carry within us.
> (p. 10)

The speaker is describing a harshly critical superego against which she must constantly struggle to fulfill her desires as an Italian/American woman who wishes to write. The internalized ancestral voices act to censor her desires and prevent her from moving away from their limited and safe world. If she moves too far and does not succeed, she feels guilty; hence, her desire "to be best." The voice within her reminds her that she might lose her family's love or she might be punished.

In the novel *Blue Italian*, Rita Ciresi tells us that Rosa, the protagonist, "had been surrounded by relatives who had the grimmest possible view of what it meant to be a human being" (p. 14). Rosa Salvatore frequently hears her mother's voice criticizing her, telling her that what she is doing is wrong. Like the mother of the speaker in Gillan's poem, who says, "My daughter, / she's ugly, but smart," Rosa's mother also seems to insult her gratuitously (Gillan, p. 10). She says to Rosa, "Who's gonna marry you? What kind of man would put up with your nonsense?"(Ciresi, p. 26). Ciresi never explains what "nonsense" Rosa's mother is addressing. Like the object of warnings and fear in Gillan's poem, Rosa's offenses are vague. Is it her humor? Her college degree? Her job as a social worker?

Throughout the novel, Ciresi uses humor to remind the reader that Rosa Salvatore is haunted by negative feelings about herself learned from her parents, in particular from her mother. I believe those admonitions and worries her mother expresses are traceable to her own immigrant parents. Like the voices in Gillan's poem, Antoinette Salvatore wants to protect her daughter and keep her from loss. Ciresi's humorous telling values as well as trivializes the emotional and psychological impact of the ancestral warnings. For Ciresi, humor becomes the defense against the grip of the painful immigrant past. Ciresi fights against the powerful fear of loss of an Italian/American identity and, with it, the love of immigrant ancestors, by supplying what appear to be trivial and insignificant causes for the struggles between Rosa's ego and superego so that, for the reader, her battles become funny rather than frightening.

In Rosa's opinion, she just never seems to measure up to her mother Antoinette's expectations, which, Rosa believes, are for her to remain like Antoinette, living, if not in her parent's house, at least nearby and keeping to the old ways as much as possible. Rosa decided early that she did not want to emulate her mother. She did not want to stay in the kitchen and wash the Sunday dishes with the other women "watching the world go by" while the men "did things" (Ciresi, p. 237). By going to college, working at Yale University Hospital as a social worker, living near the hospital in an ethnically diverse neighborhood, and dating Gary, a Jewish man, Rosa constantly transgresses these maternal boundaries and fails to meet her mother's expectations. Her life's obvious difference from her mother's expectations causes Rosa anxiety and guilt.

In her first conversation with Gary, Rosa tells him "she was worth nothing—absolutely nothing—in her parents' eyes because she was single and had no kids" (Ciresi, p. 59). When Rosa spends a Sunday with her parents, they reveal that they know she has been dating someone and ask his name. The name, Gary Fisher, immediately demonstrates that Rosa is dating a non-Italian. Her admission produces anxiety, as evidenced by Rosa's sharp and funny responses to her mother's questions and her subsequent actions.

Antoinette insists that Rosa bring Gary to Sunday dinner the following week, and then asks what Gary likes to eat. Rosa replies, "Food" (p. 69). Her mother asks where they met, and when Rosa responds "[a]t work," her mother indicates her displeasure by making hissing noises and offering the *non sequitur* that when Rosa took the job, she told Rosa to watch out because "at Yale Hospital they do abortions" (p. 69). Rosa's determination to enter the world beyond Pizza Beach frightened Antoinette, and she felt compelled to warn against dangers she could not articulate but that she imagined existed and threatened Rosa's Italian/American cultural identity. Antoinette continues to project all her fears of the larger world onto the fact that abortions are performed at Yale University Hospital. Abortions become the symbol of all that is different and dangerous.

Although Ciresi's handling of the situation is funny, this reminder of the dangers inherent in ignoring her parents' injunctions makes Rosa anxious, and she dumps the rest of her ravioli into the trash. The tomato sauce splashes on her new lace sweater. Ciresi tells us that Rosa can't wait to get home to wash out the tomato stain. The point the novel makes is that the stain of an immigrant past and the guilt and anxiety it causes can't be washed out. They become an internal voice.

In the car traveling to dinner at her parent's house with Gary the next week, Rosa feels so uncomfortable that she develops "a throbbing headache, an aching bladder, a sore throat, and the initial abdominal rumblings that always signaled the prelude to a spastic colon attack" (p. 71). Ciresi has supplied a funny but accurate list of symptoms caused by fear and anxiety, which lead Rosa to imagine ending up in the hospital and being diagnosed as having Italian parents.

Freud argues that a psychic state is written directly on the body, albeit in a covert form, and that illness can be an expression of lack of an independent position when an individual believes those circumstances cannot be changed. In Lacan's interpretation of Freud, symptom becomes metaphor. In his terms, there is a substitution of one signifier, the body's pain, for another that is unavailable to consciousness because it is repressed. Rosa wants to move away from the culture of Pizza Beach, but she feels a responsibility to it. This conflict causes her anxiety, guilt, and symptoms. Rosa obviously feels uneasy and uncomfortable with her family's ways. She cringes when she thinks about her parents' side yard that is filled with plumbing supplies (including a pristine white toilet bowl), the photo of Mussolini on the garage wall, or their table manners. Antoinette embarrasses her daughter because she pulls the Italian bread apart instead of slicing it. Despite all the psychic turmoil that the visit causes for Rosa, she obeys her mother's demand that she bring Gary to dinner. She rebels against and is acquiescent to the ancestral voices embodied in her mother.

On the drive home, Rosa tells Gary, "My family is ridiculous," and then dissolves into tears. Ciresi then recounts "the hardships and horrors" of Rosa's childhood, which seem to consist of trivial and humorous ways in which Rosa's family differed from what Rosa feels is the norm (p. 90). She was forced to eat escarole and beans on Fridays; she wasn't allowed to shave her legs until she was sixteen; she had homemade clothes rather than ones from a department store; she was told not to read too much because glasses were expensive. Ciresi uses little things to depict, in a metonymical way, a larger and more important cultural conflict. Because, since childhood, Rosa has constantly resisted the Italian/American culture of Pizza Beach, she has been criticized by her mother for what her mother sees as her inadequacies. Eventually, Rosa sees herself as inadequate.

Like the speaker in Gillan's poem, Rosa's superego, shaped by parental and cultural mandates, is constantly judging her and finding her wanting. Rosa does not need her mother to identify ways in which Rosa is inadequate. She has internalized her mother's opinions and thus is compelled to criticize herself when her mother is not present. Sitting by Gary's family's pool, Rosa "was afraid she would spill something on her clothes and was all too aware that she had neither worn the right outfit nor had she brought the proper wardrobe for tomorrow. . . . Rosa felt like a slob, some kid from the Fresh Air Fund brought in to get a taste of the more genteel life" (pp. 105–106). When Rosa is praised by Gary's dad because he admires what he believes is the selflessness her career as a social worker implies, she says, "I push papers" (p. 107). She has internalized her parent's negative attitude toward her work.

The speaker of Gillan's poem internalized her mother's condemnation that she was ugly; Rosa is convinced she is unworthy because she is fat. The emotions caused by her mother's criticism and the lack of maternal hugs, kisses, and support are displaced and appear as an obsession with weight. At her father's grave, as Rosa plants flowers, she imagines "her backside was monstrous" (Ciresi, p. 225). When Rosa goes to the psychiatrist to discuss her husband's imminent death, she says to the doctor, "Look at me. I'm fat" (p. 247). When she meets Gary's parents for the first time, she images that the little black dress, for which she paid $220, is not becoming: "The model in the catalog had looked chic and thin and elegant. Rosa looked like something out of steerage, a *paesana* walking down Grand Avenue to seven o'clock Mass on a summer morning, who had to don a black crocheted sweater to cover her flabby upper arms before she entered the church" (p. 168). Innumerable times throughout the narrative, she sees herself as fat and therefore unacceptable.

The voices in Gillan's poem internalized the degrading epithets *wop* and *guinea* and "whispered" them back to its speaker. In Ciresi's novel, Rosa imagines her fatness to be embodied by an Italian immigrant who arrived in this country in steerage. She, too, has internalized a degrading mainstream perception of Italian immigrants, and now she identifies with it. Like the speaker in Gillan's poem, Rosa could say to herself, "you aren't really very much / you guinea, you wop" (Gillan, p. 9).

In both works, the speaker or character identifies those qualities within herself that connect her to an immigrant past. Immigrants were made to feel inadequate because they were different. This speaker and the character, Rosa, continue to judge themselves as inadequate when they no longer possess those markers such as language, customs, and education that indicated the immigrants' difference. Yet, in fact, they struggle to move away from the immigrants' cultural identity.

In an as-yet-unpublished paper, Elizabeth Messina offers the psychoanalytic term *transposition* to describe the process whereby trauma is transmitted cross generationally. In her clinical practice, Messina has observed symptoms of anxiety and depression in the children, grandchildren, and even great-grandchildren of Italian immigrants that can be linked directly to an "unrecognized history of trauma and unresolved grief that has been transmitted across the generations" (p. 3). Messina argues that the descendants of the immigrants become the receivers and absorbers of a never-discussed psychic trauma that is the direct result of the migration experience.

I would suggest that the superego judges, criticizes, and condemns the ego's actions but expands the criticism to include the injunctions of the dominant culture as well, so that the character frequently feels a compelling sense of inadequacy, especially in new situations. The speaker of Gillan's poem is uncomfortable at the current reading and has been uneasy before because she had read:

> ... with the poet
> of the beautiful hair who keeps tossing
> her hair back, that glorious mane,
> while I huddle in my chair
> and think of having to follow her
> . . .
> How my insides quake
> . . .
> but I get up and turn the joke
> against myself before they can
> My mother tells me I'm beautiful
> but I know she means inside.
> (p. 10)

Rosa's mother implies that her daughter does not fit because she transgresses her mother's values. Having internalized Antoinette's perception of her but not Antoinette's cultural mandates, Rosa sees herself in American society as a misfit who is always revealing her ethnicity and thus exposing herself to more alienation. Ciresi's novel humorously tells the story of Rosa's triumphant effort to move beyond Pizza Beach literally and philosophically. It also dramatizes the emotional cost of that journey. Ironically, Rosa loses her husband and her baby in the adventure. What is Ciresi saying in this hilarious but tragic novel? Is her message a dark one: that transgression is met with punishment? Or is her message that transgression is essential even if it is fraught with disappointment and pain? The text remains ambivalent.

Similar to Gillan and Ciresi, Mary Cappello, in her memoir *Night Bloom*, recognizes that the immigration experience with its culture of poverty and otherness has inheritable effects and that these effects can be vague feelings of fear and phobia in second- and third-generation individuals whose lives can thus be restricted and limited. Cappello's memoir recounts that her maternal grandfather, John Petracca, immigrated to American when he was sixteen, became a shoemaker, learned English, and kept a journal. This document, now in Cappello's possession, embodies the immigrant voice in her memoir and recounts the bodily effects of poverty on the immigrant. Petracca explains that his home was extremely cold in the winter and that he was unable to provide enough money for fuel, food, or dentistry for his mother, wife, and children. The physical pain of poverty led to a psychic injury as well, and Cappello believes this damage is inherited in what she calls "habits of being":

> And yet there are ways that we inherit the pain or deformation caused by the material or laboring conditions of our forbears . . . of habits of being that cause one to lie, rest, love, move, speak in one's body in certain ways.
> (p. 43)

Cappello tells us that she "began to be attuned to the ways in which poverty manifested itself" in her mother's body and her mother's work. She claims that certain effects persist even if one experiences "upward mobility" (p. 45). In the memoir, John Petracca's fear of further loss because of his precarious state of poverty and alienation reappears in his daughter's life as a series of phobias, among them, agoraphobia. Cappello tells us that her mother did not leave her house for seven years. Cappello believes that her mother's childhood "living with the threat of losing one's heat, water, electricity and not having enough food to eat can easily engender states of terror" (p. 127).

As Cappello sees it, her mother's agoraphobia has its source in her immigrant father. The author explains a dream her mother has shared by saying, "My mother's agoraphobia might be a sign that something terrible was happening in the immigrant household. To go outside would be to announce it, but its expression is prohibited" (p. 133). She suggests that there was some "unnamable hurt experienced by the immigrant" that was "dangerous to share with mainstream culture" and that her mother's body might announce it even if she were silent (p. 134). Although Cappello does not offer an explanation of what that hurt could be, I would suggest it is the psychic trauma caused by immigration and alienation in the new country, with poverty being the chief maker of outsider status. In her adulthood, John Petracca's daughter overcomes the poverty but retains the fear of being found out if she leaves the house.

Cappello says of herself: "That I have left the working class does not mean that I am not heir to familial repetitions. I did not rise above and beyond some form of familial ailment" (p. 53). What she has learned from her family is "what they didn't expect [her] to learn" because it was not taught but absorbed, just as the fear in Gillan's poem is ingested with the baby's milk. For Cappello, fear is also her inheritance, which she describes as "a fear that the body remembers but the mind forgets." Like the speaker in Gillan's poem and Rosa in Ciresi's novel, she no longer knows what to fear, but she responds to life, via her body, with fear (Cappello, p. 84). She says that in her family, "Fear [was] worn as an amulet" (p. 87).

Cappello tells us that the actual events of her childhood are a "backdrop" or "padding" for what she sees as her inheritance of fear. She claims that the source of her childhood fears was "maternal inheritance" (p. 86). On childhood walks Cappello, absorbed her mother's fear of dogs and, with it, the habit of being afraid. She tells us that the habit of fearing has spread to her nephew who, although he is ten, has become afraid to take a bath alone since he saw *Jurassic Park*. It isn't the specific fear that is inherited; it is a way of imagining the world and events within it. In Cappello's family, as in Rosa Salvatore's family, the world outside is perceived as dangerous and is, thus, approached fearfully. Cappello tells us that "depression and agoraphobia of her family are not failings but responses, conditions, ways of saying" (p. 75). They are psychological responses to the trauma of immigration and alienation, and they are inherited ways of being.

Cappello herself names her own fears, and they also are connected to a view of the world as a place of potential loss: "I realized that I wasn't so much afraid of not getting tenure as I was afraid of getting it. For if you weren't in thrall to the past, where would you be? 'Nowhere,' I would tell myself . . ." (p. 91). She sees the acquisition of tenure as a marker that separates her from her second-generation family: "As I climbed higher and higher up the ladder of middleclass-dom, I surmised, I feared losing my working-class family. Tenure was a pinnacle that would release me, but who wanted to be released? I wanted to be embraced . . ." (p. 91).

Cappello believes that to prevent her family from yet another loss, in particular the loss of her mother, she developed some of her mother's phobias: "I had been trying to re-embrace my family via my mother, by identifying not with her pleasurable and pleasure-giving self but with the readiest marker of her suffering, of her detachment from me: her phobias, her terror. If I could become my mother, I would not lose her" (p. 92).

Freud suggests that we fear loss of love if we disobey our parents. Cappello claims that she developed phobias so that her mother would love her: "If I could become her in her pain, not only would I not forget her, but she would remember me because she would remember that I loved her" (p. 92). Cappello says: "Maybe none of us has 'our own' memory, but each of us inherits the memories of our ancestors, while what distinguishes us is our interpretation of those pasts" (p. 118).

Recent studies on the anatomy of fear have concluded that nerves from an area in the brain, the central nucleus in the amygdala, carry messages that control heart rate, blood pressure, respiration, and other bodily functions, which respond to the emotion of fear. Two neural routes lead to the amygdala: one to the thinking part of the brain and the other to the emotional part. What is most significant about Dr. Joseph Le Doux's recent research is the discovery that the circuitry transmits information to the emotional part first. Research reported in the *New York Times*, 28 February 1999, suggests that all it takes is one terrifying experience to form a lifelong emotional memory, one that is extremely difficult to erase.

People experience, learn, and unconsciously commit to emotional memory many fearful situations without ever being aware of what has triggered the racing heart and quick pulse. The implication of fear-conditioning experiments in animals is that we have a separate memory of a fearful stimulus lodged in the amygdala and informed by things we have heard or seen but do not consciously remember. Freudian analysts who have followed the work of Le Doux point out that neuroscience's version of unconscious fear strongly corresponds with the Freudian notion that it is indelible and never goes away.

Further research suggests that the amygdala gets activated not only when a person experiences a fearful situation directly as the immigrants did, but also when a person experiences trauma indirectly through "learning, hearsay, rumor: word of mouth, or subliminal suggestion. Even the empathetic horror we sometimes feel listening to details of a plane crash might create a hand-me-down sense of fear" (*New York Times*, p. 70).

Mary Cappello has suggested that although each of us inherits the traumatic memories of our ancestors, we interpret them differently. By way of contrast, for Maria Fama, the immigrant voice imparts a legacy not of fear and anxiety, but of resiliency and hope. Two poems by Fama, "Tablecloth" and "Nonna Mattia," contain conversations between the speaker and a dead female ancestor. In "Tablecloth," the speaker hears her great-great-grandmother's voice speaking to her each May when placing her ancestor's handmade embroidered tablecloth on her Philadelphia table. In "Nonna Mattia," the speaker addresses her great-grandmother directly and asks for the woman's strength. Although each poem alludes to ancestral hardships, the speaker does not focus on the trauma and the suffering caused by them. Her poems repress the misfortunes and afflictions of the migration experience.

In a phone interview, Fama told me that her poems reflect her actual experience with her immigrant relatives. She knew her great-grandmother, Mattia, for whom the tablecloth was made. Fama feels that the hard times the women in her family experienced—her great-grandmother spent World War II in Italy—"are balanced by their resilience and the happy moments all lives have." She says of her ancestors' experiences: "It was not unremittingly grim. I heard about some of those happy moments along with the hardships."

Messina argues that for Italian immigrants, "their survival needs required a denial or minimization of the trauma and its subjective impact" (p. 4). She suggests that:

> too much emotional awareness of their anguish and loss, while adapting to a hostile environment, would have diminished their confidence in their ability to prevail in the future, and might have distracted them from their immediate task—surviving one more day. (p. 4)

Fama's poetry reflects a repression of the devastating effects.

"Tablecloth" begins: "Nonna Angela speaks to me in May" (Fama, *Identification*, p. 9). Although Fama repeats that line four times, she never reveals the actual words of Nonna Angela, her great-great-grandmother. Instead, Fama recounts the woman's history by telling the story of the tablecloth. Hidden within the story is the message from the ancestor. The grandmother's voice is embodied in her actions, and her body becomes a talking one. In a Freudian sense, it reveals what is not spoken. Fama tells us:

> Nonna Angela grew cotton from a seed
> She spun and wove the fabric on a rickety loom
> She washed and rinsed it in a mountain stream
>
> Nonna Angela pounded the cloth on rocks
> and let the hot Sicilian sun bleach
> the tablecloth a gleaming white
> for her daughter's wedding day. (p. 9)

Fama depicts a patient, caring woman who must go through the agrarian artisan process before she can even begin to create the gift of the tablecloth. Later in the poem, we learn that when she was making the tablecloth, she was "still young and twice-widowed" and had five children. Fama glosses over the harsh realities those images suggest and instead focuses on the woman's resilience: her "sun-struck face [was] hopeful / for five children to find a good life" (p. 9). For this woman, Fama denies the power of traumatic experiences to destroy the psyche.

For Fama, the ancestral voice is one that expands, encourages, and survives with psyche intact despite hardship. Notwithstanding her own losses, Nonna Angela embroidered the cloth with flowers, pea pods, and blossoms symbolizing long life and fertility. Her labor became "embroidered wishes, / for her oldest girl" (p. 9). The covert message she speaks through her actions is that people must continue living with hope, love, and self-sufficient creativity despite traumatic external events. At the poem's end, the speaker acknowledges that she has heard the message—read the talking body—inscribed in the woman's life:

> Nonna Angela speaks to me in May
> I answer in gratitude
> for her long-ago labor of love
> and of hope. (Fama, *Identification*, p. 10)

In Fama's "Nonna Mattia," the speaker begins by addressing the great-grandmother:

> Nonna Mattia
> great grandmother
> large and generous
> I ask for your strength (Fama, *Identification*, p. 11)

The rest of the poem demonstrates the great-grandmother's strength in surviving four ocean crossings (one during which she was "alone and pregnant"), living in a mining town in Ohio, and picking crops in New Jersey. Nonna Mattia also "scrubbed laundry, took in boarders / nursed the sick and dying" (Fama, *Identification*, p. 12).

Although these situations imply a suffering equal to that endured by the people named in Cappello's memoir, no mention is made of pain, anxiety, or fear. The speaker's memory of this woman is during one of those moments of joy:

> I remember you elderly and brave
> caring for me with smiles and laughter
> your coal black eyes watching the world
> as you sang in clear Sicilian cadence (Fama, *Identification*, p. 12)

Nonna Mattia's apron, which wraps around the speaker twice, becomes a symbol for the woman's strong faith, compassion, and courage. The speaker reads the largeness of her great-grandmother's body as representative of her spirit:

> I wrap your apron around me twice
> as I look for cover in your
> largeness of body and heart (Fama, *Identification*, p. 12)

For Fama, the voices of the ancestors are life-giving. Their values, like the tablecloth or the apron, can be carried from Italy to America and utilized in both countries. The speaker identifies with them and does not imagine a conflict between their values and hers. She sees a powerful connection between Nonna Angela, the maker of the tablecloth; Nonna Mattia, the daughter who received it; and herself. She accepts and emulates their messages of hope and love. Her ego is comfortable with the ancestral injunctions that create her conscience. She validates their message.

Although I have written about women who openly discuss their Italian American heritage in their creative work, I have explored their writings in search of ways that the psychological attitudes and ailments of the speakers in the poems and the characters in the prose reveal a connection to an immigrant ancestor and to the trauma that individuals experienced. I am not offering a formula for identifying Italian/

American literature, but rather a location where Italian/American signs can be found. I am not suggesting that a highly judgmental superego— a fearful, phobic, or overly anxious character in a creative work—will always signify Italian/American writing. In fact, it does not in Maria Fama's poetry. However, it still is important to examine patterns of thought in fictional characters and in poetic speakers for ways that their expressions of conscience reveal a connection to the injunctions and prohibitions of immigrant ancestors.

Julia Kristeva tells us that "literature represents the ultimate coding of our crises, of our most intimate and most serious apocalypses" (p. 208). The experience of immigration embodies some of these crises. Italian American writers continue to represent such apocalypses in their literature, sometimes overtly but often in covert ways. It is up to the critic to discover the Italian accent in their works.

Works Cited

Cappello, Mary. *Night Bloom*. Boston, Massachusetts: Beacon Press, 1998.
Ciresi, Rita. *Blue Italian*. Hopewell, New Jersey: The Ecco Press, 1996.
Comfort, Bob. *Dogfight*. Directed by Nancy Savoca. Warner, 1991.
Fama, Maria. "Nonna Mattia." In *Identification*. Philadelphia, Pennsylvania: Allora, 1996, 11–12.
———. "Tablecloth." In *Identification*. Philadelphia, Pennsylvania: Allora, 1996, 9–10.
———, telephone conversation with author. 8 February 2000.
Freud, Sigmund. *Civilization and Its Discontents*. Translated and edited by James Stachey. New York: W.W. Norton, 1989.
———. *The Ego and the Id*. Translated and edited by James Strachey. New York: W.W. Norton, 1989.
Gillan, Maria Mazziotti. "The Crow." In *The Voices We Carry*, edited by Mary Jo Bona. Toronto: Guernica, 1994.
Gioia, Dana. "What Is Italian American Poetry?" *Poetry Pilot* (December 1991): 3–10.
Giunta, Edvige. "Narratives of Loss: Voices of Ethnicity in Agnes Rossi and Nancy Savoca." *Italian/American Writing*, Special issue of the Canadian Journal of Italian Studies 19, no. 53 (1996).
Hall, Stephen S. "Fear Itself." *New York Times Magazine* (24 February 1999): 42–47.

Kristeva, Julia. "Powers of Horror." In *Powers of Horror: An Essay on Abjection*. Translated by Leon S. Roudiez. New York: Columbia University Press, 1982.
Messina, Elizabeth G. "The Recovery of Traumatic Memories: Revisiting Italian Migration." Paper.
Rossi, Agnes. *The Quick: A Novella and Stories*. New York: Norton, 1992.
———. *Split Skirt*. New York: Random House, 1994.
Tamburri, Anthony Julian. *A Semiotic of Ethnicity: In (Re)cognition of the Italian/American Writer*. Albany: State University of New York, 1998.

Justin Vitiello

Beyond Tautologies?*

Poetics of Female and Feminist "Italianità" in Four Anthologies of Italian American Women's Literature

Casting about like Joseph Grand in Camus's *The Plague* for an opening so flourishing that all my interlocutors would declaim "Hats off," I agonized for months in search of a way to creatively construct palingenetic responses to the issues embodied in my title. I already had some ballast in steerage to sail this ocean of possibilities: (1) what the Indian philosopher Bibhuti Yadav called "the tragic optimism" of the poet's quest for "identity by placing questionability at the heart of Being, wondering whether even Being knows what it is, where it is and how it is"[1]; and (2) my study and teaching of Helen Barolini's *The Dream Book*, which, for the purposes of this specific discourse, contextualizes questions of "literary hegemonies and oversights" and "literary apartheid" in

---
*Used with permission of Justin Vitiello, Temple University.
[1]"Methodic Deconstruction." In *Interpretation in Religion*, edited by S. Biderman and B. A. Scharfstein. Leiden: E. J. Bull, 1992, 163, 139.

most lucid ways to vindicate Italian American women's literature for the first time in the history of the world.[2]

Yet, regarding means to interpret both forementioned rites of passage toward cultural mainstreams or along the borders of alternative forms of artistic creation, I still cogitate as to how to deal with my subject(s): *The Dream Book* (1985) and the three other anthologies dealing with, among other genres, poetry published in the last two decades: "Il Viaggio Delle Donne" in *Sinister Wisdom* (1990), *la bella figura: a choice* (1993), and *Curaggia* (1998).[3] So, as a point of departure here, I would like to return to an essay printed as Chapter I of *Beyond the Margin: Readings in Italian Americana*,[4] where I tried to explain why Barolini's seminal anthology was so radical in the fields of American literature and multicultural studies:

> (1) generally speaking, it establishes à la (Wole) Soyinka that "redefining the self in one's own authentic terms is essential for an integrated literary expression" . . . ; (2) it responds head-on to "the pressure of pluralism" . . . in America from the perspective of "recombining two cultures" to engender "a third realm of consciousness and expression" with an Italian background and an American foreground . . . ; (3) it challenges the pundits of both American and Italian American studies by providing an artistic vehicle of that "eternally" silenced, repressively archetypified creature Man called Woman, revealing that She (Pandora? Eve? Ave Maria?) is authentically many voices in many psychosomatic valences; and (4) it raises a question also posed by Robert Scholes in his fine essay "Canonicity and Textuality" about the relation-

---

[2] See the 1985 New York Schocken Books editions, here on pages 36–40.
[3] See *Sinister Wisdom* 41 (Summer/Fall 1990); *la bella figura* (San Francisco: Malafemmina Press, 1993); and *Curaggia* (Toronto: Women's Press, 1998).
[4] "Off the Boat and Up the Creek Without a Paddle—or, Where Italian Americana Might Swim: Prolepsis of an Ethnopoetics." In *Beyond the Margin: Readings in Italian Americana*, edited by P. A Giordano and A. J. Tamburri. (Madison, New Jersey: Fairleigh Dickinson University Press, 1998, 23–45.

ship between literary judgments and ethical/political/poetic justice. (pp. 37–38)

Like Hamlet in Act I, I would prefer to stop here and take no further action. However, Ezra Pound, as much as I hate to acknowledge him, rattles "the brain in my skull"[5]: "The critic who doesn't make a personal statement, in re measurements he himself has made, is merely an unreliable critic."[6] Furthermore, I suspect I am moving—in an attempt to rend the veil of my socially constructed gender identity—toward the kind of apprehension Mary Cappello writes of in *Night Bloom:*

To understand might require an act of willed detachment, to comprehend is to willingly let go. My mode is more one of apprehension: 1. to take hold of; 2. to grasp; 3. to fear; 4. to understand a little.[7] In addition, I hope, to embrace, in brotherly solidarity, the sensibility of the sister subjects I am studying.

So here I stand with Barolini, who makes a crucial Blakean argument in her essay "Differences, Identity and St. Augustine"[8]

Without contraries there is no progression.... Creativity is the force that deals with a changing reality as one emerges from a family or national or religious identity into a newness of self. Creative ethnicity uses one's background as a point of departure and is outward facing, evolving, tolerant, adaptable. Above all, it allows for self-definition, yet is not exclusive of relationships with other groups. (p. 108)

---

[5]*Tante grazie* a Bob Dylan!
[6]*ABC of Reading*. New York: New Directions, 1960, 30.
[7]Capello, Mary. *Night Bloom*. Boston: Beacon Press, 1998, 66.
[8]Barolini, Helen. "Differences, Identity and St. Augustine." In *Chiaroscuro: Essays of Identity*, West Lafayette, Indiana: Bordighera, 1997, 102–113.

On the one hand, creative ethnicity acknowledges Cappello's *angst* of awareness regarding her *Italianità*:

> Now I try to understand the pathological sense of loss (in the form of depression) and fear (in the form of phobia) that characterizes my ethnic heritage. . . . I can locate the source of disjunction in the immigrant status, the initial anomie of being out of place . . . in the light of the patriarchal history of Mediterranean culture aided and abetted by the misogynist spirituality of the Catholic Church. (p. 73)

On the other hand, the creativity that is the flip side of manic depression and one high of female and feminist consciousness[9] embodies an integral sense of fluid being/becoming that Edgar Wind identifies in his *Art and Anarchy*:

> A certain amount of turmoil and confusion is likely to call forth creative energies. . . . Dissatisfaction and discontent, far from being inimical to the arts, have often been their tutelary genius.[10]

In this context, we must face additional oxymora. As Edvige Giunta indicates in her editorial introducing *VIA*'s Fall 1996 "Special Issue: Italian/American Women Authors," although there is no "cohesive and homogeneous principle for defining a quintessential Italian/American female identity, there exists a "diversity of voices that have been forging an Italian/American literary tradition" within and around "a space that is continuously re-invented by a community of writers, artists, critics, and readers" (p. i). In fact, the existence of the four anthologies in question here attests to the cultural and literary legitimacy

---

[9]See the various works of Kay Redfield Jamison.
[10]Wind, Edgar. *Art and Anarchy* 3rd ed., London: Duckworth, 1985, 1.

of such a *locus amenus*, or what Mary Jo Bona has described in concrete, nonphantasmic terms[11] as the

> culture of *italianità*: customs and rituals specific to the local villages from which they [fathers in Bona's context, but, more generally, most Italian Americans] or their parents emigrated.[12]

As we know ad nauseam, cultural and historical conditions regarding such migrations of the many forms of *Italianità* led to the original dominance in the United States of male voices. After all, a woman's place, like a child's, was to be seen and not heard. What irony! It was, in the Old Country, the responsibility of Italian women—and other women since the Sumerians and other ancient peoples[13]—to preserve culture via an orality also deemed sacred, and to perform noble functions in the artisan/artistic milieus of storytelling. Traditionally, then, it was the women who kept their folk cultures alive, at home and abroad, by doing what Krzystof Wodiczko has lucidly identified in re the role of storytelling as "creative manipulation":

> To create a performance, dramatize, make a humorous story out of a painful tragic experience, find metaphoric ways to explain the unexplainable, find the words for unbelievable facts, construct. . . .[14]

Enfleshing what Walter Benjamin called "the revolutionary energy of the new"—"based on transporting personal experience into the

---

[11] See my review of *From the Margin: Writings in Italian Americana*, edited by Giordano Tamburri and Gardaphé. West Lafayette, Indiana: Purdue University Press, 1991) in *Italica* 69, no. 4 (Winter 1992): 528.
[12] See "Mater Dolorosa No More?: Mothers and Writers in the Italian/American Literary Tradition" in *VIA* 7, no. 2 (Fall 1996): 17.
[13] See *A Book of Women Poets: From Antiquity to Now*, edited by Aliki and Willis Barnstone. New York: Schocken Books, 1980.
[14] Wodiczko, Krzystof. *Critical Vehicles: Writings, Projects, Interviews*. Cambridge, Massachusetts: MIT Press, 1998, 115.

historical"[15]—women vates have, from time immemorial,[16] been the builders of "an aesthetics of self-creation and recognition."[17] In doing so, women have, as Mary Ann Vigilante Mannino says, been the innovators in "crossing borders" to empower themselves as self-confident, nurturing, and wise vehicles to root traditions and revitalize visions of female agency.[18]

Reviving this ancient role, Italian American women in the past fifteen years have shouldered the rock not only of orality but also of authorship in the fulfillment of the Rimbaudian prophecy quoted by both Sibilla Aleramo[19] and Simone de Beauvoir[20]:

> There shall be poets! When woman's unmeasured bondage shall be broken, when she shall live for and through herself, man—hitherto detestable—having let her go, she, too, will be poet! Woman will find the unknown! Will her ideational world be different from ours? She will come upon strange, unfathomable, repellent, delightful things: we shall take them, we shall comprehend them.

And via their preservation and rejuvenation of oral tradition, Italian American women writers have actualized and are still narrating and poeticizing that "viable and creative culture of a (folk) people" that Antonio Machado appreciated so deeply:

> It is very possible that the erudition of our academies can never compete with our folklore, with the native insights of our people. The people are better informed and wiser than we are. A man

---

[15]Quoted in Wodiczko, 131.
[16]See, again, the Barnstones' anthology.
[17]Wodiczko, 131.
[18]I thank Mannino for allowing me to quote from her manuscript, "Revisionary Identities: Strategies of Empowerment in the Writings of Italian/American Women," now published by Peter Lang.
[19]Alerama, Sibilla. *Diario di una donna, 1945–1960*. Milan: Feltrinelli, 1978, 280.
[20]Beauvoir, Simone de. *The Second Sex*. New York: Vintage, 1947, 795.

who knows how to make something perfect in its own way . . . is . . . an artist who puts all his soul in his work.²¹

Without being naive or delusional, we must ask ourselves why women's age-old cultural contributions have been ignored, denied, suppressed, and exploited by most men, even some who would simultaneously sacralize them. Sibilla Aleramo, profoundly aware of this timeworn paradox of women's sacred place in the creation and preservation of culture versus her systemic cultural and historical oppression and repression, spoke poignantly to this issue in her prophetic, radically feminist 1906 novel, A Woman:

> nearly every . . . poet up to now had glorified an "ideal" woman: . . . Beatrice was a cypher and Laura a hieroglyph. The women poets praised were all unattainable. . . . They idolised one set of women in verse, while the prosaic reality of their lives was that even if they married them they turned the women they lived with into domestic servants.²²

Although this is not the place for a reiteration of major feminist texts that elucidate this basically male problem, to respond to the following issue raised by Aleramo strikes me as a first step toward a cure for a certain cultural pathology (misogyny) we have all been living for millennia: "surely it was possible for a woman to take the core of her experience and create a masterpiece from it—the equivalent of a life?" (p. 122).

Answers to the above queries might seem obvious, yet seventy years after Aleramo created her own autobiographical novel, Dacia Maraini protested in *Donne mie* (1974) that female creativity of a "Sibillan" nature was still not being taken seriously by the male-dominated literary establishment:

> *"Le poesie delle donne sono spesso*
> *piatte, ingenue, realistiche e ossessive"*

---

²¹Machado, Antonio. *Juan de Mairena*. Berkeley: University of California Press, 1963, 27.
²²Aleramo Sibilla. *A Woman*. Berkeley: University of California Press, 1980, 156.

> *mi dice un critico gentile dagli occhi a palla . . .*
> *"Non c'è garbo, scioltezza, estro;*
> *sono prive dell'intelligenza maliziosa*
> *dell'artificio". . . . .*
> *(Ma) una donna non può fare finta*
> *di non essere donna. Ed essere donna*
> *significa conoscere la propria soggezione,*
> *significa vivere e respirare la degradazione . . .*
> *La sua voce sarà forse dura e terragna*
> *ma è la voce di una leonessa che è stata*
> *tenuta pecora per troppo tempo assennato.*

> "Poems by women are frequently
> flat, naive, realistic and obsessive",
> a kindly round-eyed critic tells me . . .
> "They have no grace, fluency, or inspiration;
> they are devoid of the mischievous wit
> of artifice . . ."
> . . . A woman is unable to pretend
> that she's not a woman. And to be a woman
> means to know her own state of subjection . . .
> Her voice will perhaps be harsh and earthen
> but it's a voice of a lioness who has been
> taken for a sheep for too much prudent time . . .[23]

Yes, it has been a voice, or voices, that Adrienne Rich saw as "betrayals of who I was and was to be . . . , split at the root,"[24] but is/are now one/many incarnating what Luce Irigaray identifies in her

---

[23]See *The Defiant Muse: Italian Feminist Poems from the Middle Ages to the Present: A Bilingual Anthology*, edited by B. Allen, M. Kittel, and K. J. Jewell. New York: The Feminist Press, City University of New York, 1986, 94–99.
[24]See "Split at the Root: An Essay on Jewish Identity." In *Visions of America: Personal Narratives from the Promised Land*, edited by W. Brown and A. Ling. New York: Persea Books, 1993, 96, 104.

provocative reflections on the differences evinced in male versus female discourse:

> With men, the I is asserted in different ways; it is significantly more important than the you or the world. With women, the I often makes way for the you, the world, for the objectivity of words and things. From that point of view, women appear to be more capable of listening to, discovering or accommodating the other and the world, of remaining open to objective invention or creation, provided that they can also say I.[25]

This is precisely what *The Dream Book*, "Il Viaggio Delle Donne," *la bella figura*, and *Curaggia* all say in diverse valencies and voices: I, you, the world. The juxtapositions of the works in these anthologies redefine concepts of selfhood, American pluralism via multicultural consciousness, radicalizing gender identities, and the poetic justice of a more inclusive canonicity. Yet *The Dream Book*, published by a mainstream press, went out of print in the late 1990s (luckily, it has been reissued), and the three other anthologies linger as productions of quality but represent marginalized cultural movements and enterprises. Thus, Maraini's 1974 poem is not a plaint dated by the progress women have made, not an evocation of some mythical age when women were really oppressed, not some die-hard, embittered feminist's lack of appreciation for the freedom men have granted to women—too much, of course, from the perspective of a male privilege that still dominates in discourses regarding cultural and literary power.

Perhaps today, more and more women have "rooms of their own,"[26] find space and money for cultural activities,[27] discover a "new

---

[25]Irigaray, Luce. *The Irigaray Reader*, edited by M. Whitford. Oxford: Basil Blackwell, 1991, 146.
[26]In Rome, there is even a Virginia Woolf University! "Naturally," it is not official.
[27]The Italian government does set aside modest funds for such activities, so the next time someone argues that BIG GOVERNMENT should not exist, tell HIM to spend OUR MONEY FOR US!

way of being together . . . , new forms of solidarity between lesbians and feminists,[28] and search, as Irigaray urges, for a common cultural heritage.[29] However, women's sexual, cultural, and literary emancipation, wherein naming who they are is so crucial as acts of self-creation, is still wrought with the fear in re "sexuality taking shape outside of permitted rhythms and forms" in social and political spaces where women might have the power to "send sex force" to each other (and perhaps to men, as well).[30]

Notwithstanding the odds against a radically free expression of cultural empowerment that could reach the mainstream, the four anthologies in question have made major strides in what Jorge Klor de Alva, in a Latino context, has called the "invention of difference with new founding myths."[31] Although some of the works in all four volumes still conceive of ethnicity in essential and totalistic terms, the majority re-envision ethnic origins and identity as "relational" within "ongoing historical processes" via "constant negotiation and reinvention" that are "contingent and unstable, not autonomous and fixed" (p. 70).

A descriptive analysis of key editorial comments and essays in the four anthologies and interpretations of some of the poems in them that I sense are most apprehending of the raisons d'être of these books will, I hope, highlight their poetics of female and feminist *Italianità*. Apropos, I already have indicated what I perceive as key foci in Barolini's *The Dream Book*; however, this ground-breaking anthology demands more attention not only for its position as an ethno-feminist palingenesis but also as a literary or historical frame of reference for the three subsequent

---

[28]See *Italian Feminist Thought: A Reader*, edited by Paola Bono and Sandra Kemp. Oxford: Basil Blackwell, 1991, 167.

[29]Ibid. 168.

[30]Sex force should not be confused with phallic expulsions or explosions, not even with Dylan Thomas's "Force that through the green fuse moves the flower."

[31]de Alva, Jorge Klor. "The Invention of Ethnic Origins and the Negotiation of Latino Identity, 1969–1981." In *Challenging Fronteras: Structuring Latina and Latino Lives in the U.S.*, edited by M. Romero, P. Hondagneu-Sotelo, and V. Ortiz. New York: Routledge, 1997, 55–74.

Beyond Tautologies? 333

anthologies. Not incidentally, in "Il Viaggio Delle Donne," Mary De Lorenzo Pelc's "Review of *The Dream Book*" acknowledges Barolini for giving other Italian American women the

> great hope that *omertà* is disintegrating, that the voices of Italian-American women will be heard, that our experiences will be taken seriously, that we will begin to identify ourselves to ourselves and to others as we write our own dream books, and songs and poems.... (p. 81)

Barolini's preface and introduction to *The Dream Book* speak most eloquently for themselves, but I want to focus on the points she makes that are most deeply interrelated to my discourse here. Departing from the premise that there were "no Italian American women writers as there are, so notably, Black women writers, Jewish, Asian" (p. ix), and from the position of being "thrice as an outsider" (Italian American, female, and a writer in a culture that resists such a *mestiere* for a woman, p. x), Barolini proceeds to compose a book affirming her gender's and ethnic group's "heritage and distinctiveness" to answer her own question: "Cannot Italian American women find strength in solidarity, and cannot solidarity itself be a means to visibility and voice?" (p. xi). Should we instead say *voices*? For Barolini conceives of female *Italianità* (as I will elaborate in speaking of the dynamics of her choices) as "complexity, difference, variety" (p. xi), not some "term unfortunately smacking of Mussolinianismo."[32]

Anticipating the passion for the emigrant grandmother figure[33] that emerges so often in all four anthologies I am dealing with, Barolini envisions how women writers can overcome their double alienation of not being wanted in Italy or in America by finding a commonality in the ancestral traditions of female creativity: the making as artisanry (art?) of stories, homes, gardens, bread, other exquisite foods, and fine

---

[32]See "Off the Boat and Up the Creek," 39.
[33]Barolini had already treated this crucial theme in *Umbertina*, first published in 1979.

needlework.[34] As her selections reveal, these crafts have begun to take shape as indisputably artistic creations in the second-, third-, and fourth-generation women writers who—enjoying "the tools of education, the confidence of language, the leisure to read, and the privacy for reflection" (p. 4)—are realizing Virginia Woolf's fundamental artistic need for a room of one's own.

With a space of their own—*The Dream Book*—the writers anthologized make literature out of what Barolini calls "Seeds of Doubt: The Internal Blocks" (p. 18). Overcoming shame for their indigenous culture—its olfactory, gustatorial, pigmentational, and societal stigmas (which they have so often internalized)—the poets included in this volume embody what Barolini sees as the "riches and glories" (p. 21) of Italian tradition, the struggle to transcend anger and the solitude imposed by familial and cultural *omertà*, and the lack of support for "public assertion" (p. 24). That is to say, Barolini and her literary sisters in this anthology confront with craft and candor their

> precarious position: . . . do you keep close to family, enjoying its emotional warmth and protectiveness, and lose your individualism; or do you opt for personal independence? Do you go against the grain of your culture to embrace the American concept of rugged individualism? Do you choose loneliness over denial of self for the family good? (p. 26)

This "questionability at the heart of Being" and Becoming focuses finally, for Barolini, on how to redefine ancient tribal laws by confronting patriarchy and matriarchy and by "self birthing" in the spirit of a border creativity whose model is provided more by Native and African American women writers than it is by Italians (pp. 27 and 33).

---

[34]Apropos of artisanry as art, in *Fontamara*, Ignazio Silone wrote: "The art of storytelling, the art of putting one word after another, one line after another, one sentence after another, . . . calling bread bread and wine wine, is just like the ancient art of weaving, the ancient art of putting one thread after another, . . . cleanly, neatly, perseveringly, plainly for all to see" (London: J. M. Dent & Sons Ltd., 1985, 9).

I would, however, dispute this point to some extent, especially in the light of the history of contemporary Italian feminism. See, for instance, Dacia Maraini's poem "Demetra ritrovata" in her 1978 volume *Mangiami pure* (Turin: Einaudi):

> *Demetra ritrovata, Prosperina ha il colore*
> *delle begonie, madre e figlia si scambiano*
> *quel nocciolo di pesca che è il cuore di donna*
> *da un petto all'altro con dita insanguinate*
> *ora madre tu sei me e tu figlia mi partorisci*
> *nel nuovo candore del mestruo glorioso*
> *ci scambiano un bacio d'amore . . . (p. 12)*

> With Demeter found once more, Persephone glows
> like begonias, mother and daughter share
> that peach pit, the heart of woman,
> from one breast to another with bloodied fingers
> now, mother, you are me and you, daughter, deliver me
> in the new candor of glorious menses
> we share a kiss of love . . .
> (translation my own)

In fact, Barolini, in spite of her ambivalence regarding Italian Americana's relationships to Italian literature, sees creative possibilities in the "reworking of the Demeter/Persephone myth with its Sicilian locus as the ultimate in the powerful mother-daughter bond" (p. 34). Furthermore the compounding of Italian and American cultures for Barolini makes functional as a source of artistic inspiration that "third realm of consciousness and expression" (p. 35)—whose sources are Italian as well as American.

To rework the canon of Anglo-American literature in this light, Barolini stresses that Italo-women critics and writers take the major initiatives. In effect, women have done so in these last fifteen years and continue to do so with greater frequency, intensity, and artistic and scholarly competence. More and more, they address key issues of gender and ethnicity in relation to the creation of art that might embrace but simultaneously go beyond these valences. Barolini, for instance, concludes her introduction by noting that "I believe that the writers represented here . . . transcend gender and ethnic group" (p. 56). Woolf would have said "hats off!" to this assertion, and Julia Kristeva reiterates it:

> I am increasingly convinced that we must avoid assigning genders to cultural productions. . . . Any generalization made about the feminine condition should merely be a way of enabling each woman to speak about her own uniqueness. This act of speaking is no more "male" than it is "female"; it cannot be generalized, for it is specific and incomparable. Only then can it be an innovation or a potential contribution to a civilization that is lucid and aware of the constraints it imposes without creating new forms of totalitarianism.[35]

Taking this quote in a relational manner, I want to narrate the poetic content of some of the authors included in *The Dream Book* and to focus on "their special tone, their special strengths, their unique vision" (p. 56). While time and space do not allow me to analyze them as "writers in their own right" (p. 56), I will try to respect (not tolerate) their "*e pluribus* variety,"[36] treating Barolini's montage as a series of shots in conflict and in harmony, as a dialectics of theses, antitheses, and syntheses, but ultimately as a healthy anarchy of creative choices where all totalitarianisms wither away and what flourishes is a chrestomathy of poems valid in their own right(s).

Perhaps appropriately, the first poem (p. 300) is a Petrarchan semisonnet (twelve verses only) by Severina Magni, born in Lucca in 1897 and obviously influenced by the *poetesse* of the Italian Renais-

---

[35]*Interviews*, edited by R. M. Guberman. New York: Columbia University Press, 1996, 112.
[36]This "twist" comes from Jennifer Lagier's poem "A Reversion to Rootstock: *e pluribus* Variety," published in *la bella figura: a choice*.

sance. However, subsequent works (pp. 303–306) by Kathy Freeperson (*née Tedesco*) and Elaine Romaine (*née Romagnano*) affirm, respectively, rebirth of tradition in radical feminism and identification with Anglo-literary tradition (the Molly Bloom Poems). In similar veins, Grace Di Santo's poems contest *omertà* ("In Defense of Plath, Berryman, Sexton," pp. 307–308), but extol the sacred "*chiesa*-large kitchen" of her ancestral culture (pp. 308–309). By way of contrast, asserting, why not?, *Americanità!*, Phyllis Capello's poetry (pp. 314–316) is clearly rooted in jazz, and Rita Valentino's (pp. 316–318) in the spirit of Walt Whitman.

Then, as tribute to Woolf, Maria Mazziotti Gillan's "Petals of Silence" (p. 319) expresses her anguish in stealing time to write. Going beyond Woolf's aristocratic individualism, Gillan bequeathes the poem to her daughter so that there will be:

> the place inside herself
> that nothing, nothing can shatter.

Tracing such a strength back to first- and second-generation immigrant experience, deeply rooted in class conflict as well as ethnic prejudice, Gillan's "Public School No. 18: Paterson, New Jersey" (pp. 320–321) recapitulates so many of the crucial themes of *The Dream Book* and of two of the other three anthologies: (1) the ambivalence—or schizophrenia—that growing up as a child of immigrants entails in one of the most Americanizing, white-washing institutions, school, where the English language is imposed as the *sine qua non* for human status; (2) the conditioning of second-generation young people to conform and be lily-white; (3) their deeply psychosomatic shame for failing to be so; (4) their intimate sense of security at home (i.e., their ethnic and linguistic pride) versus their visceral and physical angst among Anglo-Saxon faces; (5) their internalized guilt for being special and their shame-faced rejection of their roots; (6) their awareness that Anglo culture has managed to teach self-hatred; (7) the revindication of ethnic pride years later when Italian Americans finally get fed up with being targets of Mafia stigmatizing; (8) the explosion of rage as a guilt-ridden but cathartic epiphany in which the dignity of heritage is reaffirmed in a militant way: the discovery of an empowered voice:

> Remember me, ladies,
> the silent one?
> I have found my voice
> and my rage will blow
> your house down.

Subsequent poems travel the spectrum from the reassertion of traditional elements of Italian culture (see Anna Bart, Jacquelyn Bonomo, and Mary Frances Wagner), through the sense of *vergogna* for such a vilified background (see Jennifer Lagier, Sandra Gilbert, Jean Feraca, and Daniela Gioseffi), to a poetic realization that Italian American women writers can interweave their ancestral traditions with bonified forms of American artistry like blues and jazz (e.g., Elizabeth Marraffino and Claudia Menza) and international frames of creativity (Rina Ferrarelli and Kathryn Nocerino). Furthermore, Sandra Gilbert asserts in "The Thoreau Pencil" that Italian American women poets can assume the agency of writing mainstream literature:

> what characters it must write
> what clean Romantic
> hieroglyphs
> pebbles from the shore of Walden pond (p. 351)

Apropos of this self-empowering-because-self-creating-discourse, Diane di Prima's "April Fool Birthday Poem for Grandpa" (pp. 370–371) epitomizes Italian American women poets' capability to go beyond what Joe Papaleo termed *native writing*, that "basically descriptive reminiscence . . . , a way of making do with the charm and uniqueness of the face of the subject that is most familiar. And nothing more."[37] In fact,

---

[37]Letter to J. Vitiello, 1 March 1992.

di Prima, better known as a Beat poet than an ethnic one, realizes in this poem what Papaleo sees as

> the constant finding of the dual identities . . . that ebb and flow with the poet's sensibility and often make for that maddening ambiguity we call ethnic identity . . . [showing] how ethnic poetry can contain the respectfully rendered portrait of the details of the immigrant world and its soul and yet be filled with intellect, be modern in language and rhythm, sharp, quick, slashing in style, and contain the modern pose and mode of irony.[38]

In short, di Prima transcends her forebears' heritage—in her experience the elite cultural one of Dante and Giordano Bruno—to incorporate the modernism of Aubrey Beardsley, Oscar Wilde, Jean Cocteau, and Sergei Eisenstein, with her immigrant grandfather's radical, international historical awareness embracing Carlo Tresca and Sacco and Vanzetti. This fusion of universal and Italian, classical and radical sources of our culture, validates a much-neglected aspect of Italian American contributions to:

> the stars over the Bronx
> that they may look on earth
> and not be ashamed.

I can think of no better work in Barolini's florilegium that expresses, in a fine, lyrical way, Italian American women's potential to radicalize the dominant culture and to claim a visibility challenging the complacency of a rigor-mortizing canon.

Unfortunately, the follow-up anthology of Italian American women's writing—"Il Viaggio Delle Donne"—a welcomed coming out of crucial aspects of ethnic as well as sexual identities—has not received due recognition beyond what is still marginalized as "the Lesbian Imagination

---

[38]Ibid.

in the Arts and Politics."³⁹ However, to adapt a phrase from a famous speech, "now is the time." Although I cannot share the optimism of Janet Capone's introductory notes ("we have arrived"⁴⁰), her argument that Italian American lesbians—with solidarity from their hetero-sisters (not to speak of some homo- and some hetero-brothers)—are moving "from obscurity to visibility" is convincing by virtue of the existence of this anthology (and the two others I will discuss). Herein, one of the strongest points of this compendium is an openness to many aspects some other radical feminist groups have vehemently rejected: (1) respecting tradition(s); (2) coming out not as a total divorce from the past; (3) not finding voice(s) via only rage and rebellion; (4) self-defining not merely as a stance AGAINST; (5) embodying compassion for those who fail to understand a radical departure from traditional gender identities; and (6) re-imaging self via a rediscovery of ethnicity so that it can be "possible to be Italian/Sicilian identified and lesbian at the same time" (pp. 3-4).

In her preface, Denise Leto synthesizes most of the above points lucidly, explaining this anthologizer's urge to:

> find what had been hidden away, silenced, oppressed. We found a meaning that transcended our individual family experience; we found a voice within ourselves deeply resonant of our ancestors; we found validation through the exploration of our her-story, Sicilian, Italian and Italian-American; we found that our own pain and joy in being Italian-American lesbians was echoed by the many women with whom we came in contact.

Leto answers her following rhetorical question as to why compose such a collection of writings (including some by nonlesbians) as a crucially elucidated strategy of survival that "depends on our ability

---

³⁹See the subtitle of this important but, for most Italian Americans, still scandalous journal.
⁴⁰With sad irony, this phrase echoes Rose Basile Green's facile and jingoist approaches in her doggerel poetry and in *The Italian American Novel* (Cranbury, New Jersey: Fairleigh Dickinson University Press, 1974).

to reassemble, to reclaim and to remember" (i.e., to embody cultural empowerments):

> Why an Italian-American women's issue? To give us the opportunity to speak, to reach out to one another, to connect, to raise consciousness about the issues Italian- and Sicilian-American lesbians face. (pp. 5–6)

Survival via consciousness raising—maybe even at grass-roots levels?—and cultural production—even "in the streets"? Yes, maybe. . . . apropos, with a refreshing touch, Leto adds a few more reasons why it makes sense to do so: "To have fun, to have a feast, to celebrate who we are" (p. 6). Herein lurk the essences of this self-empowering anthology in which "each word, each image . . . is an act of courage". *Touché!* Also because the editors have included, as one of the first liminal poems and as a celebration of their grandmotherly tradition, Gillan's "Public School No. 18" (pp. 8–9).

In subsequent works chosen scrupulously by the editors, the theme of the wisdom of their female predecessors is developed in various feminist experiential contexts with deep cultural roots. For cases in point, see Mary Russo Demetrick's "Legacy" (p. 54) and Kathy Freeperson's "Munda" (p. 66), both of which eulogize matriarchal agency roles: witchcraft as healing and midwifery as the art of giving life; Diane Gravenite's "Shadow Sister" (pp. 67–70) which, from Sicilian roots, affirms women's global liberation in harmony with the tremors of "Kali, Shiva, Medusa"—all monsters in male culture but goddesses in this context; Chris Cuomo's "The Wax Problem" (pp. 114–15), an ironic poem that turns out to be a paean to certain female filaments growing, according to certain standards, where they are not supposed to grow; Elizabeth Fides's "Salsa di Pomodoro" (p. 121), a good, old-fashioned recipe that turns out as a postmodern poem.

As capstone to this anthological construction of a poetic herstory, Capone's "In Answer to Their Questions" (pp. 122–27) recapitulates the major issues of "Il Viaggio Delle Donne." From the outset, Capone pops the question: as a lesbian, "what/would you write about being

Italian-American?" The poet's responses are first aimed at deflating stereotypical balloons: she is not a Capone from Chicago but is deeply committed to and proud of her participation in the June 1989 Gay Pride March in San Francisco (see the related photos on page 7). Furthermore, her dignity is not only individualistic; it is also collective in sexual and ethnic valences, "mostly for myself and my commare [sic] *lesbiche/per la maggior parte per noi.*"

Apropos of Capone's employment of Italo-lingo, she proceeds to express what it means to come from that "booted country"[41]:

> ... I'm understood,
> loved, and included,
> ... (and) *aglio e oglio*
> is Neopolitan
> for soul food.

Subsequently, Capone elaborates as to what her deep sense of ethnicity means in specifically religious, racial, historical, linguistic, geographical, economic, genetic and generational, neighborhood and culinary, ghettoized and stigmatized terms. In the poem, she re-creates self-defining images of "ceremonies filled with tradition," "skin color ... olive, not white," "hair ... [like] ... a dense garden cultivated for centuries / by Neapolitan peasants," "the boat from the boot-shaped country," "the syllables and vowels / of our long and tuberous family names / lopped off on Ellis Island," "the Northerner's boot in Sicily's ass," "my Neapolitan grandparents," "our neighborhood / laid out like a village in Naples," "Sunday morning sausage and meatballs / foaming in oil," "those dagos, garlic breath bastards, stupid wops," "the entire Mafia / looking over my shoulder." Then, as a coda, she lashes out against the various forms of *omertà* wherein Italian Americans grin and bear their history of oppression, their victimization via racial stereo-

---

[41]See, again, Gillan's "Public School No. 18," 8.

typing, and, most appropriate to this anthology, the heterosexist stigmas against her self-realization:

> But, second generation American-Italian
> also means I do what I must to survive,
> means I won't keep my mouth shut,
> won't shrink to fit
> someone else's definition of our lives
>
> Italian-American
> means my living habits
> are cultural ceremonies, not quirks
> my skin is olive
> and the hair spreading . . . over
> the top of my lip
> grows thicker and thicker
> the more I resist,
> the more I insist
> on possessing
> entirely who I am (p. 127)

From such apparent Chaos of "dissatisfaction and discontent," avatars of Lilith find their tutelary genius in poems like this. For here, dramatically expressed, is a new energy that keeps "forging an Italian/American female literary tradition" (see, again, E. Giunta in VIA, Fall 1996).

Rose Romano has often stressed in conversations shared with me that feminists scorn Italian American ethnicity and that she is estranged from the radical lesbian communities around the country. However, her own composing of *la bella figura: a choice* belies her claims. This anthology, published by her self-run press Malafemmina, has no explicit editorial statement of a *raison d'etre*, but it can be understood via the selection of poetic fragments that serve as epigraphs, a brief introduction by the radical feminist scholar and godmother Lucia Chiavola Birnbaum, and Romano's own selections for this volume.

In a letter dated 3 October 1991, Romano asked me a provocative question: "If you say we don't have poetry, aren't you saying we don't have a soul, that we don't exist as a people, that we're just a bunch of individual wops who'd better get American if we want to accomplish anything worthwhile?"[42] Relieved that she said "soul" instead of "blood," I guessed that she saw *Italianità* as individual and collective quintessences voiced by writers (men included in this instance) of Italian American pasts and presents in terms of specific themes and images that emerge in their writings.[43]

Skeptical of such a tautology and all fear and trembling in re the ironicizing of the obvious,[44] I tried to understand Romano's editorial criteria for her anthology by meditating on its four epigraphs: (1) the conclusion of Gillan's "Public School No. 18," which asserts, in defiance of the dominant Anglo-American cultural milieu, that one Italian American has found her voice and "my rage will blow / your house down"; (2) Gigi Marino's metaphor of a culture reclaimed in her grandmother's act of sewing her "broken rosary / back together again"; (3) Rina Ferrarelli's attempt to describe her father to her son characterized as "a bad translation" (i.e., a limited way of preserving Italian Americans' true heritage due to loss of language and of historical and cultural roots); and (4) Maria Fama's empathetic reading of her past via Nonna Angela, who speaks to her in the month of the Madonna (May) via "her long-ago labor of love / and of hope"—and through arts and crafts, too.

Myths of soul notwithstanding, in the spirit of the above-mentioned poets, Lucia Chiavola Birnbaum underscores the key criteria for the composition of this anthology. She reminds us, first and foremost, that *la bella figura (lbf)* is "the literary journal devoted to Italian-American women" to remember "the deep cultural history of Italian Americans" (p. xi). Rejecting the traditional canon as a way to read the poetry of

---

[42]See another discussion of this in "Off the Boat and Up the Creek," 24–25.
[43]In my review of F. P. Alfonsi's *Dictionary of Italian American Poets* in *Italica* 68, no. 1 (Spring 1991), I questioned the simplistic, racialist notion of ethnicity as blood.
[44]For my opposition to certain mythologies in re ethnicity, I have received hate mail.

lbf, she asserts that "none of the dominant categories fit" (p. xii) and that, in the spirit of Barolini, "our task is to try to remember our own history, and then, along with all the other uprooted others, transform culture and politics" (p. xii).

Chiavola Birnbaum's brief introduction to *lbf* might have been even more appropriate as a preface to "Il Viaggio Delle Donne" or *Curaggia* because the political perspective in the latter two cases is deeply radical. In contrast, Romano's autobiographical sketch to her own poetry in *lbf* makes it clear that her approach to ethnicity is predominantly conservative. Even her rebellion against her patriarchal family is informed by a nostalgia for another traditional configuration of group identity and by a typically American rugged individualism:

> the anti-Italian bigotry I found in the lesbian, progressive, and literary communities . . . inspired me to start my own literary journal. . . . The only reason I had to believe there were any Italian-American writers was that I'm an Italian-American writer. (p. 34)

Notwithstanding this ill-informed approach to the richness of Italian American radical feminist writing, Romano, perhaps guided by the good intuition of the poet, has put together an anthology with remarkably rich dialectics of themes and images of creative ethnicity.[45] As prelude to her own seminal poems, "Vendetta" and "To Show Respect," she has judiciously chosen Jean Rosalie Pidala Webster's beautifully evocative "Brooklyn Neighborhood" where

> This was no melting pot,
> this street, a small town
> surrounded by city.

---

[45]While the question of what is good poetry would take many more centuries never to define, I refer my readers to Terry Eagleton's lucent *Literary Theory: An Introduction* (Minneapolis: Minnesota University Press, 1983, 1996) for an intelligent discourse on the issue.

> The old country fought asphalt
> and streetcars here.
> Grapevines stretched beside brick houses.
> Fig trees hung over sidewalks, their purple
> fruit tasting of another place. (p. 2)

Furthermore, the insertion of three effective poems by Lenore Baeli Wang sets up a context—the distortion of images of Italy through Italian America nostalgia—that is so poignant in Romano's poetry, as well. In the cases of Baeli Wang's works, imprecise memories, in contrast to Romano's, are sweet: "Permanent Residence" (pp. 5–6) evokes the Ragusa [Sicily] where grandma "played" (?); "A Day in Ragusa" (p. 7) fantasizes the poet's return to Sicily to die in a land that no longer exists; and "Last Night's Ravioli" (p. 8) waxes eloquent over the "more piquant" taste of leftovers (things, by the way, that Sicilians would not be caught dead eating).

"Vendetta" (pp. 35–42), which sounds best when recited with the Brooklynese accent of someone who has grown up on or around Fort Hamilton Parkway, is an angry tour de force, vindicating Italian American victims of stereotypes against their real, imagined, and internalized victimizers. Epitomizing the vitality of oral tradition in Italian American culture, it tells HER STORY with caustic irony. Unfortunately, it does not balance its aggressive tone with self-irony and, thus, smacks too much of the victim's scapegoating of her victimizers with little awareness that she too is complicit in her oppression.[46] In fact, every section of this compelling poem is constructed as a Manichean struggle of bad versus good. The theses and antitheses are present in all thirteen sections of the poem, but the only synthesis is vendetta against who-knows-what fabricated demon of sterile American nonculture: "the bland, apologetic, / constipated, gutless white culture." The opposi-

---

[46]See the cover of the first edition (San Francisco, California: Malafemmina Press, 1990), where Romano, at seven or so, smiles lovely and innocent from under her first communion veil.

tional structure goes as follows: (1) dehumanized "modern American women" only interested in "having a career" versus heroic Italian grandmothers who "endangered . . . life, . . . / sanity, . . . dignity" to emigrate "for freedom and the opportunity / to work eighteen hours a day . . ."; (2) the "colorless" America versus the exotic stereotypes of the Italian as cute and spicy but not human, just "a plum tomato"; (3) American feminist spirituality recognizing "African Goddesses, Asian Goddesses, / Native American Goddesses" versus Italian women worshiping "the Virgin Mary, Blessed Mother, Madonna" of the "oppressive church of / organized religion"; (4) the media exploitation of the Mafia image stigmatizing "all Italians" versus the poet's one refreshing moment of irony: "I'm tired of not knowing anyone / in the Mafia"; (5) again, insensitive "women into radical causes" trying to propagandize via media versus the ideal grandmother who "knew / what was happening / to every other woman on the block, / and responded as though / it was happening to her?"; (6) a recapitulation (formulaic?) of contradictory images of Italians as cute or gangsters; (7) the myth of Italians' emigration as a glorious adventure wherein they "chose this land of opportunity" versus the exploitation of this oppressed and brutalized ethnic group (by their own kind, too); (8) that pseudo-land-of-opportunity versus her father's experience of Jim Crow laws in a motel; (9) discrimination Italians have suffered versus a justified *omertà* to protect their families and their culture merely to exist; (10) the wisdom of the poet's immigrant aunts, expressed in linguistic and culinary terms versus the second generation's ignorance, defined as 100 percent American, of Italo-essences; (11) the U.S. government conspiracy to negate Italian culture and history versus the justifiable *omertà* to protect the Italian soul; (12) the dominant message of mainstream media "that Italians / have no history, no culture / beyond pasta and wine" versus a need to assert that they are "a real people"; (13) the pressure to Americanize versus the poet's grandmother's apotheosized choice: "she'd rather be Italian."

Romano's follow-up, "To Show Respect" (pp. 43–45), is a refabrication of a past that validates in fantasy her choices as a gay "rooted" in "a room full of Italian- / American Lesbians, eating." This poem celebrates an imagined—not historical—community of women of several generations finally now, in history, honoring their oppressed matriarchs. The latter, in hindsight and in herstory, have come out (at least in the poet's imagination) and passed on to their descendants the wisdom of the "Crone" and her magic and the customs relating to a state of being "round, like a meatball" and still clad in "black/dresses, black stockings, square black/shoes." Thus, for Romano, these women devolve "from Madonna / to Virgin to Goddess" in a Dionysian/Sapphic ritual that they never experienced in history but might have subconsciously longed for in their captivity—at least according to Romano's regressive mythology.

Although Romano herself indulges in certain myths spuriously claiming historicity, for the rest of her anthology she has chosen a majority of works elaborating more subtle and balanced discourses related to women's *Italianità*. In contrast to Romano's nostalgic view of "the Old Country," Jo Quici's autobiographical sketch provides a more balanced way to understand an ethnic "vehicle for self-expression. My psyche is both Italian and American, not separate at all, but a merging," an interweaving where, "far from being an embarrassment, my ethnicity was an avenue to adventure and discovery" (p. 47). Herein abides a transcendence of shame, rage, dualism, schizophrenia, resentment, and hatred of Self and Other(s).

To digress for a moment, I still ask myself why it has taken Italian Americans so long to come to such a mature and balanced awareness. Many answers have been offered to the question, and I eschew banality here by not repeating them. Personally, I would like to highlight Mona Toscano Paschke's work (pp. 52–55) incorporating her Etruscan, Abruzzese, Ovidian, Mediterranean, Homeric strains of heritage and mystery; Gigi Marino's celebration of her grandmother (pp. 61–62)— so dignified in the preservation of folk artisanry and so lovely as elegy; and Jennifer Lagier's fine poems (pp. 74–83) encompassing grandmotherly storytelling and tribal lore, the brilliant intuition that America is a land dreamed as (not founded on) the principle of "*E Pluribus Variety*," where "The Mute Muse Delivers" and, in a "Matriarchal Momento," "Behind this photo [of three of her female relatives] / lie travels and troubles / which could overflow volumes" (pp. 82–82).[47] So I still wonder why the shame for this rich culture exists.

The trials and tribulations, triumphs and joys of Italian journeys to America are, in effect, being asserted as integral parts of an extraordinary cultural heritage, folk and aulic—in *lbf*, too. This anthology, in this affirmative vein, includes ample selections of works by four of the strongest and subtlest voices of Italian American poetry today: as no surprise, Maria Mazziotti Gillan (pp. 84–105) and Rina Ferrarelli (pp. 108–116), but also Maria Fama (pp. 117–131) and Barbara Crooker (pp. 144–151).

It would take a book or two to do justice to these poets' *opera omnia* in order to analyze in depth what Italian American women are doing to revamp and revitalize American poetry from the perspective of a double or multiconsciousness. My scope, however, demands, like a Critical Destiny, that I indicate the female *Italianità/Americanità* montage/dialectics in these anthologized writers.

I need not repeat why Gillan's "Public School No. 18" has been included so many times in anthologies. I can proceed to "Arturo," a poem that crystallizes her re-search for an inner and outer denied identity as a struggle to "take back our names"—in linguistic terms, as well as historical ones. Thus, it embodies Gillan's key idea expressed in her autobiographical blurb:

> Increasingly my sense of myself as an Italian-American has informed my work. I think of my acting as a way of giving voice to people who could not speak for themselves, a way of making the Italian-American real for other Americans who are influenced by stereotypical images of what it means to be Italian-American. (p. 84)

---

[47]See Howard Zinn, *A People's History of the United States* (New York: Harper Perennial, revised ed., 1995), 50: "The country . . . was not 'born free' but born slave and free, servant and master, tenant and landlord, poor and rich"—and man over woman?

What that means for Gillan is never escaping certain voices within ("The Crow") that still echo via inferiority complexes and ghosts (or talismans), striving to exorcise inner demons of the immigrant past, and recapturing "the magic at the heart of ordinary lives" that conserves even in generations enjoying upward mobility "the charm of those moments where I rested / in the luminous circle of love." Moreover, most concretely, these are moments perpetuated by material culture produced by "My Grandmother's Hands" that gives Italian Americans a precious sense of continuity in a most humble but dignified way:

> The skein of the past spun from . . . love,
> stretches back . . . to me, to my mother,
> the old country, the old language lost,
> but in this new world, saved and cherished;
> the tablecloth my grandmother made . . .
> and the love she taught us to weave
> a thread of woven silk
> to lead us home (p. 94)

Home, of course, is no longer for most Italian American women writers that ancestral village to which Tina "returns" in Barolini's *Umbertina*—only to realize she can't belong. Rina Ferrarelli clarifies this crucial point: "I'm surprised that no distinction is made between me and Italian-Americans born here" (p. 108). In fact, many of the poems by this immigrant from Calabria are emblematic of women's vital roles in the preservation of a genuine, contemporary Italian culture (via, again, artisanry as art). To cite one, I want to reemphasize how so very often women pass on the most positive aspects of heritage, here true gifts to the poet's daughter:

> She'll also inherit
> these linens—towels, tablecloths
> and napkins, and a pillows' cover
> long and delicate as an altar cloth . . . (p. 111)

Women writers, more than men, have preserved the ancient Italian (pre-Christian) sense that sacred and profane are one, a cultural valence more matriarchal than patriarchal. Maria Fama's bio-sketch reconfirms such a view, for she

> believes that the predominant force in her artistic development was her upbringing in a Sicilian immigrant household, where she learned of a Sicilian culture where women are powerful in the home and heard the ritual prayers, traditional teachings, and oral poetry which was transmitted through the generations in this ancient culture. (p. 117)

As proof of the pudding, every Fama work in this anthology evinces American influences but embodies one or another aspect of this *educazione*: "The Werewolf Story" (pp. 118–120), which deals with a Sicilian/American/global archetype; "A Mediterrarnean Walking Riff," which captures Fama's mythic and intellectual roots in Sicily and Italy via jazz rhythms; "Fig Tree in the Yard," where the poet preserves "our displaced blood" via the transplanting of this typically Mediterranean source of Edenic fruit; "Sicilia," where the poet connects intimately to a plausible history in harmony with its myths; "Caffè Espresso," where her love of coffee connects her to Italian culture and female loved ones, wherever she may transport the real stuff; and "Every Christmas" and "Tablecloth," where rituals and artisanry provide spiritual connections and onenness "of love / and of hope" (p. 127), always assuring that "The Goddess has sprung to life" (p. 129).

This Goddess is reborn even in people who have lost their original name.[48] Barbara Crooker, whose father changed his name and married a Smith, could not eradicate the poet's appreciation for "My Grandmother's House" with its

> . . . doilies
> of almonds in nylon net
> and palms crossed

---

[48] Another poignant discussion of this problem can be heard—with an ear to more dissonant tonalities—in James Baldwin's *Nobody Knows My Name*.

> on pictures
> smells of spice & garlic
> like a good ragout
> on the back burner,
> a simmering of wine & secrets (p. 145)

As Mary Ann Vigilante Mannino has indicated, Crooker's "Knitting" (one of the finest poem's in Romano's anthology) is a tour-de-force for its comprehensive vision of four generations of Italian American women in their struggle to preserve ancestral culture and adapt it in terms of their American needs of female fulfillment.[49] To the credit of this fine poem, it dignifies the first generation of illiterate immigrants who managed with their needles to "force the soft gray yarn / into patterns as old as Europe" with "stitches . . . perfect, / cabled with love" (p. 150). Then the poem shifts to the second generation, not as deft in artisanry but still intent on being craftswomen:

> My mother also knits
> from patterns and pictures. (p. 151)

In this process of preservation and loss of artisanry (and oral history and culture), the poem shifts to the third generation, famous for abandoning ancestral cultures and languages and accepting the concept of Americanization as a rejection of ethnicity:

> My older daughter tries to knit, too,
> but her hands can't master the needles.
> . . . She is already a maker
> of emperor's cloth. (p. 151)

Hope still lives though. The fourth generation—Barbara Crooker, especially—will transform her artisan heritage into art, "clicking my pen across the page": "I take words and knit them back in poems" (p. 151).

---

[49] See her forthcoming book to be published by Peter Lang.

Such an individualistic affirmation is appropriate in Romano's anthology. However, when we deal with *Curaggia*, the concepts of Italian American women writing are collective, and sexually and politically radical.[50] The introductory pieces by the three editors of this provocative and energizing anthology make this clear.

Domenica Dileo's "Understanding Oneself as Oppressor and Oppressed" (pp. 11–15), paying tribute to "Il Viaggio Delle Donne," stresses how this anthology is a struggle in class and feminist consciousness raising and an assertion that women—in this context, predominantly lesbian—can seize means of cultural production to combat the status quo Mafia, "the white, middle-class patriarchal / heterosexist social formation" (p. 13) and to "eradicate the injustice being done to other social groups" (p. 14), especially here to all "Italian women" (p. 14). Although "the political meaning" of the anthology "is left to the reader," this essay invites us to reflect on the whole book's audience: "the Italian community? . . . The feminist . . . ? The academic . . . ? . . . The larger social political context?" (p. 14). Or all of the above?

In "The Moon Only Howls When Hands Leave Lips and Words Spread Like Dew to Conspiring Minds" (pp. 17–20), 'Nzula Angelina Ciatu has different, albeit complementary, dialectical foci: (1) the crucial issue of the traditional family, one of the strongest institutions "conforming to sexually oppressive realms" versus women's self-realizations and totally liberated voices in feminist/lesbian communities; (2) the recognition, via the publication of this anthology, of

> the survivors [of this conflict]: those of us who are outcast, beaten, or threatened upon coming-out; the numerous Italian women whose families have severed contact because they chose to leave the home unmarried or because they did not conform to sexist dictates; . . . the women who have no choice but to stay,

---

[50]In Italian, one says "*coraggio*," and in Sicilian "*curaggiu*." Here, in defiance of grammar, the editors have chosen *curaggia*: "We have used dialect and feminized the word to pay tribute to women's courage, to acknowledge our strength, our ability to survive, and to acknowledge our faith that we will get through, we will through it all" 25.

and those who stay out of choice, and who continue to confront and survive; . . . the women treading new ground . . . in celebration . . . of our *Italianita* [sic]. (p. 18)

In this all-inclusive-and-embracing context, Ciatu reminds us that there already exists such a female and feminist literary tradition of *Italianità* and the manifestos of constantly innovated changes in print to create an ongoing, radicalizing culture: *The Dream Book, la bella figura, The Voices We Carry, Sinister Wisdom,* and the Fall 1996 issue of *Voices in Italian Americana* (p. 19), all of which allow "our voices . . . to reach one another across geographical boundaries" so that "community is forged with new invigorating boundaries on old familiar ground" (p. 20). Personally, I can think of few more optimistic views of how to foment nonviolent cultural revolution than Ciatu's conclusion:

> The Italian women's reality within North America with all of our diverse tongues, ethnicity, class statuses, skin colours, divergent historical origins, and sociological placements that fall under the umbrella "Italian" will only add depth to the ongoing necessary discourses on racism and classism within feminist and mainstream communities. (p. 20)

The last editorial, Gabriella Micallef's "Curaggia, Writing by Women of Italian Descent" (pp. 21–23), elaborates on the book's compositional criteria in personal, psychological, experiential, relational, ethnic, racial, and cultural terms. Echoing Klor de Alva's notion of identity as a construct based on myth, legend and history to self-validate and empower, it zooms in on "our desires, our sorrows, reflections of our lives" (p. 21). Thus reminded of Sibilla Aleramo, we can read this anthology with a relish for a "risotto marinara, a little bit of this and a little bit of that" (p. 22) with the empathy that it demands, taking the risks—pain and joy, laughter and tears, curses and blessings, struggles and moments of serenity—that it challenges us to imagine and enact.

Perhaps a useful way to read this anthology in empathy (true respect, not tolerance?) is to focus on the major sections, polemically and poetically entitled, and to identify major inter- and intra-themes and images framed as collective discourses: (1) "The Spread of Air Between Us" (pp. 29–70), which plays variations on the generational themes of family guilt versus female rebellion, profound love of grandparental heritage (via artisanry, too) versus the grandmotherly rejection of young women in their brood who try to break away from gender and social roles, the struggle of women to validate themselves as individuals (artists, too) versus their persistent need to find strength in female ancestors who might never understand their drives; (2) "Just Two Dagos Getting Some *Gelati*" (pp. 73–109), where the poets evoke and invoke "Sicilia *terra-cuore*," the strong matriarchal figures of ancient myths (witches, goddesses, grandmothers with abundant facial hair), (i.e., images that validate their androgyny); (3) "Dimi [sic], when are the Lesbians coming for coffee?" (pp. 113–151), where the poems are militant in their comings out via the symbols of their crucial rebellion against traditional roles: motorcycle boots worn to clean house, the dancing of the tarantella at the Bay Area Sicilian Italian Lesbians (BASIL) "March at Lesbian and Gay Pride in San Francisco" (June, 1992), the defiance in dreams of ancestors who negate their granddaughters' search for happiness in the discovery of their true sexual identity; (4) "What If Someone Found Out We Wash Dandelions, Cook Them in Olive Oil and Garlic, Eat Them with Thick Crusty Bread?" (pp. 155–190), where the radical lesbian stance proudly integrates peasant culture into its own frame of reference and way of being (not lifestyle!); (5) "Her Tongue the Culprit" (pp. 193–239) where *Italianità* is correctly identified as multiracial and multicultural in terms of its real history, its "psychic diaspora" (pp. 204–205), and its "confluence of ancestries from the Arab, North African, Semitic, Greek, and Spanish . . . , a compelling mix of ethnic and cultural forces" (p. 213); (6) "The Story in her Bones" (pp. 242–262), where the "intersection of gender and (this rich) ethnicity" (p. 213) is validated as a way to foster the "process of authorial self-birth" (p. 275); (7) "Her Garden Asks for Water" (pp. 265–295), which deflates the grand illusion that women have arrived at the points this revolutionary anthology wants to see them arriving at and which stresses that they are always ready to push their revolution farther because, still, after centuries of struggles, defeats, and moments of apparent triumph, "I am the woman who always rewrites / I am / the woman" (p. 265); (8) "Life Is Theatre" (pp. 299–352), where the poets are still contemplating "How to Kill Your Father (p.299) (see "Life Is the Theatre or To Be Italian in Toronto Drinking Cappuccino," pp. 320–321) why women are still prey, and why Italian American women writers still find a "pen heavy to lift" (p. 325).

A poignant image in a poem by Giovanna Patriarca brings us toward a conclusion of this essay that is realistic but hopeful about Italian American women's literature.[51] She writes regarding the inspiration of her illiterate peasant ancestors, her birth as a writer in spite of their much-maligned heritage. Here Patriarca honors their strength in passing on an empowering female folk, then literary culture:

> i will leave my poems
> somewhere
> in time they will be
> stumbled upon . . .
> my dying aunt
> will never hear my poems
> but i know her life
> helped me to write them
> *
> my heart is strong . . .
> women's hearts grow stronger
> with each rupture
> maybe
> women's hearts never die

In fact, in this new millennium, women's hearts, intellects, and creative talents are very much alive. Via poetry, among many other

---

[51]Patriarca, Giovanna. "Notes on Aging," 324–328.

forms of cultural expression, they embody what Terry Eagleton sees as a real hope for human survival in this genocide-ridden world:

> If literature matters today, it is chiefly because it seems . . . one of the few remaining places where, in a divided, fragmented world, a sense of universal value may still be incarnate; and where, in a sordidly material world, a rare glimpse of transcendence can still be attained.[52]

To put this cosmic wager in another way, I would query: If Rimbaud were alive today, would he see his prophecy being fulfilled? Would he say, "Sisters of the world, continue to unite in your diversity! You have nothing to lose but the rest of your chains!"?

---

[52]See Eagleton, 20.